Praise for *Teaching Preschool and Kindergarten Math*

A true confession: teaching preschool and kindergarten has always been a terrifying thought for me. I began my teaching career by teaching ninth graders and, over the years, moved down the grades as I became curious about misconceptions that students showed. When I got to second grade, I knew I was on the edge of my comfort zone. And while from time to time I'd visit a kindergarten class and teach a math lesson, I never felt completely comfortable or successful. If I had had access to Ann and Brenda's book, I might have felt differently. Their delight in and commitment to teaching young children shine throughout their resource. It's inspiring.

—Marilyn Burns, Founder, Math Solutions

Teaching Preschool and Kindergarten Math celebrates the competencies and learning processes of young children. Throughout the chapters, the explanations, teacher reflections, and thought-provoking questions lead educators to a deeper understanding of the math work they do with children and how to make it even more meaningful. I've made lots of notes and can hardly wait to begin some of these processes in my own classroom.

—Kirstin Rasmussen, Santa Clara Head Start, Tucson, Arizona

Take a random look at any of these materials and you know in an instant they were created by great teachers. The first clue is their abiding and inviolable respect and faith in the developing minds of young children. They start with the children, understanding and respecting them, and from there provide the experiences that embed the content they will need to succeed in school and, more importantly, to become mathematically adept adults and citizens. Secondly, while the materials, activities, and teaching tips are theoretically sound and supported by research, the theory and research are always presented in a way that makes sense and works in a classroom.

—John Snyder, Dean of Bank Street College, New York, New York

The hands-on, developmentally appropriate (and fun!) activities in *Teaching Preschool and Kindergarten Math* encourage children to make mathematical connections to the real world around them. In their shared commitment to provide our youngest learners with challenging yet sensitive opportunities for learning, Ann and Brenda have provided us with a resource that we should not be without.

—Paul J. Ohm, Principal, Ocotillo Learning Center,
Sunnyside Unified School District, Tucson, Arizona

Drawing on many years spent carefully observing young children in their own exemplary classrooms, Ann and Brenda deliver just what they promise: a guide that focuses on the essential mathematics that needs to be experienced by children in the early grades.

—*Nancy Litton, author,* Getting Your Math Message Out to Parents, This Is Only a Test, *and* Second-Grade Math: A Month-to-Month Guide

Clear understanding and acceptance of how young children think is complimented by insightful questioning techniques that encourage learners to take the next mathematical steps. Engaging photographs, video clips, and reflective journal entries all contribute to thinking more deeply about important issues like assessment and how to keep young learners engaged in meaningful mathematics.

—*Vicki Bachman, curriculum/mathematics consultant, Grant Wood Area Education Agency, Cedar Rapids, Iowa*

Teaching Preschool and Kindergarten Math captured my attention instantly! This resource is brilliant! The video will make your teacher heart smile. From jars and rocks to nuts and bolts and tweezers, Ann and Brenda will inspire you to provide purposeful, engaging, and developmentally appropriate math experiences everyday! As a former kindergarten teacher and a mother of a preschooler and a soon-to-be kindergartener, these are the opportunities for learning I dream about for my daughters . . . and for all young mathematicians.

—*Beth Terry, parent and math specialist, Alexandria City Public Schools, Virginia; 2004 PAEMST Awardee—Colorado*

Ann and Brenda's work in *Teaching Preschool and Kindergarten Math* shows a commitment to the belief that children are mathematicians from a very early age. The experiences these dedicated professionals offer are a confirmation that mathematical ideas can and should be developed through exploration and inquiry as young children strive to make sense of the world around them.

—*Kay Thill, teacher in residence and student teacher supervisor, University of Arizona*

As a teacher who works with struggling students and students with special needs, I appreciate the myriad of opportunities this resource offers for students to equally develop both sides of the brain during their learning. In the high-quality text and videos, students are constantly working with objects in their environment and challenged to discover the relationships between those objects by using their fine and gross motor skills, vision, and verbal skills. An equally important aspect is the emphasis on math talk to help children justify and make generalizations. Teachers are sure to walk away from each chapter with ideas they can immediately implement.

—*Lisa Ann de Garcia, author,* Elementary Mathematics Is Anything But Elementary *and mathematics specialist, Department of Defense Schools, Atsugi Japan*

Teaching Preschool and Kindergarten Math is laid out in a user-friendly format with math vocabulary and icons in the margins that highlight activities such as circle time, children's literature, and home-school connections. One of the strongest components is the video clips; the video clips of students bring the text to life. This is a valued resource on my bookshelf as well as many other teachers with whom I work.

—*Joan Barrett, math professional developer, Collinsville, Illinois*

Teaching Preschool and Kindergarten Math extends the work of Marilyn Burns and the use of manipulative mathematics for early childhood education. This hands-on, easy-to-follow approach is a must read for educators who hope to establish mathematical thinking in young children. It offers practical guidelines that engage and inspire.

—*Emily Vance, international early childhood consultant, researcher, and author*

Teaching Preschool and Kindergarten Math brings the language of mathematics to life for teachers of young children through its thoughtful, thorough, and user-friendly format. The video clips, reflection questions, and reproducibles support teachers in developing their own observational skills in order to better understand children's thinking. This is an easy to use, fabulously rich resource.

—Eleanor Droegemeier, University of Arizona College of Education Advisory Board member; former preschool teacher and preschool program coordinator, Tucson Unified School District; 2007 Arizona Early Learning Award of Distinction

Teaching Preschool and Kindergarten Math provides opportunities for teachers of three-, four-, and five-year-olds to understand the big mathematical ideas that are developing in their students. It gives effective guidance to observing this development by naming learning progressions to look for and assess. The authors thoughtfully guide the reader through the complexity of developing mathematical ideas with the use of videos, Teaching Insights, and Math Talk support.

—Connie Lewis, mathematics specialist, K–5

Finally, a teacher-friendly resource for creating professional discourse about young mathematicians! *Teaching Preschool and Kindergarten Math* provides educators, parents, and administrators with a comprehensive look at the importance of developing numeracy in young children. Ann and Brenda share their expertise through carefully crafted lessons; their passion for teaching and learning is evident throughout and the video clips are priceless.

—Mary Ann Warrington, math specialist/coach and educational consultant, San Francisco, California

Teaching Preschool and Kindergarten Math

More Than 175 Ideas, Lessons, and Videos for Building Foundations in Math

Ann Carlyle and **Brenda Mercado**

With Video Streaming

Math Solutions
Sausalito, California, USA

Math Solutions
www.mathsolutions.com

Carlyle, Ann.
Teaching preschool and kindergarten math : more than 175 ideas, lessons, and videos for building foundations in math: a multimedia professional learning resource / Ann Carlyle, Brenda Mercado.
pages cm
Includes bibliographical references and index.
ISBN 978-1-935099-44-4 (acid-free paper)
1. Mathematics—Study and teaching (Early childhood) 2. Mathematics—Vocational guidance. I. Mercado, Brenda. II. Title.
QA135.6.C367 2012
372.7'049—dc23 2012041076

ISBN-13: 978-1-935099-44-4
ISBN-10: 1-935099-44-2

Math Solutions is a division of Houghton Mifflin Harcourt.

Editor: Jamie Ann Cross
Production: Denise A. Botelho
Cover and interior design: Susan Barclay, Barclay Design
Composition: MPS Limited and Barclay Design
Cover and interior images: Amelia Maldonado Elementary School, Tucson Unified School District, Tucson, Arizona, USA

Printed in the United States of America.

5 6 7 8 9 10 11 2266 22 21 20 19 18
4510005540

A Message from Math Solutions

We at Math Solutions believe that teaching math well calls for increasing our understanding of the math we teach, seeking deeper insights into how students learn mathematics, and refining our lessons to best promote students' learning.

Math Solutions shares classroom-tested lessons and teaching expertise from our faculty of professional development consultants as well as from other respected math educators. Our publications are part of the nationwide effort we've made since 1984 that now includes

- more than five hundred face-to-face professional development programs each year for teachers and administrators in districts across the country;
- professional development books that span all math topics taught in kindergarten through high school;
- videos for teachers and for parents that show math lessons taught in actual classrooms;
- on-site visits to schools to help refine teaching strategies and assess student learning; and
- free online support, including grade-level lessons, book reviews, inservice information, and district feedback, all in our Math Solutions Online Newsletter.

For information about all of the products and services we have available, please visit our website at *www.mathsolutions.com.* You can also contact us to discuss math professional development needs by calling (800) 868-9092 or by sending an email to *info@mathsolutions.com.*

We're always eager for your feedback and interested in learning about your particular needs. We look forward to hearing from you.

Contents

Reproducibles

Acknowledgments

We first thank the children in Brenda's classroom. Their conversations were so inspiring and purposeful. Then we thank Brenda's colleagues in PACE, Ann Sanchez, Artemisa Aguilar, and Maria Barajas, for their continuing support and wisdom. It would have been impossible to do this work without them.

We are grateful to Mary Mercado, principal of Maldonado Elementary School, for creating a school environment that allowed us to work with children in appropriate ways, and Pat Delaney, PACE Program Coordinator, for her countless hours of encouragement.

We really appreciated the expert editorial guidance and work of Jamie Cross, Sheri Willebrand, and Denise Botelho, who were able to take our collection of thoughts and blend them into a readable and cohesive whole.

Of course, none of this would have been possible without twenty-five years of inspiration and vision from Marilyn Burns and the Math Solutions organization (too many to name individually!). Marilyn has consistently helped us with our own understanding of mathematical knowledge and a respect for children's thinking.

Finally, Tom Carlyle, David Mercado, and David Antonio Mercado have been our continuing support and home team guys. They have helped make possible our long-distance collaboration in many practical and helpful ways. We can't thank them enough.

Connections to the Video Clips

The classroom shown in the video clips in this book is an inclusive room. There are children with special needs and speech and languages challenges, and the majority of these students are learning English as a second language. The culture of the classroom is bilingual, and indicative of the Southwest. For example, the home center is called the *casita*. This is a child-centered classroom, inspired by the Reggio Emilia approach to preschool education.

Demographics

The students in PACE (Parent and Child Education) Preschool at Maldonado school in Tucson, Arizona, are 93 percent Hispanic; 45 percent are English language learners; 100 percent of the student qualify for free and reduced meals as established in the guidelines of the USDA Child Nutrition Program.

Chapter	Page	Topic	Title	Length
How to Use This Resource	xix	N/A	Introduction	1:31

Chapter	Page	Topic	Title	Length
2	22	Small Group Time	2.1: Sorting Various Colored Buttons 	1:43
2	24	Small Group Time	2.2: Sorting White Buttons 	1:15
2	26	Small Group Time	2.3: Sorting Nuts and Bolts 	1:12
4	58	Circle Time	4.1: How Old Are You? 	:22
5	64	Assessment Opportunities	5.1: Mason Counts Rocks (age 3 years, 10 months) 	1:30

continued

Chapter	Page	Topic	Title	Length
5	67	Assessment Opportunities	5.2: Imanol Counts Rocks (age 4 years, 9 months)	1:11
5	69	Assessment Opportunities	5.3: Danitza Counts Rocks (age 5 years, 5 months)	1:57
5	71	Assessment Opportunities	5.4: Counting Practice During Snack Time	:44
5	72	Assessment Opportunities	5.5: Isabella Counts Rocks (age 4 years, 10 months)	2:00
5	75	Assessment Opportunities	5.6: Jenny Counts Rocks (age 4 years, 9 months)	1:34

Chapter	Page	Topic	Title	Length
5	77	Assessment Opportunities	5.7: Michael Counts Rocks and Cubes (age 5 years, 6 months) 	2:05
5	81	Assessment Opportunities	5.8: Mia Counts Rocks and Cubes (age 5 years, 7 months) 	4:20
5	85	Assessment Opportunities	5.9: Sendes Counts Rocks in Spanish (age 5 years, 7 months) 	2:15
5	89	Assessment Opportunities	5.10: Abbie Counts Rocks (age 5 years, 8 months) 	2:10
5	91	Assessment Opportunities	5.11: Abbie Plays the Hiding Game (age 5 years, 8 months) 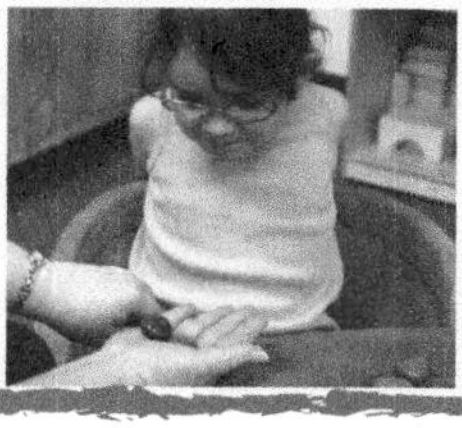	1:26

continued

Chapter	Page	Topic	Title	Length
6	102	Circle Time	6.1: The Counting Song 	:54
7	116	Circle Time	7.1: Counting Beads on the Bead Board 	1:44
7	133	Small Group Time	7.2: Counting Snack Cups and Snacks 	1:48
7	138	Choice Time	7.3: Taking Surveys 	2:49
8	149	Circle Time	8.1: How Many Are *Not* Here Today? 	2:54

Chapter	Page	Topic	Title	Length
8	153	Circle Time	8.2: How Many Are Here Today? 	1:09
8	165	Circle Time	8.3: Do You Have an A in Your Name? 	3:03
9	211	Small Group Time	9.1: Exploring Shapes Using a Light Table 	3:53
9	243	Choice Time	9.2: Building with Blocks 	3:22
10	285	Choice Time	10.1: Dramatic Play in the Hospital 	1:56

Mathematics is a participant sport. Children must play it frequently to become good at it. They do need frequent modeling of correct performance, discussion about the concepts involved, and frequent feedback about their performance. Both modeling and feedback can come from other students as well as from adults, and feedback also sometimes comes from the situation. All children must have sustained and frequent times in which they themselves enact the core mathematical content and talk about what they are doing and why they are doing it. In mathematics learning, effort creates ability.

—National Research Council's Early Childhood Math Report

How to Use This Resource

To view the clip, scan the QR code or visit mathsolutions.com/TEACHPKintro

Watch the video clip "Introduction." Talk with a friend or colleague; what do you see in the introduction that makes you the most excited about *Teaching Preschool and Kindergarten Math*?

Why This Resource?

We designed this resource to support the efforts of teachers, supervisors, program coordinators, and private/in-home caregivers in creating a more focused, successful mathematics program across and within early childhood classrooms while simultaneously deepening their understanding of the mathematical ideas that need to be developed at an early age.

As teachers of young children for more than fifty years combined, we have studied the needs and interests of three-, four-, and five-year-olds. This resource reflects the best of our studies, featuring lessons, math talk ideas, investigations, formative assessment opportunities, routines, insights concerning student misconceptions, research-based strategies, and more. We use video clips, classroom stories, photos, student work samples, and teacher reflections to share student learning. The 26 video clips were filmed in an actual early childhood classroom, giving you the unique opportunity to see these practices in action with young learners.

We know that high-quality preschool education is crucial for all students. Unfortunately, there exists a well-documented gap in mathematical knowledge within the group of children first coming to school. This gap in mathematical knowledge not only applies to preschool children; in our many conversations with our preschool and early childhood colleagues we hear teachers lament their lack of mathematical content knowledge and the lack of mathematical professional development available to early childhood teachers. We intend for this resource to facilitate change for all involved.

We believe that a rich and focused early childhood program is fundamental to children's success in their future studies. We hope to deepen teachers' understanding of the mathematical ideas that they are teaching. We want teachers to engage their students in mathematical talk that demonstrates what children are learning. We want young children to use their voice to share their thinking, their mathematical ideas, and their growth over time. We believe that all children bring to their learning awareness, competence, capability, and a potential for learning. They have their own theories about why and how things happen, and they are curious about their world. We also know that children learn in many different ways. Children are visual, tactile, kinesthetic, and/or auditory learners. Some children see things geometrically; others see things numerically. This resource shares ways we have found to help all kinds of learners make sense of the mathematics in their world.

Teaching Insight

Instead of Cut-Outs

We want early childhood teachers to understand that young children are willing and excited about interacting with math. We know that young children do not learn mathematics through pencil/paper tasks or worksheets. Neither do teachers have to buy cute counting objects or spend tons of time cutting out charming figures. Instead of cut-out monkeys, we suggest teachers use connecting cubes to represent monkeys—children will then be engaged in symbolic play much like they will be when they learn that numerals represent quantities. Remember: Young children are very competent! They also have wonderful imaginations.

Connections to Curricula

There are numerous preschool curricula on the market. Most have curricular themes that are interesting to young children: school, family, community, animals, and nature. Most have a strong emphasis on literacy, oral language development, and learning about school skills and behaviors. What we believe is largely missing from these programs is an in-depth focus on the essential mathematics that needs to be experienced in the early grades. The Common Core Standards, while not specifically addressing preschool, describe *Standards for Mathematical Practice* that have guided us in writing this resource. It is our hope that teachers with one of the popular preschool curricula already in place at their schools will turn to this resource and these practices, to enhance and make more focused the work they are doing in developing mathematical thinking and math conversations with their students.

Why Young Children Inspire Us

People who work with children in the early years are familiar with the poignant and amusing things that young children say and do. Children during these years find all sorts of ways to play with most any object, from a box to a stick. As teachers of young children, we are inspired by their notions and behaviors.

We are charmed by the young children who cover their eyes while playing peek-a-boo and honestly think that we cannot see them because they cannot see us. They have a strong sense of themselves.

We admire the child who comes to school wearing a superhero cape and stays in character throughout the entire school day. This child has an imagination that can serve her well as she negotiates challenges throughout the day.

We respect the imagination of the child who climbs inside a washing machine box and transforms it into a bear cave. He makes connections between his world and the world of the animals he is learning about.

We understand the significance of counting when we hear how a child who loves to count will show you five fingers for how old she is. She proudly associates her age with counting, as Gabi does in Video Clip 4.1.

We have also seen how young children cannot make sense of numbers without a meaningful context. Consider this dialogue between the teacher, Brenda, and four-year-old Maybaleve:

Brenda: *How many is four and one more?*

Maybaleve: *Six.*

Brenda: *How many is four balloons and one more?*

Maybaleve: *Five.*

Brenda: *How many is four dogs and one more?*

Maybaleve: *Five.*

Brenda: *How many is four candies and one more?*

Maybaleve: *Five.*

Brenda: *So how many is four and one more?*

Maybaleve: *Ten.*

The young child can make sense of *one more* with a context, yet makes no sense at all of the same numbers when there is no context.

Because of these special perspectives about young children, and because of the importance of the role of mathematics in their future lives, we were inspired to create this resource.

"Everything around us can be better understood with mathematics. Preschool is a good time for children to become interested in counting, sorting, building shapes, measuring, and estimating."
—Clements (1999)

Five Steps to Getting the Most from This Resource

1. Read "Why This Resource?" It only takes fifteen minutes to do this. Congratulations! You're partway there.

2. Observe mathematics in an early childhood classroom. Use the questions outlined in Reproducible A, Observation Questions: Mathematics in an Early Childhood Classroom. If you are a teacher, think about these questions as they apply to your own classroom.

   Become familiar with how this resource is organized (see pages xxiii–xxvi). We recommend you start with Section I and proceed next to Section II and then to Section III. We have tried to build ideas about how children typically develop mathematical thinking beginning with looking at real objects, then seeing the need to count them, and eventually looking for relationships in their world.

See Reproducible A.

3. Pay special attention to the series of *Learning Progressions* reproducibles (Reproducibles C1–C7). Take a moment to look them over before exploring the ideas within the chapters. These reproducibles will help you observe and assess children's thinking and learning.

See Reproducibles C1–C7.

4. Read, watch, and reflect. Read the chapters. Watch the video clips as they come up in each chapter. Continually reflect on the observations you made in Step 2.
5. Put the practices in this resource into use. Give yourself and your colleagues time. Determine a date to check back in with your observations. Revisit your responses to the observations questions—are you seeing change? Let us know. Email us at info@mathsolutions.com.

How This Resource Is Organized

This resource is divided into three sections: Young Children's Mathematical Ideas: Getting Started; Understanding How Young Children Count; and Developing Young Children's Number Sense. For maximum benefit, we suggest reading the sections in order because they build on one another. Each section is divided into topic-specific chapters. The chapters offer an abundance of lessons, math talk ideas, investigations, formative assessment opportunities, routines, insights concerning student misconceptions, research-based strategies, classroom stories, and more. Each chapter adheres to similar friendly elements as follows.

Connections to the Video Clips

The accompanying video clips are a look at early childhood math experiences. Brenda Mercado, author and preschool teacher, takes educators into her classroom in PACE (Parent And Child Education) Preschool in Amelia Maldonado Elementary School for a *seeing is believing* look at young children experiencing math. The clips have been chosen to help readers think about what the actions and words of children might mean in their development as young mathematicians. Throughout the book, a play button icon appears when there is a corresponding video clip. The video clips are organized by chapter and by topic (Circle Time, Small Group Time, Choice Time, and Assessment Opportunities).

Reproducibles

The Reproducibles

Whenever possible, we include reproducibles to facilitate the implementation of the suggested ideas and activities. When a corresponding reproducible is included, it is noted with an icon. Pay special attention to the series of *Learning Progressions* reproducibles (Reproducibles C1–C7). Take a moment to look them over before exploring the ideas within the chapters.

Math Talk

At the heart of this resource is an emphasis on promoting and supporting student *math talk* in various settings. Chapter 1 is devoted to math talk, *Math Talk* sections in every chapter highlight definitions, suggestions, learning scenarios, and math content for supporting math talk in early childhood classrooms.

A Child's Mind

This resource informs teachers about common student errors and/or misconceptions so they can teach more purposefully. Teachers need to think about what goes on in a child's mind and then find ways to address how the child reasons. These reflections are highlighted throughout so that you can easily refer to them time and time again.

Teaching Insights

Throughout the chapters we share insights that we feel will be especially helpful to teachers in managing their classrooms and/or successfully implementing the activities and lessons. We include explanations of key math manipulatives from pattern blocks to connecting cubes, and share our best practices in managing classroom space, from the studio to the light table.

Literature Connections

Children's literature brings another voice, or part of the outside world, into classrooms. Because children are naturally drawn to books and stories, we provide numerous ideas for using these resources. Reproducible D is a bibliography of children's books that support mathematical thinking.

Home/School Connections

Since the child's world is broader than the classroom, we want to help teachers, supervisors, and program developers extend the classroom learning to the child's home and neighborhood. We are careful to include how teachers can do this, and support family efforts in helping children become mathematical problem solvers. Although there is mathematics in everyday life, parents and caregivers may not know how they are supporting it every day. We hope to encourage family efforts by sharing with them things they are already doing that help develop mathematical thinking. We also share documentation of what the child can do with families so they can celebrate the child's progress.

Key to Additional Icons

The National Academy Press report stresses "children need a great deal of practice doing a task, even after they can do it correctly." This kind of meaningful practice will lead to fluency and confidence. For this reason, we offer an abundance of learning opportunities throughout this resource. The learning opportunities are identified by the following icons (key features of an early childhood curriculum). These learning opportunities are also in Quick-Reference Lists at the end of this resource. Each list features the opportunities by type as another user-friendly way to access them.

Circle Time Circle Time, an activity for large groups of children, has been around for about a century. Every individual in a circle is equal and belongs to the whole group. Each member of the circle can see and hear every other member of the circle. Children express feelings and ideas to the whole group, take turns listening and speaking, and listen to stories or participate in songs and games.

Teachers use Circle Time when they want to share something with the entire group. It is difficult for young children to listen and focus for long periods of time, so these Circle Time activities are kept short and lively. Often during Circle Time we ask children to share their ideas about interesting mathematical ideas and problems. We ask them to share their strategies so other children can hear. These conversations act as sources of knowledge for the children who are listening.

Small Group Time In Small Group Time, groups of four to six children move through rotations until eventually all children have the opportunity to complete a task or receive specific instruction. The activities are planned and either teacher-directed or teacher-supported. Teachers may slightly alter the instruction to meet the needs of each small group, knowing that some children may complete an activity and move on to another activity, while other children may need teacher support. This is not a rigid use of time. Sometimes students in one group "finish" the activity and move on to their choice activity. In the same time, some students may need more time within the supportive environment with the teacher to complete the task.

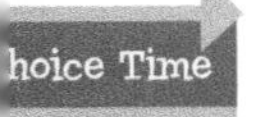

Choice Time Choice Time is an opportunity for children to choose where they want to work. There are usually areas of the classroom designated for specific choice time purposes: the writing area, block area, housekeeping area, studio, light table, reading nook, take-apart area, and science area, for example. (The Classroom Map on page 333 shows how Brenda's classroom is designed to accommodate Choice Time areas and more.) During Choice Time children are self-directed and often have particular preferences. Choice Time is one of the most important times of the day as we watch children negotiate, investigate, and experiment with their peers and materials. Their personal choices really matter to them. It is important for them to find a part of the day where they can truly make a personal choice about how they want to spend their time.

Teaching Insight

Using a Choice Board

Use a "choice board" to help children plan their choice time. Take photos of the areas in the classroom open for choice time. Place the photos in a column on the viewer's left side of a pocket chart. Ask each child to decide where he or she is going to go during choice time; the child then places his or her photo in the pocket chart, next to the corresponding classroom photo. A choice board helps deter children from wandering around, not knowing what to do during choice time—most importantly, when children make the choice they become invested in the activity. Children are welcome to make different choices during the time allotted.

Angelica places her photo on the choice board, next to the classroom area she has decided to go to during choice time.

Teaching Insight

Cleaning Up During Choice Time

It is important that children learn that they need to clean up their choice time area before they move on! Practicing moving from one choice activity to another needs to be part of the process for introducing this classroom procedure. Once children have practiced this, it becomes easier to manage.

A Note About the Research

There is clear documentation that high quality preschool education is important for all students (Espinosa 2002). Further, the emphasis and improvement of the mathematics education for our youngest and most needy children who first come to school is crucial (Bowman, Donovan, and Burns 2000).

Research supports the recommendations and practices in this resource. We draw particular inspiration from the NCTM and NAEYC Joint Publication *Curriculum Focal Points* and the National Research Council's Early Childhood Math Report that emphasize coordinated learning paths for children to move within and across the grades. These documents clarify for pre-K teachers how foundational and necessary it is for them to work more deeply on pre-K mathematics goals.

How to Access Online Video Clips

Readers have several options for accessing the video clips. Either scan the QR code (with a QR code reader app of your choice) that appears within the video clip section in the text or enter the corresponding URLs in your browser. To access all the clips at once, follow these instructions:

1. Go to mathsolutions.com/myvideos and click or tap the Create New Account button at the bottom of the Log In form.
2. Create an account, even if you have created one with the Math Solutions bookstore. You will receive a confirmation email when your account has been created.
3. Once your account has been created, you will be taken to the Product Registration page. Click Register on the product you would like to access (in this case, *Teaching Preschool and Kindergarten Math*).
4. Enter key code **TEACHPK** and click or tap the Submit Key Code button.
5. Click or tap the Complete Registration button.
6. To access videos at any time, visit your account page.

Key Code: TEACHPK

Section I

Young Children's Mathematical Ideas: Getting Started

Overview

This section explores what children understand about math ideas and bring to the classroom. We support the teacher in being able to view the big ideas from a child's point of view. Chapter 1 focuses on math talk, an essential for developing mathematical ideas. The suggestions shared in this chapter can and should be applied to every chapter in this resource and beyond to maximize discussion and exploration opportunities. Chapter 2 looks at collecting, sorting, and classifying. These collections lead to counting. These skills support children in exploring multiple ways to arrive at a solution. They encourage children to make generalizations, which are powerful mathematical ideas. Once children are able to notice differences and likenesses in materials we use in the classroom, we can begin to help them use that information to make patterns, which are explored in Chapter 3. Young children begin to think algebraically by exploring shapes, making their own patterns with a variety of materials, grouping things according to a rule, or noticing patterns they see in the environment.

Grace: Well, I know there's more here 'cuz yesterday there's four absent and today there's three absent, so there's more. I don't hafta count to know that.

Teacher: Can someone explain what Grace just said?

Daniela: She's talkin' about yesterday, but we're talkin' about today.

Teacher: Grace, would you tell us again about what you said?

Grace: We don't have four absent today, we have three. So there's more of us here today. I don't even hafta count to know it.

Teacher: I think you are right. Yesterday we had four absent and twelve were here, and today we have three absent and more are here.

Daniela: Let's count 'em.

Five Suggestions for Engaging Young Children in Math Talk

Chapter 1

Overview

In the dialogue on the opposite page, children are talking about meaningful events that happen during their daily school routines. The conversation reveals their thinking about mathematics in their lives. Because they talk about their attendance data every day, these girls are beginning to make connections between the results from one day to the next. The numbers are beginning to have relationship and meaning.

A crucial part of getting young children started with mathematical ideas is to engage them in mathematical talk. The authors of *Classroom Discussions* describe five reasons why talk is critical to teaching and learning:

1. Talk can reveal understanding and misunderstanding.
2. Talk supports robust learning by boosting memory.
3. Talk supports deeper reasoning.
4. Talk supports language development.
5. Talk supports development of social skills. (Anderson et al. 2011, xvii)

Early childhood teachers know from experience that young children learn best by doing and talking about what they are doing. However, teachers may not know how to establish productive conversations about mathematics. With a focus on early childhood, this chapter provides key suggestions for engaging children in math talk. These suggestions apply to everything in this resource. "Math Talk" special features further highlight the importance of mathematical conversations and the role of mathematics content learning in the development of the young child. Video clips show math talk in action in the classroom. We encourage you to think about math talk in everything you do in your early childhood mathematics curriculum.

Your Experiences with Math Talk

How can teachers encourage *math talk* (as well as other conversation) in the classroom? Think back to your own memories of math classes. Was talking about mathematics part of your experience? Many adults remember their math classes as being quiet, a time when children listened to the teacher, practiced procedures that the teacher showed them how to do, and demonstrated their understanding by filling in worksheets or responding to multiple-choice questions. In contrast, early childhood teachers know from experience that these strategies are not appropriate for young children. However, they may not know how to establish productive conversations about mathematics. Why do you think it may be difficult for teachers to find ways for children to do the talking instead of teachers doing it themselves?

Five Suggestions for Engaging Young Children in Math Talk

1. Create a stimulating environment through objects and tools.
2. Create a safe environment through routines.
3. Ask questions.
4. Make play situations learning opportunities.
5. Know the mathematical content.

Suggestion One: Create a Stimulating Environment Through Objects and Tools

For more on creating a stimulating environment through objects and tools, see Chapter 2, Sorting and Classifying and Chapter 10, the Dramatic Play section.

The environment is significant for mathematical learning. The physical and social environment itself in the classroom can become *another teacher.* A rich and stimulating environment increases the learning opportunities. Children are naturally curious and interested in learning when they are provided with a supportive physical and social environment. It is not sufficient to expose children to interesting materials by showing and telling. To engage in making meaning, children need opportunities to *show* what they know about mathematics and numbers through their play, language, drawings, and constructions. They also need the opportunity to converse with others in a classroom community where math talk is nurtured.

A rich physical environment has many objects and tools to capture the imagination of the child and stimulate discussion. See Video Clip 10.1, for example—in this clip we see children at play in a classroom hospital. The pretend play with dolls stimulates conversation.

See Video Clip 10.1.

Suggestion Two: Create a Safe Environment Through Routines

The classroom should not only be stimulating; it should also be a safe place for children. An environment in which children feel safe and comfortable is also an environment conducive to talk. One of the best means of creating this is through routines. Establish routines so children know the expectations and feel comfortable in their shared space. For example, children should know how to form a circle on the rug for whole group activities, how to put their photo on the pocket chart to select their choice time activity, where to find writing and drawing tools for their journals, how to use the restroom and wash up at the sink independently, and so on. See Video Clip 7.2, Counting Snack Cups and Snacks and Video Clip 8.2, How Many Are *Not* Here Today? for filmed examples of routines in action in Brenda's classroom.

See Video Clips 7.2 and 8.2.

Suggestion Three: Ask Questions

The teacher has an essential role in promoting math talk. Ask questions and listen with full attention to student responses. Make eye contact with children and get down on the child's level to speak with them. Keep the following in mind as you engage in conversation with children.

Encouraging Conversations with Children

1. Ask questions that require more than one-word answers.
2. Use the expansion technique.
3. Make comments.

Ask Questions That Require More Than One-Word Answers

Your questions should encourage children to explain their thinking. Ask, "How should we make sure the bears have enough space for their beds?" "Why do you think those blocks make the best boat?" "What ways could you sort these buttons?" Children's explanations give a window into their thinking. These conversations in turn provide formative assessment opportunities throughout the day. For example, use the story "Goldilocks and the Three Bears" and have children sort bowls, spoons, and chairs for the mommy, daddy, and baby bear. Ask children to tell you why they decided the baby bear should have the smallest bowl. Record your observations of how children used length, weight, and volume to sort objects (see Reproducible C3, Learning Progressions: Early Childhood/Measurement).

See Chapter 8, *Three Bears Sort and Compare.*

See Reproducible C3.

There are often different ways to explain the same idea. Encourage adults and children to look at multiple ways to think about problems, and learn multiple strategies that can be used to solve problems. When children are describing how to make sure they have half of a lemon for their lemonade recipe (see the activity, *What Is Half?* in Chapter 10), they present different explanations about how halves are a fair and equal way to divide one lemon for two people. This information helps us with the child's understanding of equivalent shapes and amounts. (Use Reproducible C7, Learning Progressions: Early Childhood/Geometric and Spatial Thinking to record your observations.)

See Chapter 10, *What Is Half?*

See Reproducible C7.

Use the Expansion Technique

One way to encourage a child to talk about something in class is to acknowledge and repeat what the child is saying, but add just a bit more information to what the child said. For example, if the child says *de* for *three,* and the teacher knows that the child is counting, she can say, "Oh, do you see three stones?" This will provide additional information about how to pronounce the word *three*, as well as demonstrate a question. This technique is known as *expansion.* When Marcos explained that sometimes his name is long and sometimes it's short during the *How Long Is Your Name?* activity (see Chapter 8), the teacher expanded with an additional example where his name is also the same length as Josiah, so his name can be long or short or equal in length!

See Chapter 8, *How Long Is Your Name?*

Phrases That Encourage Conversation with Children and Let Them Know You Are Listening

"I see."

"Oh."

"Mm hmmm."

"How about that!"

"Really?"

"Tell me more."

"Say that again. I want to be sure I understand you."

"No kidding."

"That's interesting."

Math Talk

English Language Learners

Children who are learning English as a second language need multiple opportunities in everyday contexts to practice English and build their vocabularies. By talking and explaining, not just by listening and watching, English language learners build an academic vocabulary. When the teacher interacts with children in contexts where the language is comprehensible, children take advantage of the English being modeled and incorporate new language into their own speech. This occurs seamlessly when conversations are thoughtfully encouraged and valued. Children also learn language effectively when the need arises in conversation with their peers.

Make Comments

Another way to encourage conversation is to comment on or describe what you are doing or what the child is doing, while the event or activity is happening. It is helpful to keep sentences short for toddlers or preschoolers who are speaking in phrases, and to use single words or two-word phrases for children who are just beginning to speak English as a second language. This is like narrating an event. For example, if a child is building something with blocks, the teacher might simply comment, "It's tall. You are being careful. It has a window. I see inside." A more expanded narration could be "I notice that you are being really careful about how you are building that tower. I think you are trying to build it so it won't fall over."

The goal is to try to understand, accept, and appreciate what the child says and does. Instead of correcting the child's speech, restate the words that the child is saying and expand on the thought; this provides a model for the child. For example, in Brenda's classroom when Jackeline was playing in the casita (house), she was singing a little song to the baby doll as she rocked her in the rocking chair. Brenda commented to Jackeline, "I can see that you are the mommy and that is your baby. She seems very sleepy." Jackeline replied, "She tired, but I help her sleep." Brenda restated, "She likes it when you sing to her. It helps her go to sleep."

Note that some children are just learning how to pronounce words, which will develop over time. It is important to listen carefully to what children are saying. They will appreciate an attentive audience.

Suggestion Four: Make Play Situations Learning Opportunities

Pay attention to children's play and find ways to use the play situation to create a learning opportunity, thus encouraging math talk. When a child is playing with a car, ask, "How fast can it go? Do you think we can make a ramp for the car?" When a child is building with blocks, make observations: "Gosh, that tower is as tall as your shoulder." Consider comparing two towers and asking, "What can we do so the towers match each other? Then they would be the same or equal."

Brenda plays alongside the child in the casita (house) and pretends that she is visiting and has brought a hot dish today to share for lunch: "Hi amigos! I brought tacos to share. I can tell you the recipe and you can write it down if you want." She knows she has made an appropriate play connection when the child says the following day, "Will you come to my house again for lunch?" or "Let's play that tower game again."

Suggestion Five: Know the Mathematical Content

It becomes less of a challenge to extend the mathematical talk with children when teachers *know* the mathematics that they need to develop for future math learning. Familiarize yourself with mathematical ideas for the early years. (Reading this resource is an ideal first step!) If teachers know more about the content and how concepts build on each other, then they will better understand our role in helping children connect these mathematical ideas.

> For more on math talk, see the following Math Solutions' publications:
>
> *Classroom Discussions: Seeing Math Discourse in Action* by Nancy Canavan Anderson, Suzanne H. Chapin, and Catherine O'Connor
>
> *Show and Tell: Representing and Communicating Mathematical Ideas in K–2 Classrooms* by Linda Dacey and Rebeka Eston

Reflection Questions

1. How would you describe the math talk you use in your classroom? How do you encourage student response?
2. Think of a child who is reluctant to speak in class, but seems to be verbal outside of the classroom. What strategies might you try to encourage this child to talk more in class?
3. Think about the daily schedule in a particular classroom. What sort of balance is there between teacher talk, student talk, and student-to-student talk? Is each child's voice heard? Why or why not?
4. What sorts of social language skills do children need to have in order to participate actively in school? How do children learn these skills?
5. How can you encourage children to talk at home about what they are learning at school?
6. How can the language used in school be made comprehensible to second-language children?

These all gots holes in 'em so
they go together. These are pointy.
I like the pink ones.

—Delicia (sorting buttons)

Collecting, Sorting, and Classifying

Chapter 2

Overview

Collecting, sorting, and classifying are key to helping children develop mathematical ideas. Such skills support children in exploring multiple ways to arrive at a solution. They encourage children to make generalizations, which are powerful mathematical ideas. Children have an opportunity to talk about their thinking as well as show what they mean using objects, groups of classmates, ideas from stories, and artistic constructions. As they communicate their thinking, children see that their ideas make sense and are valued.

This chapter describes how teachers can use *stuff* to bring meaning to mathematical ideas. We explore the creation of collections—groups of items that become valuable tools for sorting and classifying in the classroom—and share ideas for a collection starter kit. We offer literature connections and activities that help children understand the concept of collections. We then move into sorting and classifying activities. To get children thinking about sorting and classifying, we believe that it's important to first present them with opportunities to justify their thinking and give a reason for their choice. Games can prompt children to think about and notice similarities and differences, as shown in several video clips of actual sorting games in an early childhood classroom.

Simple sorting and classification are fundamental concepts that help children to organize their thinking about the real world. Young children naturally find ways to make sense of things in their world by looking at all kinds of differences and similarities.
—Reys et al. 1995

Continued

Creating Collections for the Classroom

We begin our description and study of mathematics early childhood curriculum, as well as our school year, by thinking about collections of stuff. We want to surround children with collections of familiar and intriguing items that they can use as tools for play. Young children seem naturally drawn to the idea of making and playing with collections. Further, the things we choose to use are just, plain interesting. These objects can be used to tell a story; they become spaceships blasting to the moon, turtles jumping into a pond, and boats racing across a lake. When children are working with a rich variety of interesting objects, they begin to explain their ideas about the qualities, quantities, and attributes of the collections. Teachers can then use collections to establish a culture of math talk in the classroom.

For more about math talk, see Chapter 1, Five Suggestions for Engaging Young Children in Math Talk.

Collections: A Starter Set

It is helpful to have some (not all!) collections of objects already in place on the first days of school to encourage children's exploration (see A Collection Museum, page 15). We have provided a list to help you get started.

Collections: A Starter Set

- **Buttons.** Button collections are sometimes passed down in families (Ann has an extensive collection of vintage buttons that she got from her mother). They can also be found at thrift stores (Ann added to her mother's button collection by scouring thrift stores for more contemporary buttons).
- **Bread tags.** The plastic closures typically found on bread bags in supermarkets come in a variety of colors and shapes, some with text and some without.
- **Lids.** A wide assortment of containers, including toothpaste tubes, bottles, and margarine tubs, have lids in different sizes, colors, textures, materials (metal or plastic), and attachment types (screw top or snap-on, for example).
- **Nuts and bolts.** Nuts and bolts in various sizes, as well as many other small items from the hardware store, appeal to children who like to take things apart and put them together.
- **Items from nature.** Smooth pebbles, seashells, nuts, and seed pods make for great classroom collections—and don't require a trip to the store!

There are many other items that inspire classroom collections: keys, marbles, stamps, and mismatched sets of playing cards. In some early childhood classrooms these items are referred to as *beautiful stuff* (Topal and Gandini 1999). When children spend time in the classroom working with these kinds of items, we like to think we are also helping children make connections to the real world. We hope they will recognize the beauty and utility of everyday items in their world.

Teaching Insight

Sorting, Arranging, and Displaying Collections in the Classroom

One of our favorite ways to sort, arrange, and display collections of objects is to use transparent jars of different sizes and shapes. We like to use clear plastic or glass canisters with wide mouth openings to allow for easy access to the objects inside. We've found that peanut butter jars, spaghetti sauce jars, olive jars, and baby food jars work especially well. Sort the like items into the see-through containers and arrange them in rainbow order: red, orange, yellow, green, blue, indigo, and violet (we purposefully choose this arrangement because of the rainbow pattern predictability in nature). The various sized containers provoke thoughts about volume. The colors are beautiful, and the materials inside look inviting.

Collections of blue objects in Brenda's classroom

Introducing the Idea of Collections to Young Children

The following activity ideas, most of them for use during circle time, introduce and help children become familiar with the idea of collections.

For more activities to use in circle time, see Chapter 6, Using Counting Books, Rhymes, and Songs.

A Collection Museum

Many teachers likely feel that they should have everything in the classroom organized and ready for the first day of school. We've learned that it is better to have the space and materials evolve over the opening weeks and months of school, and purposefully introduce materials to children in a meaningful and organic way over time. One way to do this is to have a Collection Museum. This is a designated place for gradually displaying and introducing collections in the classroom. An ideal location for such a museum is near the door, where parents drop off their children. Display the jars (collections) on an eye-level shelf that will catch children's attention. Use the museum to gradually bring items into the classroom, putting them on display for investigation and study over a period of time instead of having the objects all present in the room on the first day of school. You'll also find that children form a special relationship with the materials they gather themselves and contribute to the class museum. Sometimes that relationship draws reluctant children into mathematical discussions and eventually into the *studio*.

For more on sorting in the studio, see page 29.

Teaching Insight

Children's Literature

Use children's literature to bring another voice, or part of the outside world, into your classroom. Children are naturally drawn to books and stories. Reproducible D lists children's literature books that we have found very helpful in supporting mathematical thinking.

Circle Time

Literature Connection

Hannah's Collections

One way of introducing students to the idea of collections is through the children's book *Hannah's Collections* by Marthe Jocelyn. Children identify with the story's main character, Hannah, who has a knack for collecting everything from barrettes and dolls to popsicle sticks and leaves. Since Hannah's room resembles a museum of collections, this book also helps introduce children to the concept of a Collection Museum. Make sure collections are on display in your classroom where all children can see them as you read about Hannah's dilemma and how she aims to solve it.

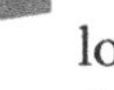

The Puddle Pail

The Puddle Pail by Elisa Kleven is another good introduction to collections. This book is about two crocodile brothers who set off for the beach. Sol, the older brother, loves to collect things while Ernst, the younger brother, loves to make things. Ernst decides to collect something too, but he can't decide what to collect. Ernst thinks about collecting clouds or stars or cookies.

See Reproducible D, Selected Bibliography of Children's Books for Supporting Mathematical Ideas.

However, Sol discourages him, saying those aren't things to be collected. Finally Ernst decides to collect puddles—but how?!

Donated Items

See Reproducible B, Letter to Families for Support in Creating Collections of Stuff.

Many classroom collections can be built from items donated by children's families. Print out and send home Reproducible B (see Figure 2.1) to each child's family. This letter explains the importance of collections in their child's development of mathematical ideas. (You might need to have this letter translated into various languages.)

When children first bring some of these items to class, ask them to help you find a place to store the objects. Most children are familiar with sorting spoons, knives, and forks in a silverware drawer at home; refer to this to help them with their sorting language. Some of the items that families donate might not fit in an already established category; in this case, create new categories or jumble the items together until there are enough to create a new collection.

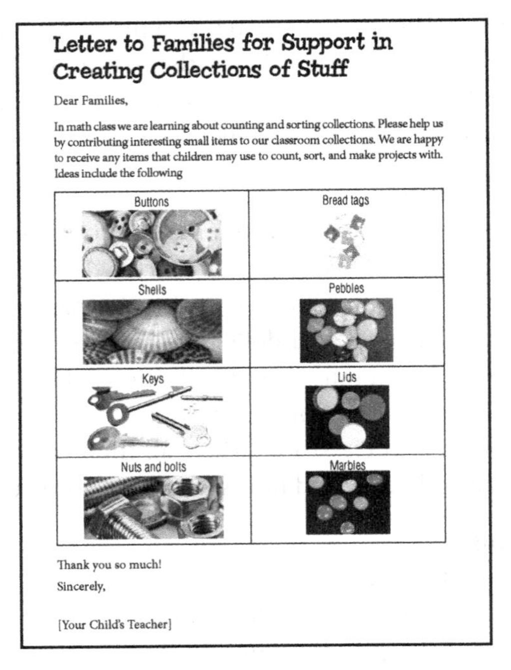

Letter to Families for Support in Creating Collections of Stuff

Dear Families,

In math class we are learning about counting and sorting collections. Please help us by contributing interesting small items to our classroom collections. We are happy to receive any items that children may use to count, sort, and make projects with. Ideas include the following

Buttons	Bread tags
Shells	Pebbles
Keys	Lids
Nuts and bolts	Marbles

Thank you so much!

Sincerely,

[Your Child's Teacher]

Figure 2.1 Sample letter to families for support in creating collections of stuff

Jumble items together until there are enough to create a new collection.

See also Sorting to Create New Collections, page 27.

Introducing the Idea of Sorting and Classifying to Young Children

Why sort things? We sort things in order to make sense of them. For example, in science we make categories of living and nonliving things, animals with and without backbones, and leaves with serrated and nonserrated edges. Geologists sort rocks by the way they have been formed. Mathematicians sort four-sided shapes into the category of quadrilaterals. Numbers can be sorted according to whether they are primes or composites, even or odd, negative or positive as well as many other attributes. We can sort objects and ideas using a Venn diagram. Since there are so many relationships in the world of mathematics, we have the challenge of making sense of this huge body of work. Sorting teaches young children about sizes, shapes, similarities, and differences. It promotes the use of different ways of looking at the same thing. Encouraging children to talk about how they sort things promotes math talk (see Chapter 1, Five Suggestions for Engaging Young Children in Math Talk). Children can also count what they sort.

See Chapter 1, Five Suggestions for Engaging Young Children in Math Talk.

Literature Connection

Would You Rather . . .

To get children thinking about sorting and classifying, we believe that it's important to first present them with opportunities to justify their thinking and give a reason for their choice. A wonderfully imaginative way to do this is through the Dr. Seuss classic *Would You Rather Be a Bullfrog?* in which children are faced with making dozens of decisions, from whether they'd want to be a dog or a cat to a bullfrog or a butterfly. The book naturally leads into a game; after reading it aloud to children, ask, "Would you rather be an elephant or an eagle?" Designate a side of the classroom for each response—for example, all children who would rather be an elephant stand on the left side; all children who would rather be an eagle stand on the right side. Ask children to tell each other why they decided to be an elephant or an eagle. Have them share their thoughts with the rest of the class. Children may reason:

> Eagles can fly and elephants can't.
>
> Elephants can pick up things with their trunks.
>
> Eagles have good eyes and can see far away.
>
> Elephants are strong.

Now pose a different question: "Would you rather be a fly or a spider?" Once again have children go to different sides of the room and talk with their group about their choice. This activity is especially valuable in helping children to justify their ideas and exercise their imaginations, as well as share factual information. Don't get discouraged if at first children have little to say. It is our experience that after children have played this game over a period of several days, they regularly ask for it, especially if the Dr. Seuss book is left on display near the rug area where children meet for Circle Time.

Math Talk

More Than One Right Answer

Playing the *Would You Rather . . .* game is often the first time children have been asked to justify their thinking and give a reason for their choice in a classroom setting. We believe it is important that there are opportunities for multiple correct answers instead of one right answer. In mathematics there may be multiple ways to arrive at an answer, and in some cases, there may be multiple solutions that are correct.

The Secret Club Game

This is a great game to get children thinking about and noticing similarities and differences in preparation for sorting and classifying activities. This game makes use of what children are wearing. It can be played in fifteen minutes. To start, the teacher picks an attribute of clothing worn by some children, and calls a few of the children with the attribute to stand in front of the class. Attributes can be such things as short sleeves, shirt collars, long pants, hoods, shoelaces, stripes, or colors. The teacher tells the rest of the class that the children standing are part of a secret club; the secret club has a rule about what all members must wear. Children must figure out what they have to wear to be in the Secret Club.

Marcos: *I think they have red on their shirts.*

Teacher: *Let's see, do they all have red? Wait, Carlos doesn't have red, so that can't be the secret. Who has another idea?*

Ana: *We have long pants.*

Teacher: *Does everyone in the club have long pants?*

Ana: *No, not everyone.*

Teacher: *I'll give you a hint. I'm looking at all the shoes.*

Ricardo: *I know! It's the laces.*

Teacher: *Does everyone in the Secret Club have laces?*

Ricardo: *Yes.*

Teacher: *You guessed it. Everyone in front of the classroom has laces—that was the Secret Club rule for this game.*

After children guess the attribute, explicitly point to it on each standing child to make clear that they all have the selected attribute. Help children determine who else might belong in the group besides the children selected.

The Secret Club Game: All these children are wearing boots.

For more game ideas on sorting and classifying attributes, see the lesson G-1 The Attribute Game in *How to Assess While You Teach Math: Formative Assessment Practices and Lessons* by Dana Islas (Scholastic 2011).

Emphasize that you want everyone to learn how to show they think they know *without* saying the attribute aloud. They can say, "I think Carlos belongs in the group [because he is wearing a shirt with stripes]."

Play another round of the game. When choosing a new attribute, try to select an attribute that includes children who were not chosen in the last round (children all want to be part of the Secret Club!). Make the game more challenging as the year goes on by choosing more subtle clues. Once children are familiar with the routine, ask each one to whisper his or her thinking regarding the rule to you; if the child's rule makes sense, have him or her help by choosing more children who follow the rule. Note that this game may take many rounds for all the children to understand how to play it.

Literature Connection

We Are All Alike . . . We Are All Different

To help get children thinking about similarities and differences in preparation for sorting and classifying, share the book *We Are All Alike . . . We Are All Different* by Cheltenham Elementary Kindergartners and Laura Dwight. This book is composed of dozens of portraits of children who have similar or different hair color, eye color, and so forth. The text reinforces diversity and ways to play sorting games.

Literature Connection

The Lost Button

The Caldecott award-winning children's book, *Frog and Toad Are Friends* by Arnold Lobel is another endearing resource for engaging children in thinking about sorting. See specifically the "Lost Button" chapter; Toad loses a button and sets out to find it with his friend Frog. The storyline encourages children to think about large and small buttons as well as the number of holes in buttons. The special project Toad ends up creating for Frog is likely to inspire children to create their own project.

The Sorting Game, Part I

To present sorting to the youngest children, start with an unsorted group of items such as shells, buttons, bread tags, lids, and small wooden blocks. Give children muffin tins, egg cartons, compartmentalized relish trays, deviled egg dishes, or clear plastic cups to facilitate sorting (we've also used velvet-flocked jewelry drawer trays and ice cube trays as sorting containers).

After children have sorted groups, tell them, "I want to make labels for these things. What can we call this group?"

Assessment Opportunity

Observe as children sort. Consider the following key questions and use Reproducible C5 to record your observations.

Key Questions

What does the student do?

What does the student notice? (color, etc.)

What items are children drawn to?

What does the student say about his or her sorting?

How does the student make use of the sorting containers?

See Reproducible C5, Learning Progressions: Early Childhood/Sorting and Classification.

The Sorting Game, Part 2

Once the idea of sorting objects has been established, focus on having children further sort a set of like objects. Consider the same kinds of questions as presented in "The Sorting Game, Part 1."

Use Reproducible C5, Learning Progressions: Early Childhood/Sorting and Classification, to record your observations of how children sorted.

These buttons are matched rather than sorted by attributes.

To view the clip, scan the QR code or visit **mathsolutions.com /TEACHPK21**

Video Clip 2.1: Sorting Various Colored Buttons

Delicia and Aracely sort pink buttons.

A Child's Mind

Sorting by Matching

Often young children will sort by matching rather than by individual attributes, thus creating a display of many different categories. Matching seems to come before the ability to sort.

In Video Clip 2.1, Brenda presents a collection of buttons to several children. The collection contains many colors, textures, shapes, and sizes. Brenda asks, "What are you going to collect?" The children decide to collect pink buttons. Brenda encourages someone to collect something different. Maybaleve says she will collect red with pink. After the children have collected their buttons, the teacher asks about their collections. Watch the clip. What questions does Brenda ask? What does each child collect?

What We Learned: When Maybaleve describes her collection she tells the color of each button instead of talking about her collection. It appears that Maybaleve has not yet figured out that her collection of buttons needs to share the same attribute. The other two girls have selected pink buttons, and they show pink on their clothing to justify why they have chosen this color button. Typically young children sort items by color and usually they persist in using color as the attribute of choice.

> **Teacher:** *(notices that Sofia is matching colors of buttons) Tell me how you have sorted these buttons.*
>
> **Sofia:** *(pointing to each group) Red, white, green, blue.*
>
> **Teacher:** *(shows a button that is both blue and white) What about this one?*
>
> **Sofia:** *Here. (Sofia indicates another group; teacher observes that Sofia has made a new category and continues to look at only the colors.)*

Brenda's Journal Page

Sorting Challenges

As the teacher, I seem to be having a hard time coming up with good questions for sorting. The children don't know the word *sort*. I've said, "How could we put these in groups so they are alike?" This doesn't seem to be useful. Maybe I should ask, "Which ones go together, or which ones are in the same family?" They can match objects easily, but they do not seem to be able to move to thinking about attributes. Maybe I should structure the sorting so fewer distractions are present?

Math Talk

English Language Learners

Identifying attributes of buttons as a way to sort them is often a challenge when English is the second language that children are speaking. When talking about buttons, the teacher may need to introduce a variety of button words using actual buttons to illustrate the words and then present a "mystery button challenge." For example, the teacher may explain and show buttons that depict the following:

These buttons are shiny.

These buttons have bumps.

These buttons are not round.

These buttons are colorful.

These buttons are soft.

The teacher then presents the *Mystery Button Challenge: Which button is not round and shiny?*

Later on the teacher might present a similar mystery for objects other than buttons (blocks, bread tags, or soft toys) to help English language learners become familiar with more descriptive words.

To view the clip, scan the QR code or visit **mathsolutions.com /TEACHPK22**

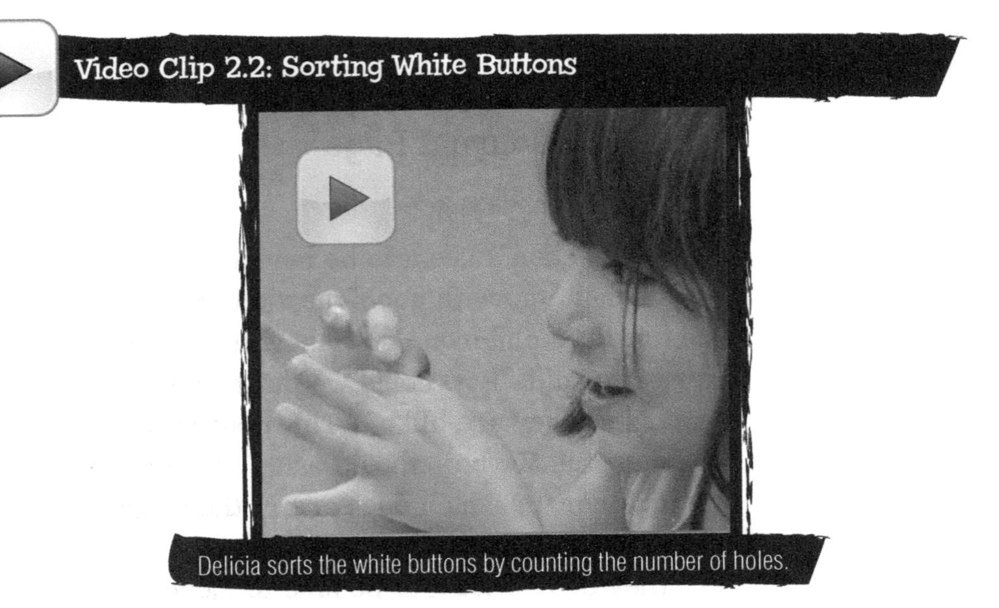

Delicia sorts the white buttons by counting the number of holes.

In Video Clip 2.2, Brenda wants the children to find a different way other than color (the attribute they habitually choose) to sort buttons, so she presents a collection of all white buttons. She guides the sorting investigation by asking children to place all buttons with four holes in one container and all buttons with two holes in another. Watch the clip. What do you observe about the children's sorting?

What We Learned: Although some of the children can tell which buttons have four holes and which have two just by looking, they do not seem to use this ability in this task. Instead, the children count each hole on each button, either because they need to count or because they think that this is a requirement for sorting. The teacher starts a set of buttons with two holes, but the children do not seem to add to it. Instead, they count four holes using other buttons in the tray.

Another Day: Sorting White Buttons

On another day, the teacher, Brenda wants to find out if Maybaleve can sort a variety of items in different ways rather than relying on using colors to discriminate. She helps Maybaleve sort the collection of white buttons by texture.

> **Brenda:** *How can you sort these buttons?*
>
> **Maybaleve:** *These are shiny. These are bumpy.*
>
> *Brenda decides to point out some different textures to see if Maybaleve has ideas about how to deal with them.*
>
> **Brenda:** *(pointing out a smooth button that has a matte finish) What should we do with this button?*
>
> **Maybaleve:** *That's not shiny, so I think it goes here. You know, it's not bumpy either.*
>
> **Brenda:** *So we can't put it with the bumpy ones or the shiny ones?*
>
> **Maybaleve:** *This one just doesn't go anywhere!*
>
> **Brenda:** *I think I agree with you. I wonder where we should put this one?*

Look to see what children will do with something that does not seem to belong in the group. When asking where such an item should go, encourage the child to explain her thinking; one of the goals of this experience is to have the child identify an attribute of an item and use it for sorting.

Assessment Opportunity

After the exchange with Maybaleve and the white buttons, Brenda recorded her observations using Reproducible C5, Learning Progressions: Early Childhood/Sorting and Classification. Brenda plans to find a way to do something similar with a different collection of items, perhaps with the lids (using all red lids, for example).

See Reproducible C5, Learning Progressions: Early Childhood/Sorting and Classification.

A Child's Mind

Modeling Thinking Strategies

To model how to sort, Brenda plays the sorting game alongside the children, thinking aloud as she sorts.

> **Brenda:** *Hmm, this one has little corners on it. I wonder if I can find some more with corners. Oh, here's another one with corners. I'm going to put these together. This one doesn't have corners, it's round. I think I'll put this one over here.*
>
> **Marcos:** *Here, Brenda, you can have this one for your corners.*
>
> **Brenda:** *Thank you, Marcos. Do you have any for my round pile? Oh, Marcos, maybe I have some for you. How are you sorting your buttons?*
>
> **Marcos:** *These are cowboy buttons.*
>
> **Brenda:** *Show me the cowboy part.*
>
> *Marcos points to the pearl snaps.*
>
> **Brenda:** *I don't have any cowboy buttons, but maybe someone else does.*

Brenda realizes that she never would have thought about cowboy buttons. To understand children, it is important to listen closely to what they say and think.

For more ideas using buttons as objects for collecting and sorting, see L-4 The Button Box in *How to Assess While You Teach Math* by Dana Islas (Scholastic 2011).

To view the clip, scan the QR code or visit **mathsolutions.com /TEACHPK23**

Video Clip 2.3: Sorting Nuts and Bolts

Children sort nuts and bolts in Brenda's classroom.

In Video Clip 2.3, Brenda shares a collection of nuts and bolts with a small group. She explains that they are going to sort the nuts, bolts, and washers in different ways, using a special tool (tweezers). Watch the clip. What do you notice about children making sense of sorting these items? What do you notice about children's mathematical thinking?

What We Learned: The special tool (tweezers) not only gives children practice with fine motor coordination but also serves as a great motivation to do this work. Interestingly, the children create a math moment out of this opportunity: they measure their tweezers using direct comparison. This investigation is of high interest; other children start to gather around the table to see what is happening.

Assessment Opportunity

After this investigation, Brenda recorded her observations using Reproducible C5, Learning Progressions: Early Childhood/Sorting and Classification. She is continually thinking about whether the children are making sense of sorting the items.

See Reproducible C5, Learning Progressions: Early Childhood/Sorting and Classification.

Sorting to Create New Collections

You'll likely receive a slew of objects from family donations (see the "Donated Items" activity, page 16). In sorting them out, you'll find that some objects don't fit in any of the designated categories/collections (we often encounter game pieces, broken toy parts, random plastic parts, and all kinds of natural items). Ask children to come up with new categories for these objects. Encourage them to explain their thinking. Some categories that children may come up with are: *things with holes, things with points, plastic junk, metal stuff, our red collection, our princess collection,* and *our wood collection.* These children are beginning to be able to use generalizations in their observations. They are coming up with attributes that make sense to them. These are the categories that they notice and also the ones that are interesting to them (the *hole* category and *princess* category, for example).

Math Talk

Generalizations

When children are encouraged to make *generalizations* about their observations, they are beginning to see that their ideas make sense and are valued and important. Children can generalize that buttons come in different shapes, sizes, and textures. A child can be shown the concept of *red* using a few toys. He generalizes this concept when he can identify anything that is red in his environment and know that it is red. Generalizations are very powerful mathematical ideas.

Sorting Our Names

This activity takes a more personalized approach to sorting. First have children make the letters in their names by gluing straws (for the straight-line segments) and yarn (for the curves) on squares of stock paper (one letter per square). Then have children sort the letters of their names into three groups: (1) straight letters, (2) letters with curves, and (3) letters with both straight and curved attributes. Children are most interested in this activity when they are sorting the letters in their own names. In addition, this activity helps them become familiar with how to write their names.

Jose separated the letters of his name into three groups based on straight/curved attributes.

Children working at a light table.

hoice Time

Sorting at the Light Table

Some items seem more interesting and engaging when examined and manipulated at a light table. We have a collection of multicolored glass beads, transparent shapes, silk scarves, colorful transparent picnic items, and manipulative shapes for the overhead projector that we present on the light table. Our students find many ways to organize these materials; we provide transparent trays with compartments.

For more on the use of light tables, see Chapter 9, Using Geometry and Spatial Skills to Build Number Sense.

hoice Time

Sorting in the Studio

A great way to get children to sort is through activities in the studio. The *studio* is a place in the classroom for children to make projects and express themselves using a variety of materials. In Brenda's classroom, paint, clay, different kinds of papers and cardboard, markers, crayons and color pencils, ribbon, sequins, yarn, and magazines are displayed near a large table (work area) in transparent containers, along with staplers, tape, scissors, hole punches, glue, clothespins, hand drills, screw drivers, and lots of newspaper and paper towels. It is important to have good light and plenty of room for work, and temporary storage as projects are set out to dry or wait for the next stage of completion. For a classroom map showing where the studio is in Brenda's classroom, see page 333.

A collection of washers, wire, and metal junk (plus a bicycle wheel!) that children turned into a sculpture.

Brenda received some interesting items donated from families that made for interesting studio challenges. She received a collection of washers, wire, and metal junk from broken appliances. Several children made metal and wire sculptures and then found a way to hang them on a bicycle wheel to finesse their masterpiece.

Teaching Insight

The Studio

This is a place for children to show their creativity and full potential as they make meaning of the world around them. As teachers we capitalize on the children's interests and provide support and resources that encourage them to show their understanding of the meaningful events in their lives. The studio provides the children with many, many materials sorted, organized, and made accessible for use.

Pablo works on his transformer in the studio.

We questioned the children and documented their work on the sculpture to share later with parents, providing insight on how their children were learning to describe their thinking. The constructions that evolve from studio activity are always imaginative and frequently involve all sorts of problem solving and measuring. Here's a sample of what children created out of the collection of washers, wire, and metal junk:

Roberto: *I made a remote controller with numbers and wire.*

Jose: *I made a tool to open stuff.*

Iliana: *I made curly hair with wire.*

Ricardo: *This machine can go on the moon.*

Math Talk

The Studio

Use studio time to document language and ideas that children use to express their thinking. Take photos of student projects and ask children to describe their work. Focus on documenting their thinking; use their words and listen for their math talk.

Pablo's transformer

Pablo made this transformer. He said it has three triangles that make it fly. He has switches to turn it on. He said it goes fast.

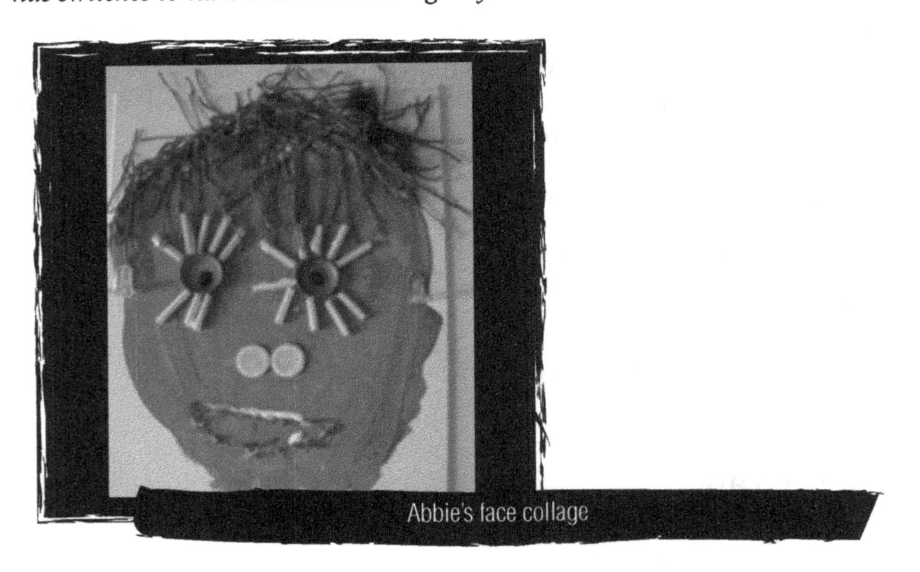

Abbie's face collage

Abbie said her face has two eyes and eighteen eyelashes. She said that next time she is going to make her mom's face and she is going to look like a queen.

Gabi works on a shapes collage in the studio.

Gabi said that her collage had messages for all of her friends. She wrote the words and names of all of her friends in the middle of the page.

Angel builds an airplane out of wood and used CDs in the studio.

Angel said that this is a face on the airplane. "The triangle is here. It is scary. This looks like vampire teeth."

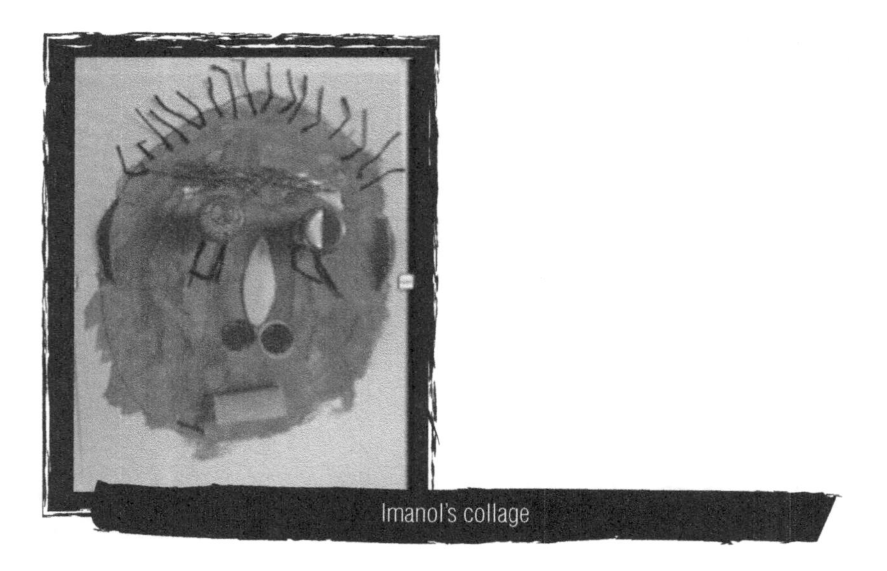
Imanol's collage

Imanol worked on a face collage. It has two eyes, a nose and a mouth. There are two ears and black hair. He said it looks like he does when he looks in the mirror.

Sorting During Cleanup Time

Cleanup time is another opportune moment for helping children learn what sorting is all about. Children like to have order in their lives. They appreciate knowing a routine and how to be independent in their classroom. Follow a predictable cleanup schedule and teach young children how to put away their things. Sorting and classification are part of this regular cleanup routine. When young children put away toys they are learning to sort, classify, match, and organize things. Silverware is sorted in a drawer, crayons are sorted by color, pattern blocks are placed in baskets with pattern block icons, and blocks are organized by size and shape. It's important to use picture and word labels to help them learn where things belong. When lots of small toys are used, provide transparent containers so children can see what is inside as well as read the labels.

Use cleanup time to encourage children to explain their thinking as well. Take a look at a mixed bin of items and chat about how to sort the items and how to label the containers. While cleaning up the room, talk about how

Cleanup time: Blocks are sorted on open low shelves according to shape.

everyone is cooperating to get the work done. To encourage math talk, ask questions, such as “Why do you think we put these things away like this? How can we sort these things? What should we do with these? Which ones go together?” Last but not least, always remember to appreciate the efforts of all the helpers!

Teaching Insight

Involving Children in Cleanup

Children can help keep the classroom tidy—and actually find it fun to put things away when they know where things belong. Sometimes it may seem like it would be easier if the teacher just put things away and did the messy chores like washing the tabletops. However, in the long run it is much better to share these chores with children, and enjoy with them the good feeling of doing a job well. Of course, we all learn ways to facilitate cleanup as we go along—we've learned, for example, the importance of assisting children in wringing out sponges so they're not too wet if we want the tables to get cleaner, not messier! Young children appreciate a thoughtfully arranged and organized environment. They learn that everyone appreciates it when they help with cleanup, too.

Home/School Connection: Cleanup Time

Parents tell us that the sorting and cleanup routines we do at school transfer to home habits, too. Families are often impressed when they hear us tell them how well their child is doing in developing responsibility and independence. They often note how the things in the classroom are labeled and organized and decide to adopt some of these ideas in their home environment.

Moving from Sorting and Classification to Counting

Moving from sorting and classification to counting can be a natural transition. When dealing with collections, embed counting in your observations and wonderings. For example, you might wonder aloud how many items are in a collection jar. Making labels and counting how many items are in each jar is a fun project that classifies and quantifies the beautiful stuff children have collected. In addition, the teacher can formatively assess where children are in their number concepts as they deal with their collections. If children are surrounded with a print-rich environment that makes sense to them, they will learn to read the words.

Literature Connection

Carlo Likes Counting

A great book to encourage the transition from sorting and classification to counting is *Carlo Likes Counting* by Jessica Spanyol. In this book, Carlo the giraffe is fascinated with groups of objects from one to ten. The groups are labeled with the name of the object and the number of items. Unlike other counting books, more than one group of items appears on each page, giving children multiple opportunities to count. Plenty of unlabeled items appear, too, for children to point out themselves.

For more on moving from sorting and classification to counting, read the next section, Section II: Understanding How Young Children Count.

Reflection Questions

1. What kinds of questions will help children think about different attributes of materials?
2. How can the youngest children learn about sorting and classification?
3. What organizational ideas can teachers use that will help facilitate student classification skills?
4. How can teachers take advantage of the sorting and classification that children already do at home? (Sorting laundry, silverware, pantry and refrigerator items, plates, cups, and pots and pans, etc.)
5. How can new sorting and classification vocabulary words be introduced to English language learners?
6. How can families help their children with sorting and classification? What do they need to know?

This is a black cat, pumpkin, black cat, pumpkin, black cat, pumpkin, black cat, pumpkin, black cat, pumpkin, black cat pattern. They're going to Halloween.

—Alexa describing the pattern she made out of cubes

Chapter 3

Patterning

Mathematically proficient students look closely to discern a pattern or structure.

—*Common Core Standards: Standards for Mathematical Practice*

Overview

Once children are able to notice differences and likenesses in materials we use in the classroom, we can begin to help them use that information to make patterns. Patterns are important to children's development of mathematical reasoning and communicating. Children need multiple opportunities to explore patterns now in order to make mathematical predictions and generalizations later on. This chapter includes ideas for introducing different types of patterns, from repeating to growing and shrinking. These kinds of patterns, which are frequently found in children's stories and poems, lead to algebraic thinking. The chapter includes suggestions for assessing children's understanding of patterns, and concludes with insights on transitioning from patterning to counting.

Introducing the Idea of Patterning to Young Children

When children notice, copy, and create patterns, they are beginning to see relationships that have a structure and make sense. Children can use their understanding of patterns to make predictions and generalizations. They will eventually be able to use their patterns to connect them to the number system. For example, when the number squares in the hundreds chart are colored with alternating white and red, every even number will be red. If they transfer an AAB pattern (red, red, green) to the hundreds chart, every multiple of three will be green. Even though teachers of young children are not working with a hundreds chart, odd and even numbers, or multiplication, they are laying the foundation for work that will come later in school.

Use Reproducible T: The Hundreds Chart and Reproducible L: Number Chart 1–20 as reference tools to explore these kinds of pattern ideas.

A Pattern Museum

Like the Collection Museum for introducing the idea of sorting to children (see Chapter 2, page 15), a Pattern Museum can introduce the idea of patterns. (You may need to move the Collection Museum to make room for the Pattern Museum.) Encourage children to add toys with patterns, flags, wallpaper pattern samples, and bead necklaces that have a pattern to the Pattern Museum. Take photos of children wearing patterns and display them in the museum. Children will enjoy discovering what has been newly added to this space.

When there are a few interesting objects and pictures in the Pattern Museum, have children represent them using connecting cubes. Children often do this spontaneously as they begin to recognize patterns. When a child makes the connection, bring the example to Circle Time to share. This sparks interest from other children. For example, children in Brenda's class noticed that Pablo's shirt had a pattern of blue and white stripes. During Circle Time they copied this pattern by connecting alternating cubes of white and blue. The entire group participated in suggesting how to do this.

When this activity is done during Small Group Time, children might also translate existing patterns from items in the Pattern Museum to a connecting cube pattern train in much the same way, only now the teacher can support children individually. In addition to Circle Time and Small Group Time, sometimes children will make patterns on their own during Choice Time and decide to place them in the Pattern Museum (see "Create Your Own Patterns" on page 45).

Since color is usually the attribute that children first notice, work with children to make repeating patterns with two different color cubes or counters.

Examples of Patterns That Can Be Represented by Connecting Cubes

Zebra pattern: white, black, white, black, white, black

King snake pattern: red, black, yellow, black, red, black, yellow, black

Tiger pattern: orange, black, orange, black, orange, black

Bee pattern: black, yellow, black, yellow, black, yellow

mall Group Time

oice Time

Repeating Patterns: Candy Canes Cubes

Bring in candy canes for the Pattern Museum in December. Hide a cube copy of the candy cane pattern in a rolled up tube of paper, and reveal one cube at a time. Tell children, "I made a candy cane pattern with these connecting cubes. Red, white, red, white, red, white; I wonder what comes next?" Have children chant the colors and predict the next color. Some children will likely be able to tell what the next color will be. Others will guess different colors. To continue the investigation, make connecting cube trains of different candy cane patterns and leave them in a basket of loose cubes to see if anyone shows interest in making these patterns on their own. Sorting out the colors sometimes prompts the children to copy patterns. A few children may begin to invent their own candy cane patterns.

Brenda's Journal Page

The Evens and Odds of a Candy Cane Pattern

Today I was looking at the red, white candy cane pattern and asked the children some questions about the number of cubes in a RWRWRWRWR train. This is the conversation I had with Ricardo:

continued

BRENDA: Do you think there are more red cubes, more white cubes or are there the same number of reds as whites?

RICARDO: There's more reds.

BRENDA: How do you know?

RICARDO: Because all the reds have partners and that one don't have a partner.

I was thinking that I would take the train apart and match up the colors to show that there were more red cubes than white cubes. Ricardo didn't need to see this demonstration, however, to know that each red cube had a white cube next to it, *except for the last one.* He is already learning something about how he can use the idea of a pattern to make sense of even and odd.

Growing Patterns: *The Very Hungry Caterpillar*

The Very Hungry Caterpillar by Eric Carle is a classic book that helps children learn about a different kind of pattern called a *growing pattern.* As you read the story (and any story with interesting patterns, for that matter), represent what is happening through cubes or other objects. For example, the story begins with a caterpillar eating one red apple; put one red cube out to represent the apple. Then the caterpillar eats two green pears; attach two green cubes to represent the pears. Next the caterpillar eats three purple plums; attach three purple cubes. The caterpillar then eats four strawberries (four red cubes) and finally five oranges (five orange cubes). This growing pattern is different from the repeating patterns that children have been creating.

Teaching Insight

Children's Literature and Patterns

In many of the books that children love to read, we find growing patterns: n, n + 1, n + 2, n + 3, and so forth. When teachers share counting books with children they are helping them develop understanding of growing patterns as well as repeating patterns. Be explicit about how something is growing by one more each time. See Chapter 6 for ideas and activities using some more of our favorite counting books.

See Chapter 6, Using Counting Books, Rhymes, and Songs, for ideas and activities using some more of our favorite counting books.

Literature Connection

Shrinking Patterns: *Five Little Speckled Frogs*

Another opportunity to act out a pattern is through reading the rhyming book, *Five Little Speckled Frogs* by Nikki Smith. In this delightful tale five frogs sit on a log, gulp bugs, and jump into a pool one by one. It is important to find a way for children to act out the story with their bodies, represent the same story with connecting cubes, and finally draw the patterns on paper. This is an example of a concrete, connecting, and abstract sequence of learning.

First read the entire story aloud. Then ask five children to sit in a row as if they are ready to jump into the pool (we use a blue hula hoop to represent the pool). Then ask, "How many green cubes will we need to represent these frogs?" Make a train of five green cubes for the five little frogs. Then begin to read the story aloud a second time. Students pretend they are frogs sitting on a hollow log, *eating the most delicious bugs, yum, yum.* One jumps into the pool. As one child jumps into the pool, place a blue cube (representing the pool) next to the five green cubes. Count how many frogs are left on the log. Say to the class, "Now there are four little speckled frogs. How many green cubes should we put next to the blue cube?" When one more frog jumps into the pool, place another blue cube next to the four green cubes and continue on in this fashion. At this point all the speckled frogs have jumped into the cool blue pool. Eventually the

Diego and Liana cross out frogs to show how some of the five frogs jump into the pool.

following pattern is created ("G" for green frog and "B" for blue pool): GGGGGBGGGGBGGGBGGBGB. This pattern decreases instead of increases, so we think of it as a *shrinking pattern.* Children may notice how the pattern is different from the growing or repeating patterns. Continue to play this frog game until everyone has had a turn to be a frog. You'll find that children delight in being frogs and doing the jumping! Extend the activity by having more children pretend to be frogs. Ask, "What if there were five speckled frogs and two frogs jump into the pool instead of one?"

For an expanded explanation and more ideas on using *Five Little Speckled Frogs*, see Lessons L-2 and P-1 in *How to Assess While You Teach Math: Formative Assessment Lessons and Practices* by Dana Islas (Scholastic, 2010). This resource also includes a video clip of the *Five Little Speckled Frogs* activity in action in a kindergarten classroom.

Clothes Patterns

Turn what children are wearing into learning opportunities for supporting the understanding of patterns. One day Brenda's class noticed that Pablo was wearing a shirt with alternating blue and white stripes. Pablo was asked to stand up and children read his shirt pattern by pointing to the stripes. Then Brenda made a copy of his pattern using the blue and white connecting cubes. The class called it Pablo's shirt pattern.

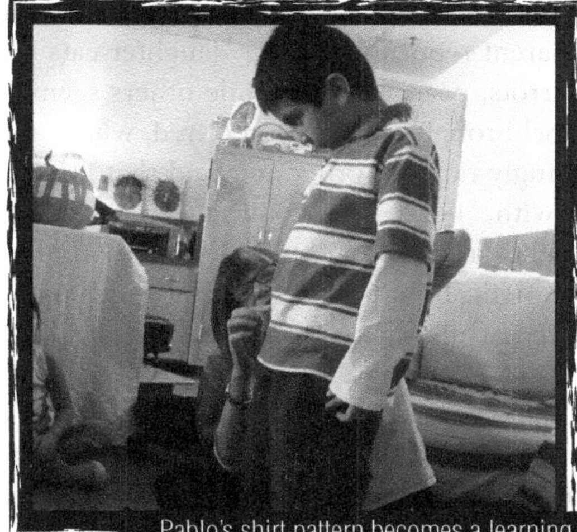

Pablo's shirt pattern becomes a learning opportunity for supporting the understanding of patterns.

People Patterns

Act out patterns by having children line up in boy, girl, boy, girl patterns, having children figure out whether a boy or a girl should line up next. Do the same thing with children standing, sitting, standing, or sitting in a pattern line. Since children are part of these patterns, they are more likely to stay engaged with the ideas. Use these people patterns to teach vocabulary as well as pattern recognition: hands on hips, hands on knees, etc.

For more ideas on having children become patterns, see the Lesson G-2 Guess My Pattern in *How to Assess While You Teach Math: Formative Assessment Practices and Lessons* by Dana Islas (Scholastic, 2010).

Create Your Own Patterns

Children need to realize that patterns are found all around us. Once they see that they can use patterns to predict what might come next in a story or a cube train, they might try to make some of their own patterns. To encourage this, first take something from the Pattern Museum and translate it into a connecting cube pattern. Do this as part of a teacher-supported small group time activity. Then sort connecting cubes into colors and let children create their own patterns. For inspiration, display patterns in the Pattern Museum that are composed of different color blocks, counting bears, buttons, and other materials. In addition to the Pattern Museum, consider placing baskets of connecting cubes and pattern blocks in various learning areas so children have multiple places to access them.

Some children catch on quickly to how to create their own patterns (and see patterns everywhere—one parent reported that her daughter eats her dinner using a pattern: peas, carrots, peas, carrots) while others seem to miss the point entirely. When Joel brought a collection of red, white, and green cubes arranged in a seemingly random order and said that it was a new pattern, Brenda responded with, "Please read your pattern to me." He correctly told her the colors in the order he had arranged them, and he seemed proud of his accomplishment. Brenda told him that she thought he had a very nice collection of red, white, and green cubes, but it wasn't a pattern *just yet*.

Alexa brought Brenda a bumble bee pattern train with yellow, black, yellow, black, yellow, black, black, yellow, black. Brenda asked Alexa to read the pattern and she did, not noticing that two black cubes were next to each other. Brenda responded with, "I think you have a trick hidden in your pattern. Do you see it?" Alexa was able to notice the two black cubes and quickly inserted a yellow cube between the black cubes. Many times children will show cube trains that are filled with all sorts of tricks, too!

Patterns made by children in Brenda's class using various objects.

Alexa creates an orange and black Halloween pattern out of cubes.

Imanol creates a repeating pattern out of heart candies.

Assessing Children's Understanding of Patterns

Finding ways to help children make sense of the patterns that they recognize and create is a challenge because children can be at so many different levels of understanding. Support each child's development by providing models of patterns for children to copy at the early stages. Then ask children to extend an existing pattern and make it longer. Begin with simple repeating patterns using only two colors and then ask children to copy and extend these.

Children who really understand an alternating blue, white, blue, white pattern can be challenged to translate this pattern from colors into some form of movement. *Let's clap for the blue cube. What movement should we do for the white cube? Wave?* Now the pattern becomes: clap, wave, clap, wave, clap, wave.

See Chapter 6, Using Counting Books, Rhymes, and Songs

We are also aware that when we share counting books with children we are helping them develop understanding of growth patterns as well as repeating patterns. We can be explicit about how something is growing by one more each time, or shrinking by one less each page. The following sections detail ideas for supporting the assessment of children's understanding of pattern.

Showcasing Children's Patterns

One way to support children in their conversations about patterns is to showcase, during Circle Time, a pattern a student has created. For example, when Alondra brought Brenda a repeating black and white zebra pattern, Brenda asked Alondra to read it to the class. Alondra did this by saying *night, snow, night, snow.* Then Brenda asked the class to study Alondra's pattern. Next Brenda put it behind her back, breaking it up into three sections. She handed it back to Alondra and asked her to choose a student who could *fix* the pattern like it was before. Alondra chose a friend to fix it and enjoyed helping her friend make it look *just right.*

Assessment Opportunity

Observe how children explain their ideas to their peers. Record children's patterning progress using Reproducible C6, Learning Progressions: Early Childhood/Pattern. Note which children can copy a pattern, which are able to continue a pattern, and which can create their own patterns.

Record children's pattern progress using Reproducible C6, Learning Progressions: Early Childhood/Pattern.

Math Talk

Describing Patterns

Adults classify repeating patterns by using symbolic notation such as AB or ABB to describe patterns. We usually begin our pattern work with simple AB patterns. Then we introduce AABB and ABB patterns. Children don't use these kinds of labels when they talk about their patterns. Instead, they use words to describe the patterns. So the brown and yellow pattern is called the chocolate banana pattern because that is what Sofia calls it when she shows it to us. The red and white candy cane pattern morphs into the hot lava, cold ice pattern when Marcos makes it with snap cubes. On another day Brenda models reading a pattern using the words mud, snow, mud, snow, instead of the colors brown and white. The children love it! If we want to expand on their math talk, we need to take advantage of their words and nudge them along using their interests. It is interesting to compare the kind of language that children use to describe their patterns. The rambunctious morning class chooses exciting words like *hot lava* and *blood* for the red cubes while the afternoon class chooses more calming descriptive words like *blue ocean* and *brown island.* When English language learners are reading their patterns using this kind of vivid language, they are trying out new labels and some new words that they are learning. It seems like it is a safe way for them to invent descriptive words to tell the class their pattern. When Diego, who didn't like to speak English in the whole group, read his pattern as lava, mud, lava, mud, he didn't have to speak very much English, but he was able to communicate his ideas to his classmates. These terms have much more meaning for children than the abstract AB language.

Brenda's Journal Page

Breaking Patterns into Periods

Today Alondra made a rhyming frog, frog, log, log pattern with green and brown cubes. Hugo, who makes a connecting cube train (but no pattern) every day, heard Alondra's rhyme and was determined to make a pattern. To help him (and others) visualize the repeating aspect of an AB pattern, I broke the trains into units—called periods—and showed the children how the cubes make stripes. The children agreed that the patterns we were making repeated the same colors again and again.

Hugo spent almost all of choice time working on making a pattern that repeated. He seems to go in and out of understanding. Children often are on the edge of understanding and seem to work very hard to make sense of what they're doing. It is so satisfying to break a pattern up into periods and see those stripes! Hugo was able to do this after chanting his words to himself: blood, guts, blood, guts.

Humberto and Nico made AB patterns using different colors. I decided to break the patterns into periods (two cubes) to show how they repeat. Both of these patterns resulted in stripes that were very clear. This seemed to help Hugo get the hang of a pattern.

continued

Amaya made an AAB that she read as kitty cat, kitty cat, princess. (The colors were brown, brown, pink.) I broke this pattern into groups of three for the periods and she loved seeing her pink stripe.

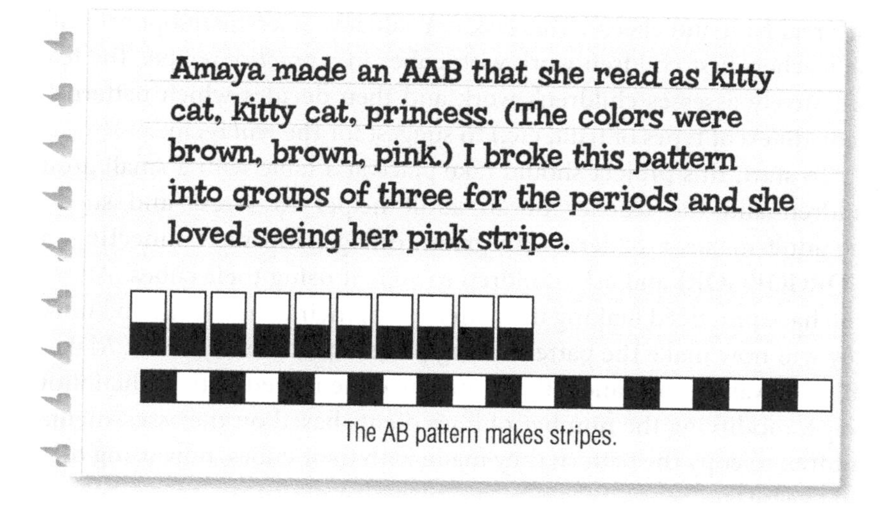

The AB pattern makes stripes.

Math Talk

Respecting a Child's Thinking

Children need many chances to show what they are learning and tell how the relationships they are building make sense to them (even if it doesn't make sense to adults!). Student misconceptions are windows into children's thinking. Misconceptions show us what makes sense for a child at that moment. This is a chance for the teacher to assess where the child is and make connections to where that child might grow. We can learn what children know by carefully watching, asking questions, and listening to them as they explore with materials. However, if the child feels like he is being tested, he will often change his answer if an adult asks a question about it. This shows a lack of confidence. For this reason, it is important to ask children to explain their thinking even when they have a *correct answer*. In order to grow confident in his own thinking, the child needs a chance to explain his thinking to someone who respects his thinking.

Pattern Snacks

The following pattern snack activity uses fruit and cheese to create a pattern. Because it is easier for children to copy a pattern that has already been established than it is for them to create one on their own, first have children copy a pattern of connecting cubes. This practice prepares children for working

Teaching Insight

Differentiating Instruction

Note that young children are much more able to copy a repeating two-color pattern than a three-color pattern. If the three-color pattern task seems too challenging, supply some alternate patterns that have only two of the items. (If there are taste preferences, some children may actually prefer to use only two of the three ingredients.)

For more ideas on using snack time to facilitate children's growth in counting, see Chapter 7 (Snack Time), Chapter 8 (Do You Like Green Eggs and Ham?, Which Juice Do You Prefer?, Which Apple Color Do You Like Best?, Which Cracker Shape Do You Like Best?), Chapter 10 (Recipes That Build Important Mathematical Ideas), and Video Clips 5.4 and 7.2.

with real fruit and cheese. This task is a valuable assessment opportunity for the teacher; first children work with cubes in a *practice* recipe. The teacher formatively assesses children's work and then decides which pattern (how many different types of fruit, etc.) to suggest for the *real* recipe.

To start, this project should take place at a table with a small group of children and the teacher or an adult helper to assess and supervise. The adult makes a pattern with green, orange, and red connecting cubes (GORGORGOR) and asks children to copy it using their cubes. After children have practiced making the pattern with their cubes, let them know that they will now make the pattern using pieces of fruit and cheese. Make sure children wash their hands; then introduce the ingredients in the following recipe, modifying the number of ingredients based on the assessment. Ask children to copy the pattern they made with their cubes, now using the fruit and cheese.

Fruit and Cheese Kabobs

Ingredients:

honeydew melon chunks (green)

reduced-fat cheddar cheese cubes (orange)

fresh strawberries (red)

Directions:

Thread fruit and cheese onto small skewers. Place on a flat storage container and chill until serving time (or up to 24 hours).

Assessment Opportunity

Record children's patterning progress using Reproducible C6, Learning Progressions: Early Childhood/Pattern. Note which children can copy a pattern, which are able to continue a pattern, and which children can create their own patterns.

Moving from Patterning to Counting

See Reproducible C6, Learning Progressions: Early Childhood/Pattern.

Over time we had a whole collection of connecting cube pattern trains in our Pattern Museum. Some were made with ten cubes, alternating two colors, and others were much longer. Children commented on how long some of the trains were. It became a logical step to count and find out how many connecting cubes were in the longest train, as well as how many of each color were in the longest train. We have found that children are interested in counting because they want to find out how many there are in their collection or pattern. Counting these connecting cube trains gave us an opportunity to think about not only counting, but also (nonstandard) measurement of length. Children began to compare the length of these pattern trains and this let us know that measurement was also on the horizon.

We have found that children are interested in counting things that they care about because they want to find out how many there are in their collection or pattern. They are not particularly interested in counting how many pencils or crayons we have because it seems like we have enough of these items. On the other hand, we have very few silver markers and highlighters, so these items have been carefully counted!

See Section II, Understanding How Young Children Count, for more on counting.

Reflection Questions

1. How can you integrate patterns into the work that children do in other subject areas?
2. What mathematical language is important for children to know and use in describing patterns?
3. Describe the difference between growing and repeating patterns.
4. How do children make sense of patterns and use them to make predictions?
5. Where are some repeating patterns found in the real world? How can you bring that real-world application into the early childhood classroom?

Section II

Understanding How Young Children Count

Overview

How do children go about counting? This section supports the understanding of counting—what children bring to the classroom, how counting is developed, and how the teacher can foster counting. Chapter 4 highlights research about this topic. Children first learn to say numbers in order and then learn number word meanings. Chapter 5 presents a series of video clips featuring preschool children counting in one-on-one assessments. Chapters 6 and 7 move into the classroom, exploring ideas for using books, songs, and other counting visuals—dot images, rekenreks, bead boards, counting bags, games, snacks, and surveys—to support children's development of their counting abilities. As children spend more time connecting number names to the real things in their world, their understanding of the meaning and utility of number grows.

I know it's three 'cuz I used to be three and that's this many. (He shows three fingers.)

—Humberto

Chapter 4

Connecting with the Research: Counting

Overview

This chapter highlights research important to an understanding of counting in early childhood. This research also addresses common misconceptions about counting. We encourage you to continually reflect on the findings in this chapter and connect them to what you see happening in the video clips in Chapters 4, 5, and 6.

Is Counting Simple?

To view the clip, scan the QR code or visit **mathsolutions.com/ TEACHPK41**

Gabi is asked, "How old are you?"

Have you ever heard someone say that counting is simple? Based on your experience with children, how true is this statement? Watch Video Clip 4.1, in which young children introduce themselves and their age. What does Gabi do differently when it comes to telling her age? Why do you think this is?

What We Learned: When Gabi tells her age, she uses her fingers to show how old she is. She counts up from one to five to tell her age. It is clear that she proudly associates her age with counting. We think this shows us that she knows there is a connection with the number of fingers she is holding up and her age. What we do not know from this clip is if she knows how many fingers she is holding up. Learning to use numbers and counting to tell what we know can be complicated!

Brenda's Journal Page

How Three Children Use Fingers to Talk About Number

In March we visited our grandchildren. I asked our youngest grandson, "Liam, mijito, tell Nana how old you are now." Enthusiastically he showed me two fingers.

When Jackeline arrived at our preschool on the first day, I asked her, "Jackeline, how old are you?" Shyly she showed me four fingers. "How many is that Jackeline?" Jackeline shrugged her shoulders.

A week later Josiah proudly walked into the classroom and announced he was five and confidently displayed five fingers.

For more insights on how young children use their fingers to talk about number, see Video Clip 6.1, The Counting Song in Chapter 6.

The Big Ideas of Counting

A great deal of research has been devoted to the topic of counting. Following are insights from the field. Read each research insight and reflect on it. Discuss with others what it means to you.

Research Insights

1. Counting can be thought of as an attribute of a set of objects in our collections. This attribute, however, is an abstract quality, and that helps explain why children use number as a category later than they use physical properties, such as color. They may only gradually see the equality of collections that have increasingly different appearances (Mix, Levine, and Huttenlocher 2001).

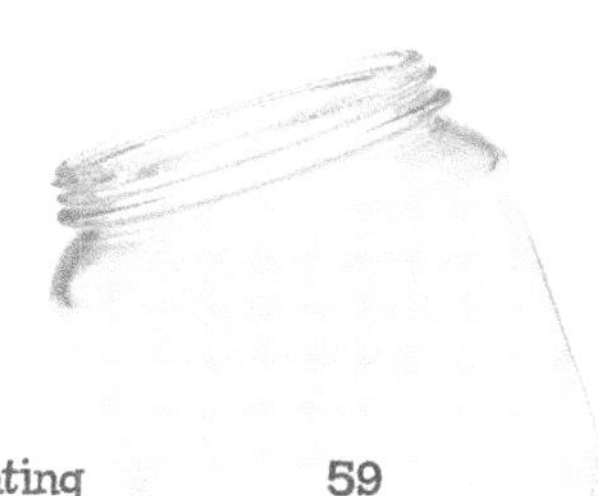

2. Counting is part of observing. Children as young as two years of age can confidently identify one, two, or three objects before they can actually count with understanding (Gelman and Gallistel 1978). This ability to instantly see how many objects are in a small group without counting is called *subitizing*.
3. There has been a great deal of research devoted to the topic of counting. For example, primates and birds can see *two*, and then choose a sign or symbol for 2. Seeing two at a glance without counting is something that babies can do.
4. By age three, children can count things without having them actually present, such as three claps or three chimes of a bell.

Math Talk

Subitizing

Subitizing is defined as seeing a small amount of objects and knowing how many there are *without counting*.

Learning Number Word Meanings

Many people think that counting is the core mathematics curriculum in the preschool years. Parents and teachers frequently ask children to count aloud. Counting aloud is very much like singing the ABC song. When children sing their ABCs they can say the letters in order, but we know they are not yet *reading* the individual letters. Even singing *l-m-n-o-p* may sound like a single word when children sing it.

Children coming to preschool may already be able to know and say some of the number words in sequence (one, two, three, four, five). This is often referred to as *rote counting*. However, children may not associate any number word meanings with this sequence.

So, *is counting simple*? Think about how children learn number word meanings. Read each research insight and reflect on it. Discuss with others what it means to you.

Math Talk

Rote Counting

Rote counting is defined as saying the number words in sequence (one, two, three, four, five, etc.) without necessarily attaching meaning to the number words.

Research Insights About Number Words

1. Children hear number words used in various ways. For example, the word *two* sometimes occurs in a list, among other number words (one, *two*, three, etc.); at other times it occurs in sentences, where it may be the only number word (you can have *two* cookies). According to research, children initially treat these contexts as separate—almost as if the words were homonyms (Fuson 1988, 1992).
2. Children learn to recite the number list up to five or higher, and to point to one object with each word, without understanding how counting reveals the number of objects in the set (Baroody 1992).

3. Children who can say the number sequence may have difficulty with the irregular patterns of eleven, twelve, thirteen, fourteen, fifteen and transitions at twenty-nine, thirty-nine, forty-nine, and so on. (They may say twenty-ten after twenty-nine for example.)

This is interesting because in some other languages the teens are regular, and young children do not seem to have difficulty remembering the sequence of the *number list* in their language. In English, ten is not one ten, eleven is not oneteen, and twelve is not twoteen. We say thirteen, not threeteen, and fifteen, not fiveteen. Only fourteen, sixteen, seventeen, eighteen, nineteen have any pattern that can relate easily to some ones and a ten, and this pattern is late in the teens. This is in contrast to East Asian number words that are said as ten one, ten two, ten three, . . . ten nine, and two ten for twenty (Fuson 2010).

Math Talk

Counting in Sequence

For very young children, counting in sequence is not at all simple—at least not at the outset. Children must learn the names of the numbers in the proper order and make sense of the patterns. In addition, a child's ability to count aloud well does not mean that he or she can correctly count a set of objects (Chapin and Johnson 2006).

Reflection Questions

1. How should we use research to inform our practice?
2. What research sources do you use in your teaching? Do you have access to journals such as *Teaching Children Mathematics* from NCTM?
3. Are you part of a professional learning community with colleagues to share thinking about current practices and findings in mathematics education? If so, describe some of the benefits of this community. If not, what steps might you take to form a professional learning community group?

I think there's three. No, no. I think there's ten . . . argh, I can't count yet!

—Michael during a one-on-one assessment

Chapter 5

Using One-on-One Assessments

Overview

This chapter describes how children go about counting. Video clips capture author and preschool teacher Brenda Mercado having one-on-one assessments with children ranging in ages from 3 years, 10 months to 5 years, 8 months. Brenda first asks each child to estimate and count rocks in a jar. As she watches how each child goes about the task, she makes adjustments to the number of rocks the child is asked to count. Brenda is trying to determine how accurate and confident the children are in their counting skills. She is gathering information about their understanding of quantity. This data is invaluable for formative assessment; it will help her plan lessons and activities to support the children's growth in counting. As you watch each clip, keep in mind the research insights and understandings explored in Chapter 4.

To view the clip, scan the QR code or visit **mathsolutions.com/TEACHPK51**

Video Clip 5.1: Mason Counts Rocks (age 3 years, 10 months)

Mason is asked, "How many rocks do you think are in that jar?"

See the research insights in Chapter 4, Connecting with the Research: Counting.

In this clip, Brenda meets with Mason for a one-on-one assessment. First watch Video Clip 5.1 in its entirety. Reflect on the research insights highlighted in Chapter 4; what connections come to mind? Then watch the clip for a second time, this time pausing at various intervals and thinking about the questions that follow.

Children are first asked to estimate how many rocks are in the jar. Chapter 10 explains the value of using a daily estimation jar and includes ideas for successfully implementing this routine.

In the first fifteen seconds of this video clip, Mason counts the rocks while they are in the jar. Listen to his sequence. Stop the clip before Mason spills the jar. When does Mason start to say numbers that are out of order? Notice how Mason gestures to the whole jar. What do you think this means?

What We Learned: We know Mason can say some number names in order. He also knows that to answer the question "How many?" he needs to count. He counts and he points to rocks in the jar as he turns the jar.

Mason is asked to spill the rocks out of the jar and count them.

Next, the teacher asks Mason to spill the rocks out of the jar and count them. Watch Mason as he does this. Stop the clip before the teacher removes some of the rocks from the group (approximately forty-five seconds into the clip). Record your observations, taking into consideration how the teacher is responding to Mason's counting attempts. What have you learned about Mason's understanding of quantity?

What We Learned: Mason touches each rock as he says a number. We call this *tagging*. Mason also touches some rocks without saying a number, and he gestures to the whole group near the end of his counting. Such a gesture usually signals that a child has run out of counting words. Mason does not keep track of the items he counts and counts some of his rocks again. This could indicate that Mason hasn't thought about the need to keep track of the rocks that have already been counted. Mason also says the number sequence correctly to four, but then he says seven, eight, nine. The teacher notes that the number of rocks he has to count is too many, so she removes some.

Math Talk

Tagging

Touching each of the objects while counting is called *tagging*. Sometimes children tag with their eyes or they may nod with their head without touching what they are counting.

The teacher removes some of the rocks and asks Mason again, "So how many rocks are there?"

Finally, the teacher removes all but five of the rocks and asks Mason again, "So how many rocks are there?" Mason counts them again. Watch the final part of the clip. Why does the teacher ask Mason the same question several times? What do we learn about Mason's understanding now?

Math Talk

Cardinality

Cardinality means knowing how many items are in a group that has been counted.

What We Learned: When Mason has only five rocks in front of him, the teacher once again asks, "How many are there?" Mason counts them correctly—one, two, three, four, five. The teacher asks again, "How many are there?" Mason counts them correctly two more times. Each time, Mason counts aloud one, two, three, four, five. Mason does not necessarily know that the last number in the set is the total. It could be that Mason thinks the question "How many are there?" means "Please count these." At the end the teacher tells him, "Five, good counting." She is helping Mason see that the last number does not name the last rock, but stands for the whole group of rocks that he has just counted. Knowing how many there are in the group is called seeing the *cardinality* of the group of objects.

Record the numbers children counted using Reproducible C2, Learning Progression: Early Childhood/Number.

Assessment Opportunity

See Reproducible C2, Learning Progression: Early Childhood/Number. Look at the first row, counting. Which numbers would you record for Mason?

Video Clip 5.2: Imanol Counts Rocks (age 4 years, 9 months)

Imanol is asked, "How many rocks are in the jar?"

To view the clip, scan the QR code or visit **mathsolutions.com/TEACHPK52**

In this clip, Brenda meets with Imanol for a one-on-one assessment. First watch Video Clip 5.2 in its entirety. Reflect on the research insights explored in Chapter 4; what connections come to mind? Now watch the clip a second time, this time pausing at various intervals and thinking about the questions that follow.

See the research insights in Chapter 4, Connecting with the Research: Counting.

Watch the first forty-five seconds of the clip. When Imanol spills the jar and counts the rocks, he ends with twenty-four. However, when the teacher asks him how many rocks there are, Imanol responds "four." Stop the clip here. Why do you think Imanol responds "four"? What might Imanol think *counting* means?

What We Learned: The teacher wonders why Imanol says four instead of twenty-four. According to Fuson's research in Chapter 4, a child may say the last word when asked *how many* instead of knowing the cardinality—how many items are in a group that has been counted (Fuson 1988).

The teacher removes some of the rocks and asks Imanol, "So how many rocks are there now?"

Resume watching the clip to the end. The teacher asks Imanol to count the rocks again; each time she removes some of the rocks from the group. What do you learn about Imanol's understanding now?

What We Learned: The teacher wants to see if Imanol will continue to say the last number he counted in response to her question, "How many rocks are there?" When Imanol has nine rocks in the group, he counts correctly to nine and reports there are nine. If there had been nineteen rocks, perhaps he might have said *nine* or *teen*.

Record the numbers children counted using Reproducible C2, Learning Progression: Early Childhood/Number.

Assessment Opportunity

See Reproducible C2, Learning Progression: Early Childhood/Number. Look at the first row, counting. Which numbers would you record for Imanol?

Video Clip 5.3: Danitza Counts Rocks (age 5 years, 5 months)

Danitza is asked, "How many rocks are there?"

To view the clip, scan the QR code or visit **mathsolutions.com/TEACHPK53**

See the research insights in Chapter 4, Connecting with the Research: Counting.

In this clip, Brenda meets with Danitza for a one-on-one assessment. First watch Video Clip 5.3 in its entirety. Reflect on the research insights highlighted in Chapter 4; what connections come to mind? Now watch the clip a second time, this time pausing at various intervals and thinking about the questions that follow.

Watch the clip until Danitza responds that there are twelve rocks in the group (approximately one minute and twenty seconds into the clip). Stop the clip. Record your observations. What have you learned about Danitza's understanding of quantity?

What We Learned: In counting the spilled rocks, Danitza pulls aside one rock at a time while saying the numbers: 1, 2, 3, 4, 5, 7, 8, 9, 10, 3, 4, 5, 7, 8, 9, 17, 6, 9, 10, 12. We can say that she is counting in *synchrony* because she says one number for each rock that she tags. Danitza demonstrates *one-to-one correspondence* because she is in *synchrony* with each of her tags and she has a way to keep track of the rocks she has already touched, but she hasn't yet memorized the correct sequence of numbers. She reports that there are twelve in the group, leading the teacher to believe that Danitza thinks the last number mentioned is the number she should report.

Math Talk

Synchrony

Synchrony means saying one number name for each object tagged.

One-to-One Correspondence

One-to-one correspondence means that there is one number for each item. That means that each item is counted only once because synchrony, tagging, and keeping track are all in place.

The teacher removes some of the rocks and asks Danitza, "How many are here?"

The teacher removes some rocks from the group and has Danitza count again by asking, "How many are here?" Resume watching the clip until Danitza responds that there are seventeen rocks. Stop the clip. What have you observed about Danitza's counting now?

What We Learned: No matter what the quantity, we see Danitza pulling the rocks to keep track of her counting. There are still too many rocks for Danitza to count the rocks accurately. Danitza consistently omits the number six in her oral counting sequence.

The teacher removes more of the rocks and asks Danitza, "Now how many rocks are there?"

In the final part of this assessment the teacher removes more rocks; Danitza counts nine. The teacher removes yet more rocks; Danitza counts five. What have you observed about Danitza's counting now? How would you continue to support Danitza's growth in counting?

What We Learned: Eventually Danitza is accurate and confident about the total of five rocks. Danitza consistently omits the number six in her oral counting sequence. She will need opportunities for guided practice with this sequence. The teacher plans to have Danitza count out six items later on in the day during snack preparation (see Video Clip 5.4).

Video Clip 5.4: Counting Practice During Snack Time

Danitza practices counting out six items (fish crackers) during snack time.

To view the clip, scan the QR code or visit **mathsolutions.com/TEACHPK54**

For more ideas on using snack time to facilitate children's growth in counting, see Chapter 3 (Pattern Snacks), Chapter 7 (Snack Time), Chapter 8 (Do You Like Green Eggs and Ham?, Which Juice Do You Prefer?, Which Apple Color Do You Like Best?, Which Cracker Shape Do You Like Best?), and Chapter 10 (Recipes That Build Important Mathematical Ideas).

In Video Clip 5.4, Brenda uses snack time to give Danitza practice counting six objects. Watch the clip. As you watch, consider how you can use snack time and other opportunities during the day to support beginning counting. How can children receive regular support for specific needs? Consider how counting *for a purpose* reinforces the child's own need for accuracy.

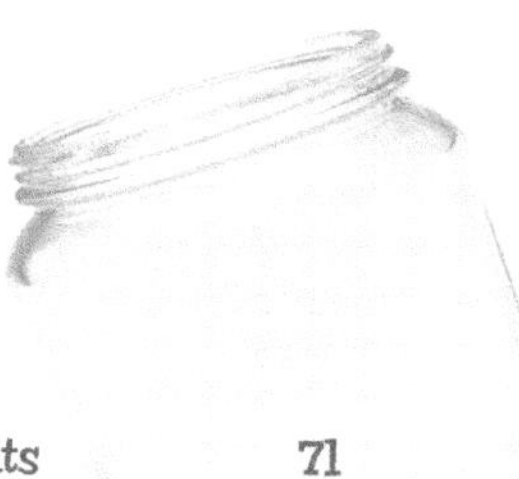

To view the clip, scan the QR code or visit **mathsolutions.com/TEACHPK55**

Video Clip 5.5: Isabella Counts Rocks (age 4 years, 10 months)

Isabella is asked, "How many rocks do you think are in this jar?"

See the research insights in Chapter 4, Connecting with the Research: Counting.

In this clip, Brenda meets with Isabella for a one-on-one assessment. First watch Video Clip 5.5 in its entirety. Reflect on everything you've learned so far, including the research highlighted in Chapter 4; what connections come to mind? Now watch the clip for a second time, this time pausing at various intervals and thinking about the questions that follow.

In the first fifteen seconds of this video clip, Isabella estimates how many rocks are in the jar by showing six fingers. Watch the clip and stop it before Isabella starts taking the rocks out of the jar. What do you think Isabella's showing of six fingers tells you about her understanding of quantity?

What We Learned: Isabella holds up six fingers but it took her awhile to say that this number was six. Because the teacher knows that Isabella is an English language learner, it is possible that Isabella might have been counting from one in her mind to arrive at six. She understood the question the teacher posed.

Isabella is asked to count the rocks in the jar.

Resume watching the clip. The teacher now asks Isabella to count the rocks in the jar. When Isabella counts, she takes one rock at a time out of the jar. The last number she counts is twenty-seven. When asked how many rocks there are, however, Isabella says seven. Stop the clip at this point (approximately one minute and twenty seconds into the clip). What do you think Isabella understands about the difference between seven and twenty-seven?

What We Learned: Isabella counts one rock at a time and has a number word for each one. She does know the correct sequence. She also reports that the number of rocks is seven when the last number she counted was twenty-seven. This is another example of Fuson's research from Chapter 4—a child may say the last word when asked *how many* instead of knowing the cardinality—how many items.

A Child's Mind

Modeling

In class, Brenda often models counting one item at a time by moving the items as the children count aloud. Some children notice her method and try to do it as well. Others have not yet figured out that this might be a good strategy. Some move the objects one at a time, but say several numbers or omit numbers as they count. So it seems that modeling does not always make sense to the child who is not ready to use this strategy.

Teaching Insight

The Difference Between Assessment and Instruction

In this type of assessment, the teacher does not spread out the rocks; she is not assessing how accurately the child can count. Instead, she is looking to see if Isabella has a way to keep track. In an instructional situation, the teacher will model keeping track as well as provide scaffolding for keeping track. It is up to the child to see the need for this strategy.

The teacher removes some of the rocks and asks Isabella how many rocks there are now.

Resume watching the clip to the end. The teacher removes some of the rocks from the group. Isabella counts the rocks and arrives at fourteen. The teacher takes more rocks away. Isabella counts nine. Even though there are nine rocks close together in the pile, Isabella is able to accurately count each one and report how many are in the group. How does the random, close arrangement of the rocks make counting more challenging for Isabella? Should the teacher spread out the rocks to encourage accurate counting?

What We Learned: The teacher removes rocks to make the task more manageable. We still do not know how Isabella would count between nine and twenty-seven rocks. Isabella uses numbers for counting, but has different ideas about the quantity she counts.

When Isabella first started counting these rocks she lined them up and seemed to be able to keep track. Later on, she doesn't use a strategy to keep track; this need to keep track for accurate counting is still developing.

Record the numbers children counted using Reproducible C2, Learning Progression: Early Childhood/Number.

Assessment Opportunity

See Reproducible C2, Learning Progression: Early Childhood/Number. Look at the first row, counting. Which numbers would you record for Isabella?

Video Clip 5.6: Jenny Counts Rocks (age 4 years, 9 months)

To view the clip, scan the QR code or visit **mathsolutions.com/TEACHPK56**

The teacher asks Jenny how many rocks there are in the jar.

In this clip, Brenda meets with Jenny for a one-on-one assessment. First watch Video Clip 5.6 in its entirety. Reflect on everything you've learned so far, including the research highlighted in Chapter 4; what connections come to mind? Now watch the clip for a second time, this time pausing at various intervals and thinking about the questions that follow.

See the research insights in Chapter 4, Connecting with the Research: Counting.

The teacher first asks Jenny, "How many rocks do you think are in this jar?" Jenny tries to count them; the teacher encourages her to spill them out and find out. Jenny spills out the rocks and counts. Listen as she counts. Stop the clip when Jenny states that there are sixteen (approximately fifty seconds into the clip). What numbers are problematic for Jenny?

What We Learned: Notice how the numbers beyond thirteen are problematic (hard to remember) for Jenny, and she uses *eleventeen* as one of her numbers. We hear how challenging it can be to say the irregular counting sequences of the numbers in the teens. Recall Fuson's research in Chapter 4—children who can say the number sequence may have difficulty with the irregular patterns of eleven, twelve, thirteen, fourteen, and fifteen.

The teacher takes some rocks away and asks Jenny to count them again.

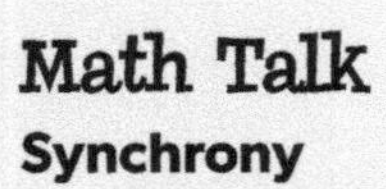

Math Talk

Synchrony

Synchrony means saying one number name for each object tagged.

Resume watching the clip to the end. The teacher takes some rocks away and asks Jenny to count them now. Jenny counts and concludes that there are eighteen. The teacher takes a few more away. Jenny arranges the remaining ten rocks in a row for counting and is accurate with this set. Notice how Jenny tags the rocks. Does she have *synchrony*? How does Jenny's organization support her counting skills? Should children be reminded to find a way to keep track to assist them in developing accuracy?

Math Talk

Tagging

Touching each of the objects while counting is called tagging. Sometimes children tag with their eyes or nod with their head without touching what they are counting.

What We Learned: Jenny tags each rock, but her voice isn't yet in synchrony with her tagging touches. She even decides to put the rocks in a line, but because she is not in synchrony with her tagging touches, she is inaccurate.

Assessment Opportunity

See Reproducible C2, Learning Progression: Early Childhood/ Number. Look at the first row, counting. How would you record Jenny's counting for accuracy?

Record the numbers children counted using Reproducible C2, Learning Progression: Early Childhood/Number.

Teaching Insight

The Difference Between Assessment and Instruction

In this type of assessment, the teacher does not remind the child to find a way to keep track of her counting. The teacher is looking to see if Jenny sees the need for a way to keep track. In an instructional situation, the teacher will model keeping track as well as provide scaffolding for keeping track. It is up to the child to make use of this strategy. When children count items for snacks we sometimes provide supports to help them count accurately, for example (see Video Clip 5.4: Counting Practice During Snack Time).

Video Clip 5.7: Michael Counts Rocks and Cubes (age 5 years, 6 months)

To view the clip, scan the QR code or visit **mathsolutions.com/TEACHPK57**

The teacher asks Michael to estimate how many rocks are in the jar, then count them.

In this clip, Brenda meets with Michael for a one-on-one assessment. First watch Video Clip 5.7 in its entirety. Reflect on everything you've learned so far, including the research highlighted in Chapter 4; what connections come to mind? Now watch the clip for a second time, this time pausing at various intervals and thinking about the questions that follow.

See the research insights in Chapter 4, Connecting with the Research: Counting.

The teacher first asks Michael, "How many rocks do you think are in the jar?" Michael answers, then changes his answer. She then asks him to count them. Michael spills the rocks out of the jar and counts. Stop the clip when the teacher asks, "Would you like me to take some away? Would that make it easier to count?" How does Michael's process of counting differ from children we've seen in previous clips?

What We Learned: When asked to estimate the number of rocks in the jar, Michael first says three. We know from research that three is a number that children from a very young age can identify instantly without counting. Michael seems to think again and then says, "No, no, it's ten."

The reason the teacher asks first for an estimate is to get an idea of what sorts of numbers the child thinks might be reasonable. This question also gives the teacher information about whether the child has an understanding of what an estimate is. Some children think this question means "Please count these."

Michael can say the numbers in order to thirteen; then he says seventeen.

When Michael realizes that he does not know the counting sequence beyond thirteen, he exclaims, "I can't count yet! " He is happy to have some rocks taken away to make the counting easier. Michael knows that he does not *know* the counting sequence for larger numbers. Some children do not know this about themselves, and continue counting with random numbers. Perhaps Michael is more reflective about his own learning.

The teacher removes some rocks and Michael counts again.

Resume watching the clip. The teacher removes some rocks and Michael counts again, stating that there are twelve. The teacher takes more rocks away. Michael counts seven. Stop the clip after Michael answers that there are seven. What have you learned about Michael's counting? What change have you noticed in Michael's attitude towards counting?

What We Learned: We notice that Michael is not accurate (there are eleven rocks) but he appears to be confident with his count of twelve. It looks like he is enjoying this opportunity to interact with the teacher. He knows that the last number he said represents the quantity. He also says one number for each rock he touches until the last rock. When he counts the smaller group of rocks he reports that there are seven when there are actually eight; it appears that he does *not* have a way to keep track of the rocks he has counted.

The teacher asks Michael, "How many cubes are in that jar?"

Now the teacher gives Michael a jar of cubes to count instead of rocks. Resume watching the clip to the end. Record your observations; what does Michael do this time when he counts? What is different than when he counted the rocks?

What We Learned: When presented with cubes, Michael lines them up. The viewer might think that this way of organizing the cubes is to facilitate his counting. However, Michael surprises us in how he ends up counting the cubes. He says six and then reports there are ten. He carefully lines up the cubes and but then glosses over them, which demonstrates that he needs to practice counting up to ten objects.

Brenda's Journal Page

Counting

I often notice that children seem to count different things in different ways when they are developing these skills. Sometimes they may line up the materials, count them back into a container, or bunch them together and count them randomly. I think it is important to have children count a variety of different items when I assess them. This way I can see a true picture of how they are thinking about counting. Some materials seem to lend themselves to being put in order while other materials do not.

Assessment Opportunity

Record the numbers children counted using Reproducible C2, Learning Progression: Early Childhood/Number.

See Reproducible C2, Learning Progression: Early Childhood/ Number. Look at the first row, counting. How would you record the way that Michael keeps track of his counting?

Video Clip 5.8: Mia Counts Rocks and Cubes (age 5 years, 7 months)

To view the clip, scan the QR code or visit **mathsolutions.com/TEACHPK58**

Mia is asked to estimate how many rocks are in the jar.

In this clip, Brenda meets with Mia for a one-on-one assessment. First watch Video Clip 5.8 in its entirety. Reflect on everything you've learned so far, including the research highlighted in Chapter 4; what connections come to mind? Now watch the clip for a second time, this time pausing at various intervals and thinking about the questions that follow.

See the research insights in Chapter 4, Connecting with the Research: Counting.

The teacher asks Mia to estimate how many rocks are in the jar; Mia silently counts the rocks and whispers six. Stop the clip after Mia says six. How does Mia try to estimate the number of rocks in the jar?

What We Learned: Mia appears to try to count (rather than estimate) the rocks in the jar by turning it and counting, coming up with six. She points to rocks with her finger in the jar. She seems shy about doing this.

Mia is asked to spill the rocks out and count them.

Math Talk

Rote Counting

Rote counting is defined as saying the number words in sequence (one, two, three, four, five). Children may not associate any number word meanings with this sequence.

Math Talk

Tagging

Touching each of the objects while counting is called *tagging*. Sometimes children tag with their eyes or nod with their head without touching what they are counting.

Resume watching the clip. Now the teacher asks Mia to dump the rocks out. When Mia spills out the rocks, she takes one at a time and arranges them in a circle. The teacher asks her to count out loud so she can hear Mia's thinking. Mia counts around the circle of rocks, stopping when she gets back to her starting point. Mia bunches her rocks back together and the teacher takes some of the rocks away, asking Mia to count again. This time Mia counts the rocks while they are all bunched together. She arrives at twelve. The teacher takes away more rocks and reminds Mia to count out loud. Mia counts eleven. The teacher removes more rocks. Mia counts seven. Stop the clip when Mia says seven for the second time. How does the teacher know how many objects she should present to Mia to count? When does it make sense to take some away? When should the teacher add some to the child's set?

What We Learned: When a child is shy, it can be more challenging to gather information about how she or he is counting. The teacher is interested to see if Mia has a way to physically tag each rock as she counts. Perhaps this number is too big for Mia. The teacher decides to take some away. At one point, Mia is inaccurate because she counts some rocks twice. If the child has memorized correctly the rote counting sequence, but does not have a way to keep track of the items that have already been counted, the last number uttered may not stand for the actual number of objects.

Mia is asked to count cubes.

Resume watching the clip. The teacher gives Mia a jar of cubes and asks her to count them. She then asks Mia to count the cubes back into the jar. She reminds Mia to count out loud. Mia states that there are twenty cubes in the jar. Stop the clip here. Why do you think the teacher has Mia count cubes instead of rocks? Why do you think the teacher asks Mia to first count the cubes outside of the jar, and then count them while putting them back into the jar?

What We Learned: Mia seems to have difficulty with her counting sequence and keeping track. The teacher persists in asking different questions and providing different objects and quantities. The teacher uses tiny cubes to see if Mia will find a way to keep track with a different kind of item. When the cubes are arranged randomly, Mia counts them inaccurately, but when Mia counts them while putting them back in the jar, she counts all of the cubes accurately. Mia has the potential for counting a large number of items accurately, but at this point in her development she does not understand that she must keep track of what she has already counted to be accurate. This idea about what Mia knows and understands is so much more useful to the teacher than knowing that Mia cannot count nineteen or twenty rocks with accuracy.

A Child's Mind

Keeping Track of Counting

It is interesting to watch children as they count, and see if they can find a way to keep track of their counting. Sometimes we see children keeping track when there are only a few items to count. When the same children are presented with a larger quantity, they seem overwhelmed with the task and gloss over the items, without tagging.

Math Talk

One-to-One Correspondence

One-to-one correspondence means that there is one number for each it em. That means that each item is counted only once because synchrony, tagging, and keeping track are all in place.

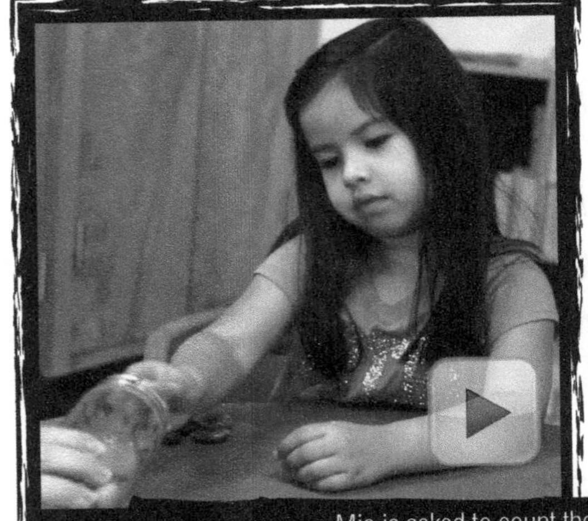

Mia is asked to count the rocks again.

Assessment Opportunity

See Reproducible C2, Learning Progression: Early Childhood/ Number. Look at the first row, counting. How would you record the way that Mia keeps track of her counting?

Record the numbers students counted using Reproducible C2, Learning Progression: Early Childhood/Number.

Resume watching the clip to the end. The teacher returns to the rocks, expressing her curiosity about how many rocks there are now that Mia has counted twenty cubes. Mia counts the rocks again and arrives at nineteen. The teacher asks Mia to slide the rocks back into the jar while counting. Mia places each rock, one at a time, back in the jar and arrives at twenty-two. What new information did you learn about Mia's counting when she was asked to do something again?

What We Learned: The teacher continues to see that Mia needs to have a way to keep track of each rock. Mia counts accurately all the way to twenty-two when asked to put the rocks back into the jar. This confirms that Mia can count accurately and with confidence. Perhaps it is the clinking sound of the rock going into the glass jar that helps Mia keep track and accurately count the rocks.

Sometimes children touch one item and say one number, thus providing a counting number for each touch. We can say that the child is showing one-to-one correspondence. To probe children's thinking, the teacher might use a material, a different quantity, and even suggest using a method to find out if it would be useful to the child. A teacher brings her knowledge about the child to every assessment situation. In Mia's case, the teacher knows that Mia is not showing a true picture of her understanding of counting, so the teacher probes a bit more. In these assessments, the procedures are not necessarily standardized. The teacher wants to find out what the child really knows.

Video Clip 5.9: Sendes Counts Rocks in Spanish (age 5 years, 7 months)

Sendes is asked in Spanish to count the rocks in the jar.

To view the clip, scan the QR code or visit **mathsolutions.com/TEACHPK59**

In this clip, Brenda meets with Sendes for a one-on-one assessment. Sendes is learning English; the teacher and student use Spanish to explain their thinking. First watch Video Clip 5.9 in its entirety. Reflect on everything you've learned so far, including the research highlighted in Chapter 4; what connections come to mind? Now watch the clip for a second time, this time pausing at various intervals and thinking about the questions that follow.

See the research insights in Chapter 4, Connecting with the Research: Counting.

The teacher asks Sendes, "How many rocks do you estimate are in this jar?" The teacher then gives Sendes the option to hear the directions in Spanish. Sendes opts for Spanish. She counts in Spanish and looks to the teacher for the numbers beyond ten. She then starts placing the rocks in a circle. When Sendes is finished with her circle, the teacher urges her to count again. Sendes counts to fifteen (quince) and then goes back and starts at eleven (once) again. Stop the clip when you hear Sendes say *catorce* (fourteen) a second time (approximately one minute and twenty seconds into the clip). What clues do you think Sendes is seeking when she looks to the teacher for the numbers beyond ten? What difference do you see in the way Sendes counts between the first and second time? Why?

What We Learned: When Sendes counts, she arranges the rocks so she can keep track. She does have the correct counting sequence to *once* (eleven).

The teacher removes some of the rocks and asks Sendes to count them again.

Math Talk

Synchrony

Synchrony means saying one number name for each object tagged.

Math Talk

Conservation of Number

Conservation of number is the understanding that the number of objects remains the same even though they may have been rearranged.

Resume watching the clip to the end. The teacher removes some of the rocks, making the set smaller. Now there are thirteen rocks; however, Sendes arrives at seven (siete). The teacher removes four more; now there are nine rocks. Sendes counts eight (ocho). The teacher removes one more. Sendes counts eight again. The teacher asks to clarify, "¿Cuantas son? (How many are there?)" Then the teacher removes another and the child counts seven (siete). The teacher adds one and the child counts again, arriving at seven (siete). How can the teacher help Sendes make sense of what happens when one more object is added? How can the teacher help Sendes touch one item and say one number in *synchrony?*

What We Learned: When the teacher first removes rocks, Sendes inaccurately counts fewer rocks and does not tag each rock as she counts. It appears that Sendes needs more opportunities to count up to eight objects with accuracy. We also learned that Sendes sees the need to keep track of what she is counting because she moves and arranges the rocks. We are not sure if Sendes and other children in this class have developed the idea of the *conservation of number.*

Assessment Opportunity

Brenda takes this opportunity to assess children's understanding of conservation of number (does the quantity stay the same?). Brenda begins by lining up seven teddy bear counters in a row. This number is large enough that the child does not know how many there are at a glance. She then asks the child to create her own row that is the same. Brenda uses one color for her row and the child uses a different color for hers. This helps make clear the different rows.

Brenda asks, "Do we both have the same?" She observes what the child does. How does the child determine that both rows are the same? Does she match them up? Does she count them? If not, the teacher matches up the rows so they are the same by putting one bear opposite each of her bears.

After the child has confirmed that the rows are the same, Brenda spreads out one row of bear counters. She asks, "Do I have more than you, or do you have more than me, or do we have the same?" If the child says one row is more, Brenda asks, "How do you know that one row is more?" If the child says the rows are the same, she asks, "How do you know that they are the same?"

A Child's Mind

Conservation of Number

Children can visually match up items from two sets of objects to see that both groups contain the same amount. However, if a child cannot count out accurately a set of objects, then that child will not grasp the idea that a given quantity of objects that are spread apart will not change if they are put close together. Young children perceive that larger amounts take up more space than smaller amounts. In order to understand that the quantity does not change unless some items are added or taken away, the young child needs to work with quantities that the child can confidently count.

Continued

A Child's Mind

Thinking Out Loud

Sometimes children benefit from hearing the adults in their lives think aloud about what the child finds confusing. Brenda acknowledges these thoughts: *It looks like there's more in this row, but, I can push the bears together and now it looks the same.*

Use Reproducible C2, Learning Progressions: Early Childhood/Number to record your observations.

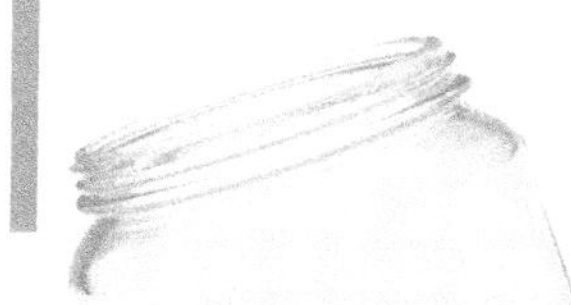

Conservation of number: Does the quantity stay the same?

The teacher then puts her teddy bear counters back into a row and asks again, "Do I have more than you, or do you have more than me, or do we have the same?" She uses Reproducible C2, Learning Progressions: Early Childhood/Number to record her observations.

A Child's Mind

Comparing

Instead of waiting until children have developed conservation of number before introducing comparing, we can engage children in using counting to describe a group of objects. Children should feel comfortable counting a group of objects and thinking about what they might *do* with that quantity, such as making small sets of matching quantities. Make one group of objects and have children create one that matches. Ask leading questions, such as, "Do we have enough? Do we have too many? Do we need more? Are they the same? What if we added more?"

For more on using comparisons to build number sense, see Chapter 8.

Video Clip 5.10: Abbie Counts Rocks (age 5 years, 8 months)

To view the clip, scan the QR code or visit **mathsolutions.com/ TEACHPK510**

Abbie is asked how many rocks are in the jar.

In this clip, Brenda meets with Abbie for a one-on-one assessment. First watch Video Clip 5.10 in its entirety. Reflect on everything you've learned so far, including the research highlighted in Chapter 4; what connections come to mind? Now watch the clip for a second time, this time pausing at various intervals and thinking about the questions that follow.

See the research insights in Chapter 4, Connecting with the Research: Counting.

The teacher asks Abbie to estimate how many rocks she thinks are in the jar. Abbie answers eleven. The teacher then encourages her to spill the rocks out and find out. Abbie spills the rocks and counts them, moving them from one pile to another. She states that there are twenty-one rocks. The teacher takes some away. Abbie counts again and arrives at twelve. The teacher asks her how many and Abbie hesitates; the teacher waits. Abbie repeats "twelve." The teacher removes more rocks; Abbie counts ten. The teacher adds one rock and asks, "What about now?" Abbie counts each rock again and arrives at eleven. The teacher adds another rock and asks, "What about now?" Abbie counts each rock yet again and arrives at twelve. This is repeated for thirteen and then fourteen rocks. Abbie continues to accurately count. After fourteen, the teacher removes a rock. Abbie counts each rock again and arrives at

thirteen. Stop the clip and record your observations. What have you learned about Abbie's understanding of counting? What happens when the teacher adds one more to ten, then to eleven, and then to twelve?

A Child's Mind

Number Relationships

A child may be able to say the number word list correctly, but not know the relationship of five to six or ten to nine. We can see this when the child counts out the objects and one more is added. Does she need to count the entire set again, or can she count on from five to get six? Even though she *knows* that six comes after five in the number word list, she must count from the beginning to determine the quantity when one is added.

What We Learned: Each time, Abbie counts one by one, tagging and moving the rocks to the side. When she first counts and gets to eleven, Abbie's original estimate for the number of rocks in the jar, she hesitates. We see how Abbie repeatedly responds to the question, "How many now?" when one more rock is added or removed from the set she just counted. In Video Clip 5.11, the teacher continues her one-on-one assessment with Abbie, this time trying to find out more about what Abbie knows about smaller numbers.

Assessment Opportunity

Record your observations using Reproducible C2, Learning Progression: Early Childhood/Number.

See Reproducible C2, Learning Progression: Early Childhood/ Number. Look at the first row, counting. What new information did you learn about Abbie's counting when one more item was added?

Video Clip 5.11: Abbie Plays the Hiding Game (age 5 years, 8 months)

To view the clip, scan the QR code or visit **mathsolutions.com/TEACHPK511**

Abbie plays the Hiding Game.

Video Clip 5.11 is the second part of Abbie's one-on-one assessment. The teacher and Abbie now play the Hiding Game with rocks. This is a revealing assessment that is presented to the child in the format of a *game. Watch the clip in its entirety.* As you watch the clip, think about the information the teacher gathers about the child's understanding of the meaning of a particular quantity.

When the teacher hides some of the five rocks, what sorts of responses does Abbie give?

What happens when the total number of rocks is four? Which combinations for a total of four rocks seem comfortable to Abbie?

What We Learned: In this game the teacher is assessing what the child can do without assistance. The teacher is interested in finding out what the child says quickly, not what the child can determine by counting or using her fingers to figure things out. Most children really enjoy this game, and since they do not know whether they are right or wrong, they do not think of this as an assessment. They just like playing the game with their teacher!

Assessment Opportunity

To play the Hiding Game with a child in her classroom, Brenda will usually begin with the quantity *five* and then open her hand and ask the child to give her five cubes.

Brenda will watch to see how the child does this. Does the child pick up one cube at a time and say the number at the same time? Does he keep on counting beyond five, or is he able to land on his target of five?

Once Brenda has five cubes in her hand, she will ask: "How many cubes did you give me?" Does the child need to recount? Or does the child remember how many there were?

Next, Brenda says, "We're going to play a Hiding Game. I'm going to hide some of these cubes and show you some. You are going to guess how many I'm hiding."

Brenda shows four and hides one. She asks, "How many are hiding?" Brenda remembers what the child says and does this again with a different combination. She does not tell the child if her answer is correct.

Some children who are successful with seeing four, and knowing one is hidden, will not be successful when shown one while four are hidden. Some combinations are just more challenging for students to conceptualize. If the child is incorrect on many of his responses, Brenda will try the same task with fewer cubes.

The same Hiding Game is then played with four. Brenda observes if the child is more comfortable with these number combinations. Brenda holds out five cubes and asks, "Will you fix it so I now will have four cubes in my hand?" She watches to see if the child takes all the cubes out and begins again, or if the child just removes one.

She asks, "Now how many cubes do I have?" Does the child need to recount? Or, does the child remember how many?

If the child seems successful with a total of five cubes, Brenda will ask the child to do the same task with six. Brenda needs to know what quantities each of her students has internalized. Can children compose and decompose different numbers in their minds? Can they think of the number flexibly? In order for children to be able to do this, they will need many opportunities counting out target numbers that match their level of understanding. Use Reproducible C2, Learning Progressions: Early Childhood/Number to record your observations.

Record your observations using Reproducible C2, Early Childhood/Number.

The Next Step: Connecting Counting to Books, Rhymes, and Songs

We have watched many children count over the years. We have learned so much about how complex it is for children to develop into *accurate and confident* counters. Seeing children count has helped us become better observers, noticing important details and skills. We realize the various aspects of counting aren't hierarchical in nature. For example, Danitza (Video Clip 5.3) demonstrates one-to-one correspondence, but she hasn't yet memorized the correct sequence of numbers. Jenny (Video Clip 5.6) tags each stone, but her voice isn't yet in synchrony with her tagging touches. Counting is complex. It is the first big step in the child's development as a young mathematician.

The next chapter describes a variety of books, rhymes, and songs that provide valuable practice to engage children in developing their counting. These activities are rich in context, so the rote sequence of numbers is embedded in the work children are doing.

Reflection Questions

1. How can the teacher engage children in finding out how many items are in a group of items?
2. How can the teacher help children count out a specific number of items without going over their target?
3. What should the teacher do if a child consistently omits some numbers in the counting sequence?
4. How can counting for accuracy be encouraged without discouraging children who make errors?
5. How can the teacher support children in developing their counting skills when there is a wide range of abilities?
6. How can children's counting skills be developed during everyday routines?
7. How can families help their child with counting? What do they need to know?

One little, two little, three little fingers,
Four little, five little, six little fingers
Seven little, eight little, nine little fingers,
Ten little fingers on my hand.

—Children's counting rhyme

Chapter 6

Using Counting Books, Rhymes, and Songs

Overview

This chapter explores activities and ideas for counting using books and songs. We share our favorite counting books and ideas for using them, then give you the opportunity to see firsthand a group of children singing a counting song using first their fingers, then a bead board. For counting to be accurate and meaningful, children need lots of repetition hearing and saying correct number sequences. We have found that numbers are remembered when they are connected to real or imaginary situations in a fun and playful manner. Children are naturally drawn to picture books with predictable text. They are enchanted with the word play of rhymes. They love learning songs that they can sing with actions and dramatic gestures. Songs and rhymes are often an English language learner's entry into English. Children regularly sing the songs and rhymes throughout the day as they play. As you are introduced to ideas and activities based on counting books and songs, think back to the research insights about counting introduced in Chapter 4.

Continued

Using Counting Books

Literature Connection

Children's literature brings another voice, or part of the outside world, into classrooms, plus children are naturally drawn to books and stories. Counting books have an important place in building mathematical ideas. Choose counting books that children want to hear again and again. The repetition of numbers one to ten, often enhanced by the use of rhymes, helps children learn and remember the sequences. They like predicting what number will be next. Children also enjoy acting out the story and taking the roles of the characters in the story. This kind of play brings the literature alive, as well as aids in reading comprehension and actively involving children in counting. Reproducible D is a bibliography of children's literature books that support mathematical thinking.

We share ideas connected to children's literature throughout this resource; for easy identification, these ideas are marked with a literature icon. Literature Connection

See Reproducible D, Selected Bibliography of Children's Books for Supporting Mathematical Ideas.

Counting in the Garden

Counting in the Garden by Kim Parker capitalizes on children's natural curiosity about bugs. Bright illustrations of a garden include hidden dreamlike insects and animals that children delight in the finding and counting. *Counting in the Garden* is best read with a small group of children, as they will want to count the creatures hidden on the pages. Once children have become familiar with the book, they enjoy making their own books with pages of ladybugs, turtles, inchworms, and ducklings. For illustrations, we have students place their thumbprints on paper to form the insect's body, then they draw legs and eyes.

Over in the Meadow

"Over in the meadow, in the sand, in the sun, lived an old mother turtle and her little turtle one." So begins this vivid counting story of animals at play in a bustling meadow. The classic counting rhyme helps children predict the next number in the counting sequence. We read this book again and again, helping children learn how the numbers rhyme with the storyline. Once students become familiar with this version, we read other versions of the same story (there are quite a few available). Students talk about how the versions are the same and how they are different. Consider posting all the different versions up on the wall and asking students to put their names by the book they liked best. In our classrooms one year the Ezra Jack Keats book had the most "votes"; another year the Paul Galdone version was the most popular. It is an interesting conversation for the children to think about how different authors and illustrators chose to tell the same story. Even though the words are mostly the same, the pictures are different. We like to think that this realization helps children see themselves as potential authors and illustrators of their own books.

Five Little Monkeys Jumping on the Bed

With this delightful book by Eileen Christelow children practice counting backward from five to zero with a rhyming, predictable text. Place a large beach towel on the floor in the center of the circle to suggest the bed; then let children take turns playing the monkeys that jump off the bed as well as the parts of the mother and doctor. The only other prop that seems necessary is a phone. Act out the story repeatedly until everyone has had a turn to jump on the bed.

Five Little Monkeys Sitting in a Tree

This companion book to *Five Little Monkeys Jumping on the Bed* provides another chance to model subtraction. Use a sock to hide a brown cube each time one of the little monkeys taunts the crocodile with, "You can't catch me!"

Brenda's Journal Page

Hiding Cubes in a Sock

We need to find many ways for children to count to five over and over again if they are not yet comfortable with that number. When reading *Five Little Monkeys Sitting in a Tree* to my class, it's so interesting to hide the cubes in the sock, especially for young children at the beginning of the year. For them, out of sight means that the cubes are gone! I wanted the cubes to be out of sight but not out of mind, so I let the children touch the outside of the sock to feel that the cubes are still there. It is challenging for a young child to think about how many are inside the sock when the cubes are hidden. Children need to take the cubes out of the sock and count them to know for sure!

Feast for Ten

What does it take to make a feast for ten hungry people? From the supermarket to the table, this book by Cathryn Falwell features a bountiful family dinner meant for counting. The cozy rhyme offers an abundance of curriculum ideas, from sequencing to number groupings to nutrition. To provide concrete examples of number words, Brenda gives each child a paper plate and has children cut out pictures of food—one meat, two fruits, and three vegetables—to create a nutritious meal.

In another activity, Brenda asks children, "How many apples would we need for ten hungry people?" Even though we think this is a pretty simple question, in our classrooms we get answers all the way from one to ten. So we put ten hungry children in front of the class and a basket of apples. Each child chose an apple from the basket and stood in front of the group. They were amazed when they found out they had ten (Josiah was amazed and Delicia said, "I told you so!").

For more ideas on counting books that also address financial literacy (such as going to the supermarket), see *Why Can't I Have Everything? Teaching Today's Children to Be Financially and Mathematically Savvy* by Jane Crawford (Scholastic, 2011).

Ten Black Dots

What can you make with ten black dots? After reading aloud this timeless book by Donald Crew, Brenda distributes a variety of objects, such as sticker dots, or other counting objects to each child and encourages them to make their own creations. We've learned that sometimes one kind of counting object is more interesting to a group of children than another. Group enthusiasm soared when we introduced a jar of flat toothpicks, a jar of pistachio shells, and a bag of blue chips to the mix. Students seemed to find that the toothpicks served as natural line segments for illustrations. The next week we included plastic drinking straws and smaller dots in brighter colors. In some cases students started penciling details into their illustrations to help others better understand their number representation pictures. Once children have made several dot pictures, they reread *Ten Black Dots* again with a focus on the counting sequence. As a final activity, they put their pictures together to form a counting book to share with families and guests.

Mia made a page for our counting book using five red sticker dots.

Josiah used five toothpicks to make a Ninja on his counting book page.

For more ideas using *Ten Black Dots* see lesson L-1 in *How to Assess While You Teach Math: Formative Assessment Practices and Lessons* by Dana Islas (Scholastic, 2011).

Silvia used five pistachio shells to represent five petals of a flower on her counting book page.

Making Class Counting Books

After children have read a collection of counting books, consider having them make their own. There are many projects that involve children making their own counting books, yet we've found that most tend to be very teacher directed. To change this, we first ask students to talk about what they notice in all the counting books they've read. Their comments include "The book shows one, two, three, four, five, six, seven, eight, nine, ten. They have that many animals there. They can go backward. Sometimes you have to count and find them hiding. We like these books."

Next, they decide on a theme for their books. In Brenda's class, children decide on monsters as their theme. Some children make pictures of five monsters, and others make pictures of monsters with five heads. Each finished page has monsters and a numeral that matches something about the monsters.

Pages are then collected and placed in *random* order to form a book. Then we read the book together as a class. Ask students, "How is our counting book different from other counting books?" Usually someone will point out that the counting sequence is not in order. Take the book apart and have children help put the pages together in order (this is a great project for a small group centered around a table). In Brenda's class students had more pictures than needed for one book, so they created a second *Monster Counting Book*.

Math Talk

Patterns

Counting books follow patterns, which can be used to develop children's mathematical reasoning. Many classic counting books have growing patterns: n, $n+1$, $n+2$, $n+3$, and so forth. See Chapter 3 for more about these patterns.

Teaching Insight

Children's Illustrations

We prefer to assemble our counting books from illustrations that children create at their own learning level, rather than have children copy the illustrations in a published counting book.

Using Counting Rhymes and Songs

For more on using rhymes and songs in the classroom, see the Total Physical Response (TPR) section in Chapter 9.

Songs also have an important place in developing mathematical ideas. Singing games engage children in counting not only because songs are fun and active but also because the songs and rhymes seem to be more easily remembered and repeated than expository text. Children often need to get their whole body moving in order to feel the rhythm and melody. Rhythm, music, and patterns are mathematical representations.

To view the clip, scan the QR code or visit **mathsolutions.com/ TEACHPK61**

Video Clip 6.1: The Counting Song

Children singing a counting song using their fingers.

Video Clip 6.1 presents a singing game in action in a preschool classroom. First children sing and count their fingers:

> One little, two little, three little fingers,
> Four little, five little, six little fingers,
> Seven little, eight little, nine little fingers,
> Ten little fingers on my hands.

For more insights on how children use their fingers to talk about number, see Video Clip 4.1, in which Gabi tells her age, and Video Clip 7.1, in which Jason resorts to using his fingers. For more ideas on using bead boards to facilitate children's growth in counting, see Chapter 7.

Then the teacher introduces the bead board. Children sing the counting song again as the teacher moves the corresponding beads on the bead board. Watch the video clip in its entirety. Why do you think children show numbers with their fingers? What connections can you make to the mathematics of our number system and the fact that we have ten fingers?

What We Learned: Some children can sing and hold up their fingers without looking at them, and others need to look at their fingers as they sing, matching the lyrics to their actions. Children who can hold up their fingers without looking have already developed the fine motor skills with a cognitive

connection to number. Children who need to look at their fingers are making sure that they are only putting up one finger at a time. It takes all their concentration as they develop the fine motor skills. Eventually some children are able to hold up their fingers in *synchrony* while counting and watching.

Math Talk

Synchrony

Synchrony means saying one number name for each object tagged.

A Child's Mind

Counting with Fingers

How do children use their fingers? Some close their fist and open it one finger at a time beginning with their thumb. Some begin with an open hand and count down one at a time; they might start with the index finger and end with the thumb, or start with the little finger and end with the thumb. Some cultures show the number of the child's age one way and use another way to add on. It is important for teachers of young children to support the way children learned to do their finger counting at home, and then be aware of how to help them generalize to other ways of counting. They will need to show that their finger counting accurately communicates their ideas of number. A great discussion happens in the class as children represent numbers with fingers. Is one finger the same as one thumb? Is there more than one way to make two? (Show all the ways they could show two.) So, we are bumping up against the idea that numbers can be represented multiple ways.

The "Me" Rhyme

This charming rhyme immediately gets children physically involved in counting—and best of all, it's naturally personalized.

I've got ten little fingers, (hold up both hands)
And ten little toes, (point to feet)
Two little eyes, (point to eyes)
And a mouth and a nose. (point to mouth and then to nose)

Put them all together, (circle arms as if hugging)
And what have you got? (put hands on hips)
You've got me, baby, (put thumbs on chest)
And that's a lot! (wiggle hips)

Identity is an important part of the early childhood classroom. Children are encouraged to draw themselves, their friends, and their families. This wonderful poem helps children remember to add details to their drawings. Children often chant the poem to their parents in the morning during journal time as they draw self-portraits and important people in their lives. We also do a great deal of drawing at the studio table. Children are especially involved in doing self-portraits. As they work on them, they again recall this poem.

One day at the studio table when Gabi and Delicia were sitting next to each other, Gabi said, "I have two eyes." Delicia said, "Well, I have two eyes." Brenda, overhearing this conversation, asked, "Well, how many eyes do two people have?" They counted and decided that two people would have four!

One More Elephant Rhyme

Small Group Time

This rhyme is about elephants that go out to play on a spider web. It's fun for children to imagine elephants jumping on a spider web as if it were a trampoline. Draw a spider web on the floor with chalk and have children play the roles of the elephants. The rhyme begins as follows:

One little elephant went out one day,
On a spider web to play,
He had such enormous fun,
He called for another elephant to come.

Two little elephants went out one day,
On a spider web to play,
They had such enormous fun,
They called for another elephant to come.

Continue until there are five (or more!) elephants on the spider web. Then there are just too many and it breaks—at this point they all fall down.

A child's drawing of elephants and spiders on the web.

Do it again! (This is our indication that this is an engaging game. It's important to change up the order of the elephants if the game is repeated. Have children draw cards to determine the elephant order.) Once children have acted out the rhyme, facilitate a conversation around the game. Review key vocabulary as needed.

Key Vocabulary

one more	first
too many	next
two more	then

Ask key questions that encourage thinking about the math behind the rhyme:

About how many elephants could jump on a spider web if it was a real game?
Why is this a funny song?
What if two more elephants jumped on the web each time?
How can we change the game?

A Child's Mind

Too Many Elephants?

Talking about too many elephants is an interesting conversation for young children. Children may first be confused with the idea of *two* and *too*. They are quick to say that an elephant is *too big* because a spider web is *so tiny* and an elephant is *so big*.

One Less Cookie . . .

This game is based on a rhyme about five cookies in a bakery shop window. Use paper cookies and real quarters for the dramatic play. Each child comes along with a quarter to pay, buys a cookie, and walks away. Eventually all the cookies are sold and the last child is very disappointed (don't worry—children actually see this as a fun ending to the play—the last child gets to put on a very pouty face and stomp away!). The rhyme goes as follows:

> There are other children's rhymes and books that focus on counting one more. See our children's book bibliography (Reproducible D) for additional suggestions.

Five little cookies in a bakery shop,
Sprinkled with powdered sugar on top,
Along comes (name of child) with a quarter to pay,
She buys one cookie and walks away.

Continue with four, three, two, and then one little cookie. Then conclude with:

> *Five Little Ducks Went Out One Day* is another rhyming book that deals with one less. See the bibliography in Reproducible D for additional counting books.

No little cookies in a bakery shop,
Sprinkled with powdered sugar on top,
Along comes (name of child) with a quarter to pay,
He sees no cookie and stomps away.

Once children have acted out the rhyme, facilitate a conversation around the game. Review key vocabulary.

Key Vocabulary

one	then
less	quarter
first	nickel
next	dime

Ask children what would happen if there were six children in the rhyme—what would change? On another day use nickels, dimes, or dollars and buy something different at the bakery shop to extend vocabulary.

> Children need many experiences in handling real money and noticing the different faces and pictures on the coins and dollars. See *Why Can't I Have Everything? Teaching Today's Children to Be Financially and Mathematically Savvy* by Jane Crawford for additional suggestions on supporting children's understanding of coins.

Reflection Questions

1. Have you ever had a song in your head that won't go away? When we sing in the classroom, we want to imprint words and melodies that children sing again and again on their own. Think back to when you learned something through song and reflect on how durable that learning was.
2. What are your favorite primary counting and picture books? Why are you drawn to them? How have you used these books with children?
3. Why do you think rhymes and repetition are so effective as learning tools?
4. How does predictable text build comprehension?
5. Why do you think a playful approach is necessary when dramatizing a song or poem?

See, five and two are seven.

—Nathaniel using the bead board

Chapter 7

Using Visual Tools from Bead Boards to Surveys

Overview

This chapter explores various tools that facilitate the development of counting skills with young children. The use of dot cards helps children instantly recognize small groups, information they can then use to help them make sense of larger groups, or how parts make up the whole. Rekenreks and bead boards provide a visual model that encourages children to unitize, or see five beads as a single group of five, and thus two groups of five as ten; a bead board lesson is shown in Video Clip 7.1. Estimation develops mathematical reasoning and number sense; this chapter includes a section on how to use an Estimate Jar and counting jars filled with various quantities of objects. Board games provide opportunities for children to count squares. Snack time can provide many opportunities for children to practice counting in a visually appealing—and tasty—way. Counting out a specific number of items in snack time activities is a different skill than counting a group of objects, as was shown in the clips in Chapter 5. The chapter concludes with the use of surveys and data collection as valuable and meaningful counting visual tools.

Continued

Quick Images

When children are able to instantly recognize small groups of items, they can use that information to help them make sense of larger groups. They are beginning to see how parts can make up the whole. Dot cards help children build these ideas; children see quickly how many dots make up the whole image.

Dots: What Do You See?

Prepare a collection of dot cards for this routine. Dot cards have familiar domino patterns as well as other kinds of dot arrangements. See Reproducible E for examples. Consider laminating the images on cardstock.

See Reproducible E, Quick Images: Dot Cards.

Choose one card and show it so that all children can see it. Ask, "What do you see?" Give children about three seconds to study the dot image on the card. Then hide the card. Ask children to tell you what they saw. Notice how children make sense of the image. Children will likely describe the image in many different ways. Acknowledge all children's ideas. Sometimes children see quantities and sometimes they see shapes; some are mathematizing the image and others are looking at form. Hopefully, children who do not yet see quantities will begin to see them when they hear their peers addressing the number of dots.

Math Talk

Recognizing Small Amounts

Very young children who spontaneously focus on number and use subitizing of small amounts are better able to learn counting and arithmetic skills. Also, children who focus on perceptual patterns and think about mentally decomposing a number, such as five is made up of three and two, are employing powerful conceptual patterns in their thinking (Clements 2009, 46).

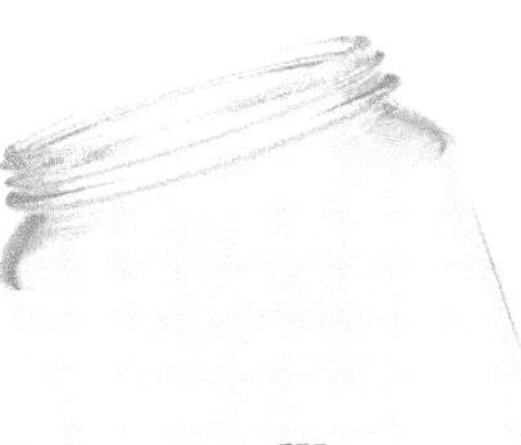

Math Talk

Subitizing

Subitizing is defined as seeing a small amount of objects and knowing how many there are without counting.

Brenda's Journal Page

Dot Cards

Today I showed children dot cards and asked them, "What do you see?" The children said, "Dots. Red dots." I revised my question to, "Tell me how you see them" but still couldn't get a numerical response. I decided to show a card that had two different-colored dots; this got some numerical responses. Once my students became familiar with talking about the number of dots, I went back to the cards with just the red dots. I showed them the following card of five dots, and asked them, "What do you see?"

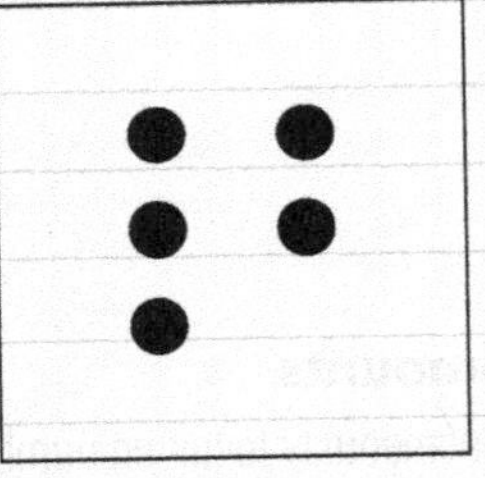

Ricardo: I see five dots.

Santos: I see four and one.

Paula: I see a P.

Marcos: I see three down and two down.

Silvia: I see a chair upside down.

Ana: I see two and two and one.

Sergio: I see six but there's one gone.

continued

I wonder if it would make a difference in children's responses if I circled groups of dots when children talked about them.

It is now week three of the dot card activity. This routine seems to now be well established in my classroom. Today I recorded some of my students' thoughts on a class chart. I collected their ideas to make a class book. On each page I intend to show the quick image of five dots and a student's thinking.

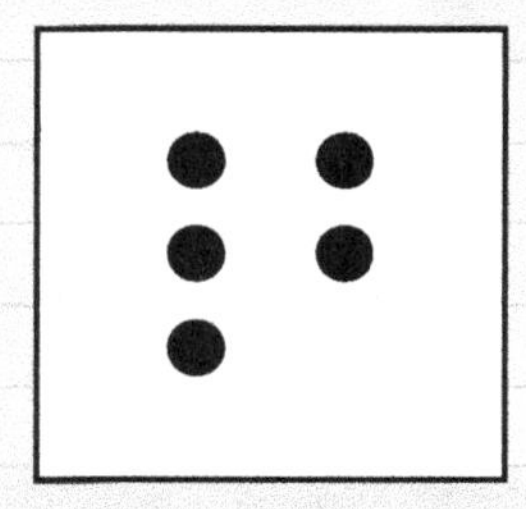

Ricardo saw 5 dots.

Santos saw 4 + 1 dots.

Ana saw 2 + 2 + 1 dots.

Marcos saw 3 + 2 dots.

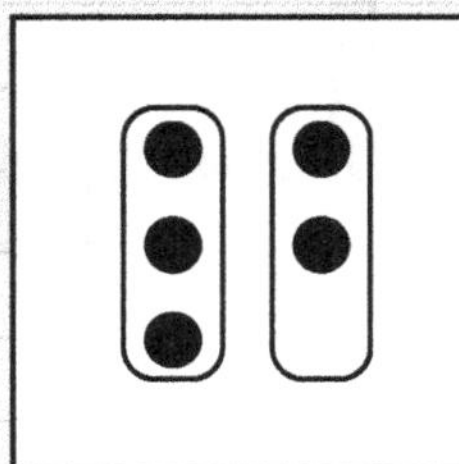

Sergio saw 6 – 1 dots.

For more ideas on using quick images such as dot cards, see *Number Talks: Helping Children Build Mental Math and Computation Strategies* by Sherry Parrish and Lesson L-1 in *How to Assess While You Teach Math: Formative Assessment Practices and Lessons* by Dana Islas. (Scholastic, 2011)

Math Talk

Unitizing

Unitizing is defined as being able to see a group as a *whole unit* and also know that it is *composed of parts.*

Rekenreks and Bead Boards

Rekenrek is a Dutch word for arithmetic rack. It combines various strengths of other manipulatives (number lines, base ten blocks, ten frames, counters) in one tool. The rekenrek is made with two lengths of ten beads each, strategically arranged into two groups: five red beads and five white beads. The lengths of red and white beads (in groups of five) provide a visual model that encourages children to *unitize*, or see five beads as a single group of five, and thus see two groups of five as ten. Sometimes this arrangement is mounted on a flat board or cardstock and referred to as a bead board.

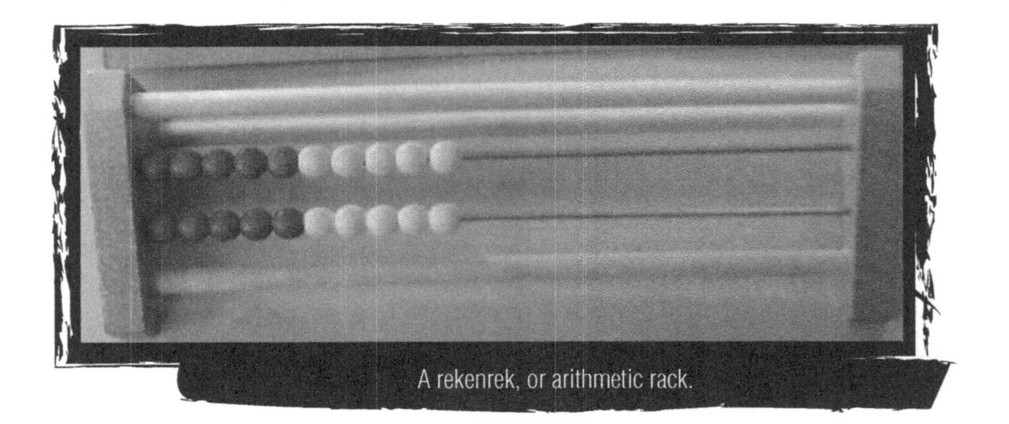

A rekenrek, or arithmetic rack.

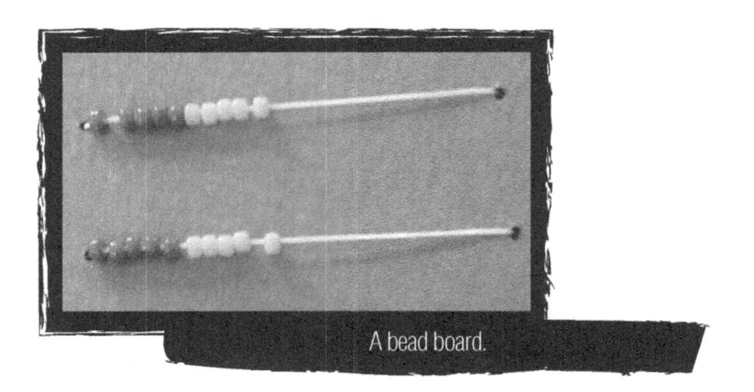

A bead board.

Ways We Can Show Five

Start this routine on the fifth day of the month. If it's March 5, for example, tell children, "Today is March 5th. There have been five days in March so far this month. How can we show five on the rekenrek?" Have children take turns coming up to the front of the class and counting out five beads. Record how they show five. For example, if a child counts out five red beads on top, record this by drawing five red circles where everyone can see them. Now ask, "Who has a different way?" Another child might move two on the top and three on the bottom. Record this using a simple illustration. Keep encouraging different ways: "I wonder if someone can show five a different way." If no one is forthcoming, show a way and record it; for example, show four on the top and one on the bottom.

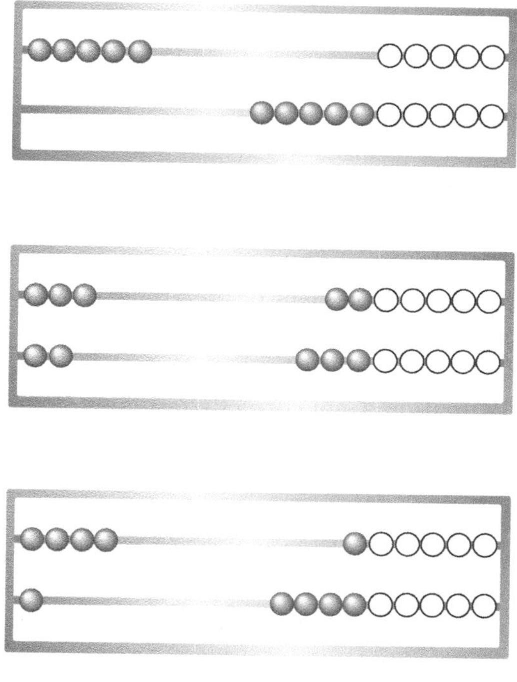

Ways to show five

Continue this for as long as you feel children are engaged. On the next day, March 6 in this example, show children how the five red beads can be combined with one white bead to make six. Children might also be excited

about the doubles, 3 + 3. Continue these experiences until the numbers become too big for the class rekenrek. Next month begin again with smaller numbers. Perhaps by late May children will be able to display twenty-three with two rekenreks.

To view the clip, scan the QR code or visit **mathsolutions.com/TEACHPK71**

Video Clip 7.1: Counting Beads on the Bead Board

Josiah counts on the bead board.

In this clip, Brenda presents the children with various bead configurations on the top row of a bead board. She is interested in how children are able to make sense of the arrangement of the groups of five beads on the bead board. Each time she asks a child, "How many is this?" and "How did you know that?" In the first part Josiah responds "ten," although there are six. In the second configuration, Gabi correctly responds "four." In the third configuration, Nathanial quickly and correctly responds "six." For the fourth configuration, Mia correctly responds "four." Jason shows his fingers to confirm that there are ten in the fifth configuration. The final child, Humberto, quickly recognizes seven in the last example. Watch the video clip in its entirety. As you see each child respond to a new bead board example, think about the following: Does the child need to count each bead, or is she or he able to unitize the five beads together? Can the child explain his or her thinking?

What We Learned: Josiah says there are ten beads although there are six (five of one color and one of the other) on the top row. The teacher asks him to count and he counts, skipping to ten after five (1, 2, 3, 4, 5, 10), indicating that Josiah is still learning the counting sequence. Gabi correctly determines that there are four beads, although she does need to count each one to know this. Nathaniel quickly and correctly responds that there are six beads. When asked how he knew this, he does not have a way to explain his thinking. The teacher asks if he counted on, "Did you go five, six?" and Nathaniel nods yes. So perhaps he was counting on from five. Mia correctly guesses four on her turn; when asked how she knew, she expresses that she didn't count—"I didn't count—I was looking at the numbers." It seems like Mia is trying to tell us that she just knew it was four, that she could subitize this number. Maybe she knew there were five beads and one was missing. Jason says that there are ten and shows his fingers to confirm there are ten. Perhaps he is remembering that ten was the ending number when all the beads were moved over in the counting song (see Video Clip 6.1). Humberto seems to recognize quickly that there are seven, but he does not have a way to explain how he knows; he points to his head as if to emphasize that he just knows. This often happens when children do not have the language to explain their thinking. It seems like he has learned that a group of five and two more is seven because he sees five without counting. This is called unitizing five.

Math Talk

Subitizing

Subitizing is defined as seeing a small number of objects and knowing how many there are *without counting.*

See Video Clip 6.1 for use of the bead board in a counting song.

Math Talk

Unitizing

Unitizing is defined as being able see a group as a *whole unit* and also know that it is *composed of parts.*

Assessment Opportunity

See Reproducible C2, Learning Progression: Early Childhood/Number. Look at the first row, counting. Which of the children in Video Clip 7.1 can instantly identify a quantity?

Counting Jars and Bags

Chapter 5 described a series of one-on-one assessments. Counting assessments like these inform the teacher about the various levels of counting abilities. Some children need to work with larger quantities, while others need to count accurately quantities less than ten. As shown in the one-on-one assessments, children are still unsure about what a large number is and use the numbers they know, like their age, to predict an estimate. We take all the information that we learn from these assessments and plan learning opportunities that meet the needs of each individual child. One way to do this is through activities using counting jars and bags. These tools also provide opportunities for us to differentiate our instruction.

See Reproducible C2, Learning Progressions: Early Childhood/Number.

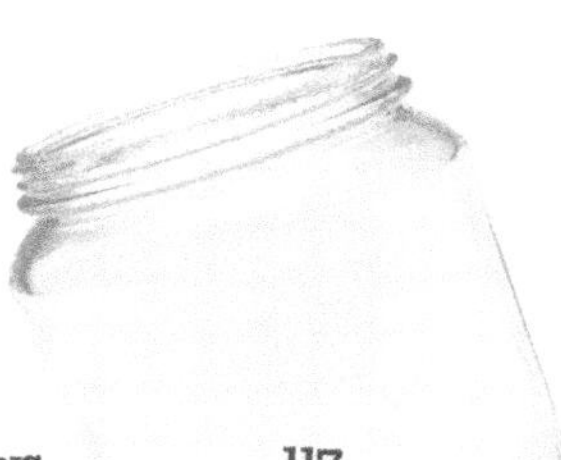

Circle Time

Estimate Jar

An Estimate Jar is at the heart of this all-time favorite routine. Each day children estimate the number of objects in a jar and then count them to find out how many are actually in the jar. This routine becomes more meaningful as children have more and more experience with it. At the beginning of the year, children seem to guess random numbers because they do not have a sense of what estimation means. They often guess their age because that is the number that they are most familiar with.

Use the same size jar all year. Children begin to get a sense of how many items (that are the size of a cube, for example) would fit in the jar. Instead of coming up with random numbers like *one million* or *eleventy-seven*, they suggest numbers that demonstrate their developing number sense. Choose large objects at first, limiting the total to less than ten objects. Record children's estimates. When they say them, hold up a clipboard and show that you are writing their number on a sheet of paper titled *Estimate Jar*. Point out that you are not keeping track of which child gives the estimate; you are simply recording the different numbers. After several children have given their estimates, encourage the rest of the class to whisper their estimate to a friend. This technique allows children to tell their estimate and then the teacher can move on. It often takes too long to record each child's estimate, and is not always necessary. Try to ensure that over time all children have an opportunity to share their estimate with the whole class.

Math Talk

Keeping Track

The Estimate Jar routine is a valuable way to model keeping track. When a child dumps out the Estimate Jar's contents and puts the items back into the jar one by one, some children make mental notes of this *keeping track* procedure, while others do not seem to notice that this is a good and careful way to count items. Eventually they will see the need to have a way to keep track.

Math Talk

Estimate or Guess?

Be clear about using the academic language *estimate* instead of *guess*. Explain to children that a guess is just a guess, but an estimate involves *thinking* and having a *reason* for the guess.

Review the estimates that you record on the sheet and note the range of the estimates, if appropriate: "Wow, we have estimates from three to twenty-six! Maybe our exact number of cherry tomatoes is somewhere between these two numbers."

Then empty the contents of the jar onto a tabletop or the rug. Have a child (see "student of the day" in the routine *How Many Days Until My Day?* on page 122 of this chapter) put the items back into the jar one by one as the class counts along. Some children find support for their counting by listening to the items as they plink back into the jar.

Cassie is estimating that there are five cherry tomatoes in the Estimate Jar she holds.

The cherry tomatoes are taken out of the Estimate Jar and counted.

After the class has orally counted the items, review how to write the number of the actual count on the clipboard estimate sheet, if it is not already there. Draw a box around the number to showcase it. Discuss the key vocabulary. Ask questions such as, "Are there any numbers on the paper that are close? Can you think of any numbers that would be close? How do we write those numbers?"

Key Vocabulary	
actual count	less
close	more
estimate	one or two more
estimation	revise

Math Talk

Estimate vs. Actual Count

With experience, children begin to understand the difference between an *estimate* and the *actual count.* Since the procedures focus on the numbers that are close, rather than on which answer is correct, children begin to feel comfortable making an estimate that is close to the actual count. Children who are proud of their estimates that are *close* are clearly making progress. Some children always want to have the exact number as their estimate, however.

Underline the numbers that are close to the actual count. Refer to a number list to support children's thinking. For example, if a child's estimate was four, use the number list to show how close the estimate was to the actual count of six. At the close of the activity, have a child take the Estimate Jar sheet home to share with family members (see "student of the day" in the routine *How Many Days Until My Day?* on page 122 of this chapter).

Teaching Insight

Making a Number List

See Reproducible F, Number Cards: 1–20.

Use the number cards in Reproducible F to make a number list. Cut each card apart and assemble them horizontally in a line, 1–20.
Tape or paste them together and place the number list on a classroom wall where everyone can see it.

Math Talk

Helping Children Make Sense of Estimation

There are several good ways to help children make more sense of estimation. One way is to place a Reference Jar next to the Estimate Jar. The Reference Jar should contain the same type of contents, but contain a different quantity, usually five or ten items. The class knows how many are in this Reference Jar and can compare it to the Estimate Jar. (For more activities on comparison, see Chapter 8.)

Another way to help extend children's thinking is to count out the contents of the Estimate Jar, then stop at mid-count, point out how many items are left to count, and ask if anyone wants to revise their estimate. Some children are able to *count on two more* in order to come up with a revised estimate. Others can count on one more, but two more is too difficult for them to consider. Occasionally model counting on one or two more for children. Have children check and see if this is a good strategy for revision.

Revisions are important. If teachers only pay attention to the original estimates and do not allow children to revise their estimate, then they are sending the message that children have to have the answer in mind before estimating. When children revise their estimates, it shows they are trying to make sense of the information they have and are coming up with a better estimate.

See Chapter 8 for more activities on comparison.

Assessment Opportunity

The estimates that children give for a particular jar can be very informative for assessment purposes. If it looks like there are many items in a jar, some children will guess what they think a large number is, such as eight or nine because these numbers are greater than their own age. Sometimes children only come up with a guess of four or five because these are the numbers that they are most familiar with. Sometimes children make up their own numbers like *fourfteen* or *eleventy-seven* because they are still learning the numbers in the counting sequence. Note the kind of estimates that children give. When children eventually begin to give a reasonable estimate, they are beginning to make sense of numbers. Record your observations of children's thinking using Reproducible C2, Learning Progressions: Early Childhood/Number.

See Reproducible C2, Learning Progressions: Early Childhood/Number.

Using Estimate Jars in Choice Time: After children have been introduced to the Estimate Jar routine, have them create their own Estimate Jars. Assemble a collection of jars, some clipboards with paper, and several markers in a basket near where other choices are displayed. Tell children to put objects in their Estimate Jar, pick up a clipboard and marker, and ask classmates for their estimates. Observe children as they write these estimates down. Are students able to write the numbers that are estimated? Then, after they feel they have enough estimates, have them empty the contents of their jar and count the items. Are they able to count the objects accurately? Do they have any idea about which numbers are close? Sometimes students go back to their classmates and report the actual count!

In the one-on-one assessments featured in Chapter 5, children are first asked to estimate the number of rocks in a jar. See the video clips in Chapter 5.

There is so much to notice when the Estimate Jar routine happens during choice time. We also find it interesting to note if they use the same tone of voice, syntax, and language that the teacher uses in the activity. Children are great observers and love to *play teacher!*

How Many Days Until My Day?

In this routine a "student of the day" is acknowledged. On each child's special day, he or she is the designated child for certain "glory" responsibilities. In our classrooms these include being the line leader, directing the counting of items in the Estimate Jar, calling on volunteers, and dismissing children to recess. Children love getting to be in charge of these responsibilities and regularly want to know when it will be their special day.

To keep track of whose special day it is, post an alphabetical list of children's first names, along with their photos, in the classroom. Help children find where their name is on the list. Every day, move a brightly colored push-pin down to the next name on the list, indicating that the child is the student of the day. Talk about why this is a fair system, because each child gets a turn before anyone has a second turn. Announce the student of the day to the class during circle time. Point out that yesterday the student who had a turn is above the pushpin. Name who will be the student of the day tomorrow. Support children in finding out *how many more* days it is until their day. Review key vocabulary as necessary.

Math Talk

How Many More?

In order for a child to figure out "how many more days until I am student of the day" the child needs to *count on*. This is a different kind of question from counting to find out "how many in all." It's important to find ways to use the language of *how many more* because children often think of *more* as being *how many are in the group that has more?*

Key Vocabulary

How many more?	tomorrow
today	fair turns
yesterday	

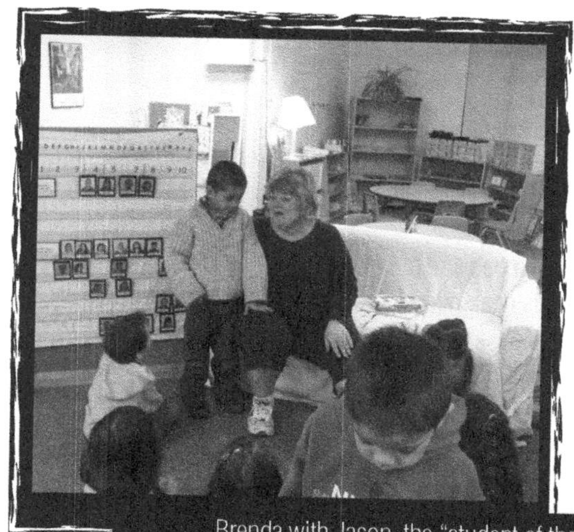

Brenda with Jason, the "student of the day" in her classroom.

Teaching Insight

Is "Student of the Day" Fair?

At first it is very hard for young students to realize that this is a fair system. They can't understand that everyone will get one turn before anyone has a second turn. They just want it to be their turn! Eventually, with repetition, each student realizes that she or he will have a turn. It's important to talk about this and help children find where their name is on the list.

Math Talk

Thinking About Time

It's important that children think about past, present, and future tense in an engaging context. Children often struggle to use the correct verb tenses to say what they mean. By regularly hearing the phrases *yesterday was* ______, *today is* _______, and *tomorrow will be* ________, children become more familiar with the language that deals with time. When the weekend is near, point to a calendar to show children that tomorrow will be Saturday, then Sunday, and then they will be back at school on Monday. For more insights on thinking about time, see the attendance activities in Chapter 8. Use daily attendance data to compare how many children are at school today with how many were at school yesterday.

See Chapter 8 for more insights on thinking about time.

Teaching Insight

Using a Calendar

A calendar is most meaningful to preschool children when it shows special events such as when there will be a guest, a field trip, or a classmate's birthday. We have found, on the other hand, that a calendar as a teaching tool is not as valuable as other graphic representations used in preschool. A calendar, with its numbers arranged in rows of seven, is not as meaningful as five- or ten-frames (see Reproducibles J and K) or hundred charts. Number patterns can more easily be seen on charts that are arranged in fives and tens. For these reasons, we keep a small (9 inch by 12 inch) calendar present in the classroom as a reference tool, but we do not address it every day. Instead, children make more sense of time in thinking and talking about when *their* day ("student of the day") is coming up.

See Reproducibles J, Five-Frame, and K, Ten-Frame.

How Many Are in the Bag?

To prepare for this routine, place various quantities of objects in sandwich bags. Use items from the Collection Museum (see Chapter 2, page 15) as well as other objects in the classroom. Label each bag with a letter of the alphabet that corresponds to the quantity in the bag (keep a key of which letter corresponds with each quantity). When it is small group time, place the bags in ABC order on the counter. Determine the appropriate bag for each child and instruct each child to get that bag. In doing this, not only is the child getting a chance to practice counting at her or his own instructional level, but she is also reviewing the letters of the alphabet. Purposefully choose quantities that students can count comfortably and accurately. For example, Danitza skips six consistently (see Video Clip 5.3). Mason can comfortably count five objects; he struggles with higher quantities (see Video Clip 5.1). In order to have a purpose for this counting, explain to children that the items they are counting will become objects for collages and other construction projects in the class studio at a later time (for insights on class studios, see Chapter 2). Have children spread out around the classroom so that their counting doesn't interfere with others (children can get thrown off when they hear another child counting while they are). Give each child one bag at a time. Show children how to open and close bags. Ask children to count the items in the bag and report to the teacher how many they counted. Continue giving them new bags as they finish counting their bag if their interest is sustained. Later on, with more experience children can use small paper numbers to label how many are in each bag; use the number cards in Reproducible F. This routine can be done again and again—it is time well spent, both in giving children counting practice and preparing materials for other projects (see *Matching Picture Cards* in this chapter)!

See Chapter 2 for use of items from the Collection Museum.

See Video Clips 5.3 and 5.1.

See Reproducible F, Number Cards: 1–20.

Games

Young children are naturally playful. We like to include games in the classroom and find that children are drawn to anything that they think is going to be a game. The positive aspect of a game is that the teacher takes a different role; now students and the teacher are all involved in the activity at the same level. Children also become teachers in their small groups. They are engaged because there might be a winner and so pay much more attention to what their friends are doing than in a typical small group activity. We also value the practical application of a game; children have an opportunity to take the

isolated bits of information that they have been learning and pull them all together for a purpose. Counting games support the development of counting skills, give children the opportunity to work with their peers, and provide moments to talk about the counting they are doing: "You moved five. No, it's six. Look, one, two, three, four, five, six!"

Matching Picture Cards

This game was adapted from the article "Early Number Instruction," by Arthur J. Baroody and Alexis Benson, in *Teaching Children Mathematics*. First assemble the picture cards in Reproducible G, Matching Picture Cards. Consider mounting and laminating each card on cardstock.

See Reproducible G , Matching Picture Cards.

Give each child the same set of two or three cards. For example, you might give each child a card with two circles and a card with one circle. Then you select a card that matches one of the children's cards. For example, you could select a card with two circles. Ask, "Which one is the same number as mine?" Children should select the card with two circles.

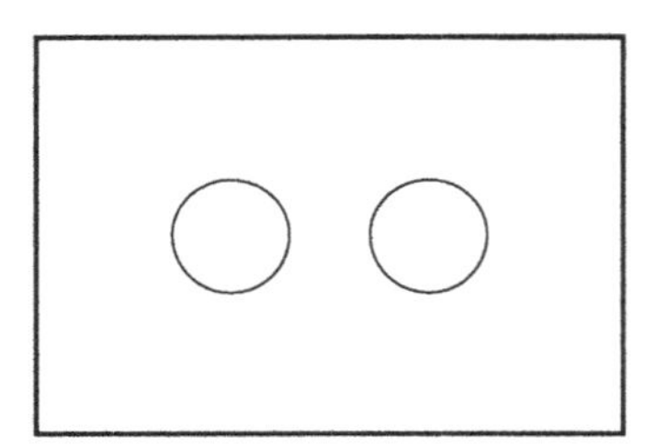

The teacher puts out a picture card.

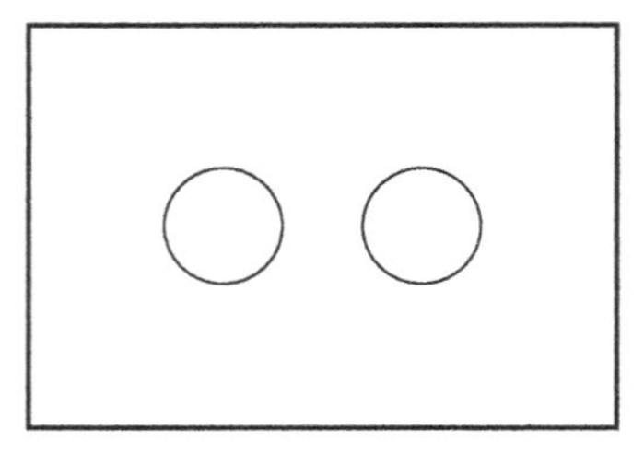
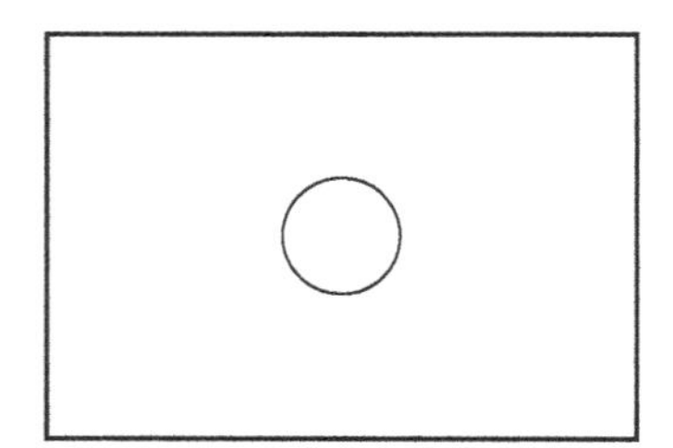

Each child has two picture cards to choose from in matching the teacher's card.

To increase the challenge, you can add more cards for children to choose from or increase the number of objects represented on the cards. Cards can also be used to develop color and shape recognition.

Some children look only at the color or shape on the cards instead of thinking about the quantity. This is an interesting assessment opportunity as well as a teaching opportunity. In a small group, the teacher can help the child focus on counting the shapes on the cards to check for a match rather than looking at the shape or the color. Number is an important way to categorize things. Another important step toward understanding number is recognizing that it is an important attribute, like color, size, and weight, for categorizing things and, thus, for identifying and comparing them (A. Baroody 2001).

The following is another example of how to play this game.

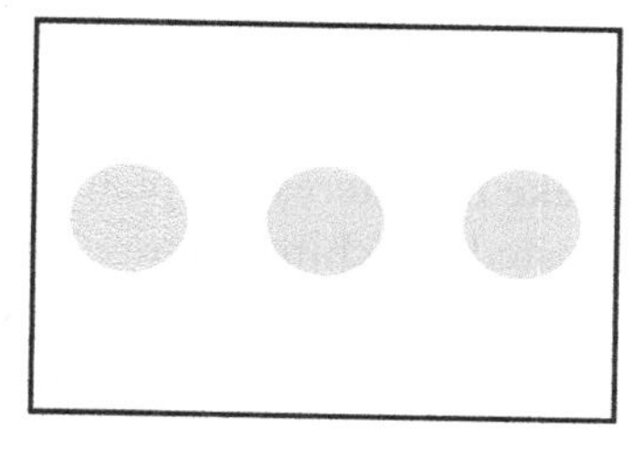

The teacher puts out a picture card with three blue circles.

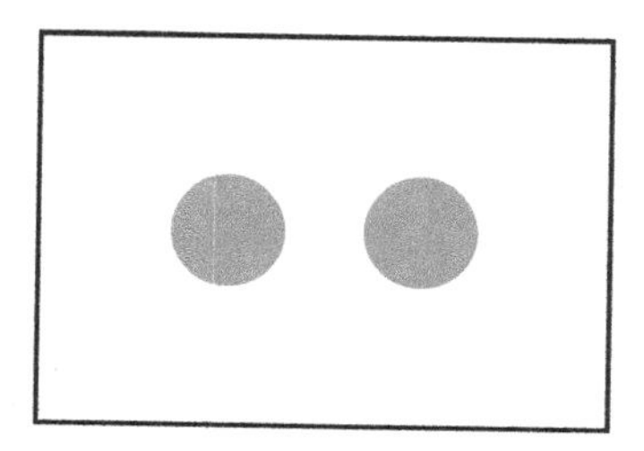

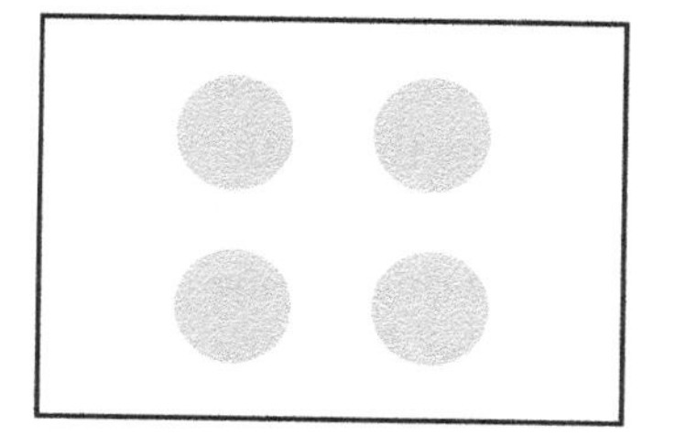

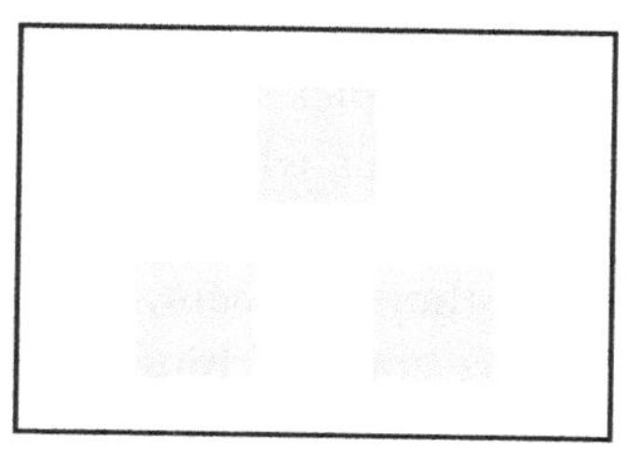

The child has three picture cards to choose from: two red circles, four blue circles, and three green squares.

Assessment Opportunity

See Reproducible C2 , Learning Progressions: Early Childhood/Number.

Use Reproducible C2, Learning Progressions: Early Childhood/ Number to record your observations.

Teaching Insight

Preparing Matching Picture Cards

See Chapter 2 for insights on class studios and collections.

Have children prepare matching picture cards during studio time. Studio materials can make for interesting picture cards—for example, in our studio, Josiah created matching picture cards using a collection of seeds (we found these more interesting than the frequently used sticker dots)! Children can also use objects from the counting bags (see *How Many Are in the Bag?*). For insights on class studios and collections, see Chapter 2.

Home/School Connections

Preparing matching picture cards can also make for a fun family activity; encourage families to help their children make these cards at home.

Choice Time

Commercial Board Games

Board games are a fun, motivating way for young children to develop counting strategies in a context. Keep a collection of counting board games in the classroom—ones that specifically use cards, dice, or spinners to generate numbers to indicate how many spaces players need to move on the board. Allow children to pick the tool that makes sense to them (dot dice for children who need to count to know the quantity, numeral dice for children who recognize numerals and the quantities they represent, tokens to practice one-to-one correspondence and matching the quantity on the die to the number of moves, etc.). Also make sure children are familiar with key vocabulary.

Key Game Vocabulary

move ahead	go back
counters	taking tur

Initially, have an adult play the game with a small group of children so that children understand how to move their marker and count spaces, with-

out counting the space they are on. Then during choice time, let children play on their own. Consider pairing up children who are working at similar levels. Keep in mind that it can be challenging for some children to play games independently. If the child has a strong sense of how to play the basic game, introduce a few motivating moves: *go ahead 3 more spaces (green), go back 2 spaces (red), go back to the beginning, go to the end of the game*. Children will usually play a game over and over again, sometimes independently and sometimes with friends. The idea of winning or loosing is usually not part of their game structure.

A Child's Mind

The Rules of the Game

Often children in small groups will change the rules of a game—this is okay! They invent ways to play the game that are more satisfying to them. Usually they agree on how the game will be played and then proceed to play the game.

Children playing the game Snail's Pace.

Teaching Insight

Our Seven Favorite Counting Board Games

The Golden Apple	Monkey in the Middle
Hi-Ho! Cherry-O	Counting Cookies
Count Your Chickens	Five Little Monkeys
Bus Stop	Snails Pace

Make Your Own Board Game

Children get especially excited about games that they help design themselves. Following is one idea for making a game board with a child.

My Own Game Board

1. Cut out colorful paper shapes (about 3 inches in size) that will create the pathway that snakes around the board.
2. Work with the child to glue the shapes in place from Start (green) to Finish (red).
3. Take photos of the child doing various things in the classroom or outdoors.
4. Glue these photos around the board and have the child tell you what he is doing in each picture. Write down these descriptions. For example, "Help Jose build a block castle," or "Help Jose find some beautiful rocks for the garden."
5. Choose a handful of small counters for the game. Decide with the child whether to use dice, cards, or a spinner.
6. Play a sample game with the child. Crown the child the author of the game and encourage her or him to teach another child how to play the game.

Snack Time

See Reproducible E, Quick Images: Dot Cards.

Snack time provides many opportunities for children to practice counting in a visually appealing—and tasty—way. Use assessment information from the various classroom activities to specifically plan the quantities each child will need to count, and then modify the "recipes" to meet the child's needs. Keep dot cards (see Reproducible E) nearby for children who may need this counting tool to scaffold their counting.

This section focuses on counting cups and counting snacks into the cups. However, counting isn't all that happens when children participate in snack time preparation; they also learn about measurement, following directions, classifying food into food groups, science (for example, how cooking can change liquids into solids), the safe use of kitchen tools, and more. Further, making their own snacks is a powerful way for children to show their independence and competence.

Even if they are not fond of the particular snack, children enjoy being the snack helper (some children expand their food preferences after regularly being involved in snack preparation!). Make sure that each child has an opportunity to be involved in preparing snacks for others. Many children do not have the opportunity to be involved in food preparation at home (understandably it often takes more time and effort to make something with a child than it would if you do it yourself). We share with families our recipes and enthusiasm for these kinds of projects. We want families to know how learning is enhanced when children are cooking.

Teaching Insight

Choosing Food for Children's Snack Time

- ☑ Does the food accommodate any allergies or special needs children may have?
- ☑ Is the food healthy?
- ☑ Is the food easy to prepare (involves a safe use of kitchen tools)?
- ☑ Is the food tasty?

Teaching Insight

Snack Time Guidelines

- Make sure children wash their hands before preparing and eating snacks.
- Begin snack time by thanking children who brought any ingredients.
- Involve children in passing out the snacks and helping to pour the juice.
- During snack time, encourage children to practice saying *please* and *thank you* and also learn how to say, "No thank you, I do not care for ______."
- Have children help with clean up and recycling after snack time.

Snack Preparation and Counting

A great way to practice counting—and prepare for snack time simultaneously—is to first work with a small group of children to figure out how many cups or paper plates are needed for the class. After the number of cups have been determined, children then count snacks into each cup. Use a snack menu like the one shown to determine food type and quantities (we keep a series of snack menus on hand that require early counting skills). Focus on a specific number each day; change the menu or recipe to match the number that a child needs to practice counting. Use assessment opportunities like those featured in Chapter 5 to learn what numbers children would benefit from counting over and over again. Some children need practice counting to a target number.

See Chapter 5 for assessment opportunities to learn what numbers children would benefit from counting during snack time.

Teaching Insight

Snack Time Menu

Day 1, Monday: one piece of apple, one cube of cheese, one mini carrot, one berry, etc.

Day 2, Tuesday: two pretzels, two stalks of celery, two raisins, etc.

Day 3, Wednesday: three cherry tomatoes, three crackers, three grapes, etc.

Day 4, Thursday: four raisins, four pretzels, four nuts, four pea pods, etc.

Day 5, Friday: five crackers, five mini slices of cheese, five olives, etc.

See Reproducible K, Ten-Frame.

See Reproducible E, Quick Images: Dot Cards.

For the larger numbers or to scaffold counting, give children tools to support their counting. For example, if children are counting snacks in groups of five, give them a visual reference, such as a five frame (see Reproducible K), a quick image card with five dots (see Reproducible E), or five paper muffin cups. After a child has counted the group, he or she places the snack in a snack cup or on a paper plate.

Video Clip 7.2: Counting Snack Cups and Snacks

Children use their classmates' photos to determine how many children need snack cups.

To view the clip, scan the QR code or visit **mathsolutions.com/TEACHPK72**

> ### Math Talk
> **Counting**
>
> It is a different skill to *count out* a specific number of items (as being done in the snack time activity here) than to *count* what is presented (as being done in the *How Many Are in the Bag? Routine* in this chapter). Sometimes it is very challenging for children to count and stop at the target number.

In Video Clip 7.2, Brenda gathers a group of four children and tells them it is their job to make the snack cups. She asks, "How many cups do we need? What could we do?" One child exclaims, "Count the people!" The teacher suggests that children use their picture cards (the pictures of their classmates on their attendance chart) to help them count. One child suggests (by pointing) taking the photos of classmates who are present back to the snack preparation table to count there. Back at the table, the children count. They conclude that they will need twelve snack cups. Brenda asks how they will count the cups. One child suggests that one cup be placed on each picture, which they do. In the second part of the clip, children begin counting snacks. Mia (age 5 years, 7 months) and Gibran (age 4) make use of quick image cards to count four and five snacks. When Gibran has his card filled, the teacher suggests they count the snacks together. Watch the clip. What do you notice about the group's ability to count? What does the teacher do? Record your observations.

What We Learned: The teacher could have told the children how many cups to use, but then they wouldn't have had this rich opportunity to solve a problem that was meaningful to them. When first told about the task and asked how many cups they need, children count only themselves at the table, concluding that they need four cups. They are counting themselves, but not thinking about the rest of the class. To encourage them to think beyond their small group of four (the whole instead of a part!), the teacher points to the class attendance

See also Video Clip 5.4; in this clip, Danitza practices counting out six fish crackers. Brenda learned from her one-on-one assessment with Danitza (see Video Clip 5.3) that Danitza consistently omits six in her oral counting practice; hence Brenda takes this snack time opportunity to give Danitza practice counting six objects.

chart. This helps the group make the connection that they need to prepare snack cups for the whole class. When the children go over to the chart and count the pictures, they skip pictures and miscount—it seems a bit confusing! Fortunately Mia suggests they return to the table with the pictures. After the children have decided the number of cups, they start an assembly line of cups, filling them with their specific number of snack items. On the video, Gibran and Mia use quick image cards to support their counting. Notice how Gibran counts the dots on his own and then with the teacher's help. It's not on the clip, but at one point it's interesting to note that Paola proclaims, "I don't need the card," as she counts teddy grahams into a cup.

Teaching Insight

A Community Snack System

Snack time becomes a chance for children to try new foods that may be favorites in other households. We use a community snack system in our class for this purpose. We send children home with a list of possibilities or guidelines, especially noting any known allergies (see "Choosing Food for Young Children's Snack Time" list). Fresh produce is especially appreciated. Interestingly, broccoli is our class's favorite vegetable, followed by carrots and cherry tomatoes. Ranch dressing for dipping is also a big hit. Encourage parents to contribute items every other week instead of preparing an individual snack for their child every day of the week. Many appreciate this, and can be encouraged to purchase food in bulk sizes, which is cheaper and more environmentally friendly than individually wrapped snacks. In our class we have chickens; they get the scraps and any leftovers not consumed. Understandably, not every class has chickens—a worm bin is another way to deal with scrap food items. In turn, the worms make compost for a class garden—and that is a real community bonus!

Teaching Insight

Healthy Snack Idea: Edamame Beans

Edamame beans are great to count—and eat! In our class children refer to edamame beans as *good to eat* and *fun to peel*. Edamame is a green vegetable more commonly known as a soybean. The word *edamame* means "beans on branches," and it grows in clusters on bushy branches. In Asia, the soybean has been used for over two thousand years as a major source of protein. As a snack, the pods are gently boiled in salted water, and then the seeds are squeezed directly from the pods into the mouth with the fingers.

For more ideas on using snack time to facilitate children's growth in counting, see Chapter 3 (Pattern Snacks), Chapter 8 (Do You Like Green Eggs and Ham?, Which Juice Do You Prefer?, Which Apple Color Do You Like Best?, Which Cracker Shape Do You Like Best?), Chapter 10 (Recipes That Build Important Mathematical Ideas), and Video Clips 5.4 and 7.2.

hoice Time

Surveys

Surveys are a way to collect data on preferences, experiences, and observations. When children interview their classmates, they become makers of the curriculum. When they put the information in graphic form, they can count and compare a visual representation of the survey information. We help them understand how charts are created from real information. In order to introduce the idea of a survey, we make many graphic representations of class information. See Chapter 8 for examples of graphs to do with the whole class to count and compare data. It is helpful to begin with yes/no questions by making a two-column chart, labeling one column *Yes* and the other column *No*. Then ask Yes/No questions, such as *Do you like strawberry yogurt?* Write children's names in the appropriate column to record their responses. This a very useful way to practice name writing. We have found that children are much more careful writing their names in this context because they want others to be able to read their names. Charts can also be created with more than two columns; for example, ask questions that can be answered by a number, such as How many letters are in your name? How many people are in your family? Children make meaningful connections and engage in mathematical discussions when they notice that they may have something in common with their friends: *Oh, my gosh, all three of us like strawberry yogurt.*

Plan to have surveys be one of the choices on the choice board (see "Using the Choice Board" in "How to Use This Resource," page xix). When

Surveys can be one of the choices on the choice board. For insights on choice time and using choice boards, see Using the Choice Board in How to Use This Resource, page xix.

children choose the questions to ask in taking a survey, they become invested in counting the data they collect. Help each child in writing a survey question and creating a corresponding graph to collect data. Once children have collected the data, discuss it with them.

In choice time surveys, not only are children finding out real information from their classmates, they are also writing for a purpose and practicing how to write their names.

In Brenda's class, numerous questions emerge from the activities and interests of the children: *Did you see* Spiderman? *Do you want to be a pirate? Do you like beans and rice? Do you think a wolf would hurt you?*

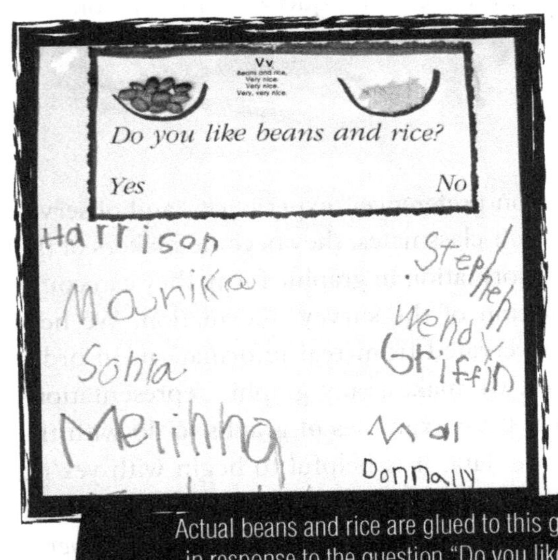

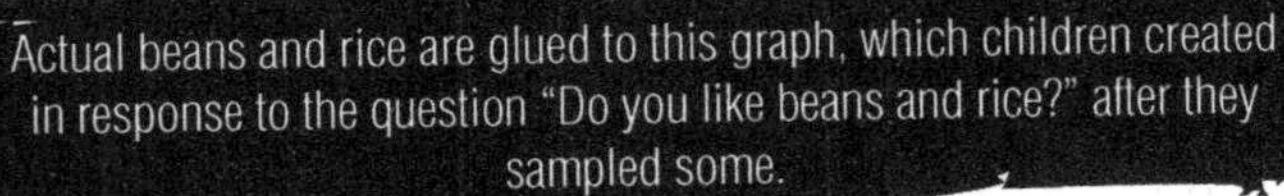
Actual beans and rice are glued to this graph, which children created in response to the question "Do you like beans and rice?" after they sampled some.

One child decided to make this graph in response to the question, “Do you think a wolf would hurt you?”—likely influenced by the class’s study of wolves.

Two children decided to make their own graphs—they copied the names of the children in the class that *did* and *did not* have the letter *e* in their names. They didn’t bother to have children sign in on their graphs!

Surveys are valuable in helping children make comparisons. See Chapter 8 for examples of graphs and more data-collection activities.

To view the clip, scan the QR code or visit **mathsolutions.com/TEACHPK73**

Video Clip 7.3: Taking Surveys

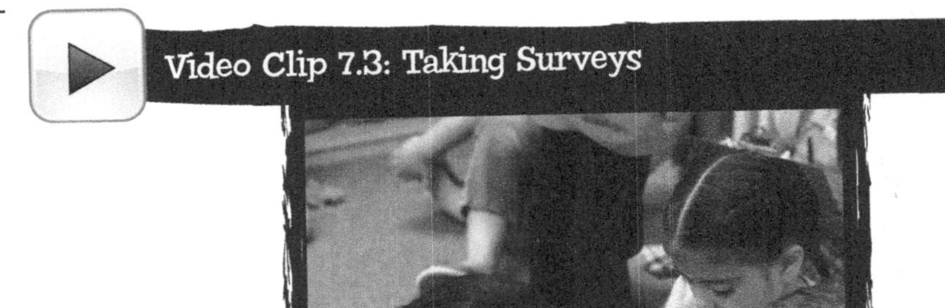

Children responding to a classmate's survey question, "Can you touch your toes?"

In Video Clip 7.3, Brenda helps children think of a survey question and create a graph. The student decides she wants to do a survey on the question "Can you touch your toes?" The teacher helps her write the question down and create a corresponding yes/no graph. Although it's not on video, the teacher does the same for the other two girls at the table. The girls then circulate with their charts attached to clipboards. We see them gathering answers from their classmates, who write their names in one of the columns. In the final part of this clip, Brenda and the children talk about their survey results. Watch the clip in its entirety. What questions does Brenda ask the children to prompt their thinking? What do you notice about the children's interaction with the surveys?

What We Learned: Some children are able to gather information from the entire class. Others end up asking only their friends for responses to their question. This may be an indication of how much they understand the purpose of the survey in the first place. It also may be challenging for some children to reach out to children who are not in their immediate circle of friends. Usually our more outgoing children choose this task.

One child asked, "Do you like salsa?" Some children responded by thinking about a sauce for tacos and others were thinking about dancing. This brought up an interesting idea of one word having two meanings.

We also learned that the data was not very accurate, but it did engage the survey taker. Some children, for example, could not tell how many were in their families, but were willing to give a number answer to the survey taker.

We also learned that keeping track of who has responded to the survey becomes problematic. It is interesting to see how they remember the survey information later on. For example, after we made our apple graph, children noticed who was eating apple snacks and connected that observation to the graph.

Reflection Questions

1. How can children's counting skills be developed during everyday routines?
2. What sorts of physical and oral counting games might help a child who has not yet learned the correct sequence for counting? Why might these be particularly helpful?
3. What kinds of questions might be posed in your class for surveys?
4. Why do you think the visual aspect of dice and playing cards is so important?
5. Why is it helpful for children to make their own game cards, board games, and surveys?
6. How can the teacher plan activities for a wide range of student needs?
7. What is the value of card or board games when children sit together around a table compared to electronic games that children play on their own?

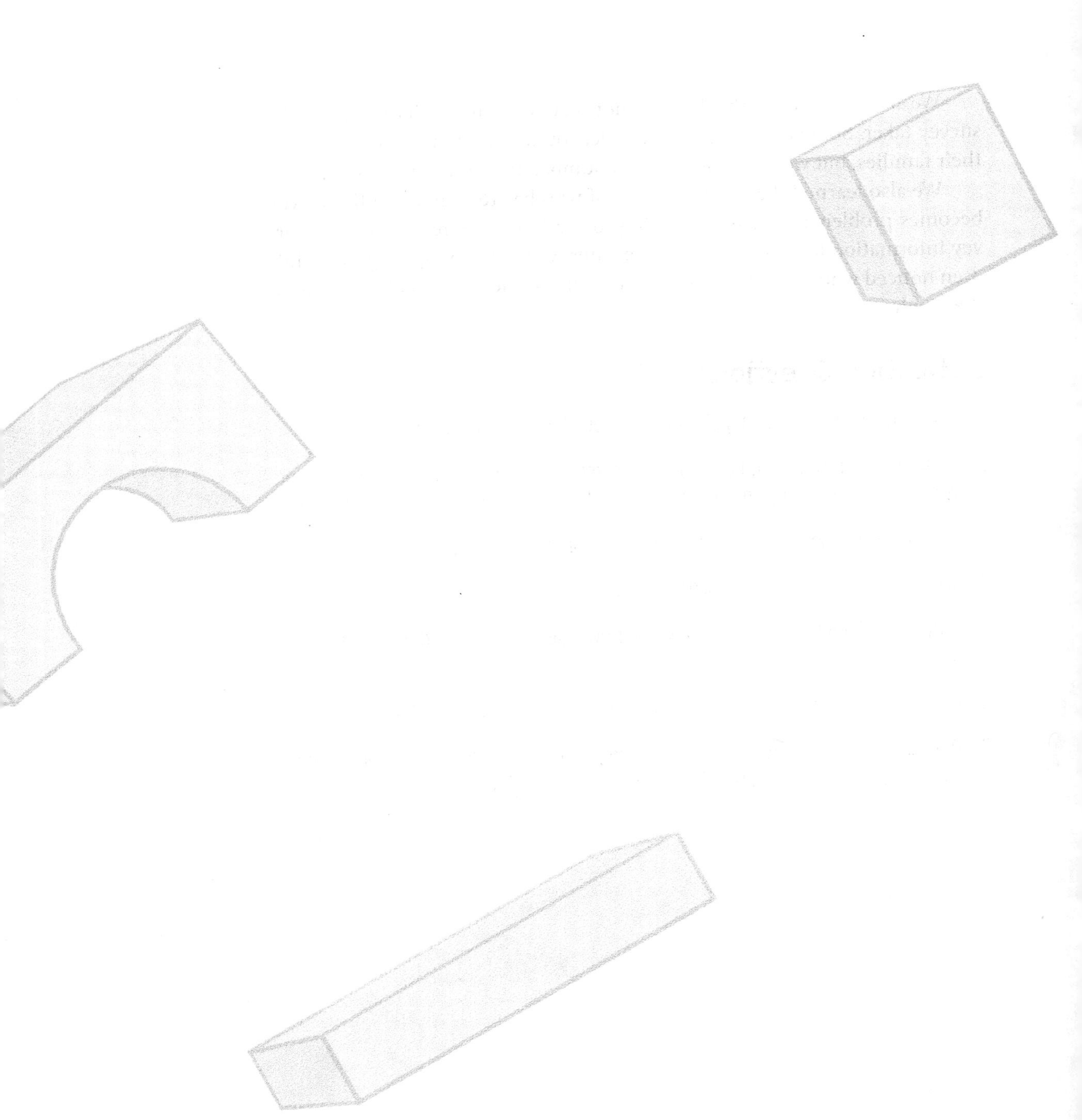

Section III

Developing Young Children's Number Sense

Overview

Section II examined the complexity of learning to count. Section III moves into number sense—what it is and ways to explore number through activities and child-centered investigations. Chapter 8 explores how children use their counting abilities to compare, measure, evaluate, and make sense of the quantities based on attendance routines, graphing, and body measurements. Chapter 9 contains ideas for encouraging children to develop and use their geometry skills in spatial orientation and spatial visualization; the ideas provide experiences that are integral to the work students do when solving problems, making projects, and describing mental maps. Chapter 10 focuses on a selection of foundational investigations—open-ended work that can be extended to other content areas when children show interest.

She says that she has more, but I think it's the same. We gotta make sure it's fair.

—Alondra

Using Comparisons and Measurement to Build Number Sense

Chapter 8

Overview

In this chapter we explore beginning opportunities for children to develop their number sense, specifically using their counting abilities to compare, measure, evaluate, and make sense of the quantities they are investigating. These ideas are especially valuable in encouraging children to "make friends with numbers." When children can compare how many cubes are in their towers or how long their own name is compared to other names in the class, they are beginning to use counting to *mean* something. Later on in school they will learn operations and procedures to do this work. Now they are using counting in a wide variety of contexts to tell their number stories.

It's important to find multiple ways for children to count and talk about comparing quantities and measurements. Children need opportunities to practice counting; they also need to make connections to how the counting that they do is useful. This chapter starts with multiple readings and dramatizations of *Goldilocks and the Three Bears*. This story sets the stage for thinking about comparisons and different sizes. Then we look at how we can take advantage of attendance routines to build number sense and number representations. Since we talk about who is here and who is absent every day, we have a familiar context to explore number relationships. Then we move into thinking about our names. We can count the letters in our names as well as look at how we might have some letters in common. Since children are also learning how to write their names, these activities are integrated into regular routines and learning to write. Finally, graphing ideas are presented to let children count and compare information that they care about.

Continued

The Big Ideas of Counting and Comparing

Following are excerpts from research important to our understanding of counting and comparing in early childhood. Read each research insight and reflect on it. Discuss with others what it means to you. How do these ideas match your own understanding of what it means to have number sense?

Research Insights

1. The word *mathematics* makes many adults think of rote procedures for getting correct answers, a holdover from our own school days. But mathematics is essentially the search for sense and meaning, patterns and relationships, order and predictability (Copley 2000).
2. Recognizing small groups or quantities is a skill children use to develop more sophisticated understanding about number. A major milestone occurs in the early grades when children interpret number in terms of part and whole relationships. A part–whole understanding of number means that quantities are interpreted as being composed of other numbers (Chapin and Johnson 2006).

Introducing Vocabulary for Comparing and Measuring

In order for children to use their counting abilities to compare and measure, teachers need to familiarize them with common related vocabulary. Literature is a good way to introduce comparison and measurement vocabulary.

More, Fewer, Less

The children's book *More, Fewer, Less* by Tana Hoban displays full-color photos of everyday objects and familiar animals—from spoons and scissors to fish and chickens—that can prompt open-ended questions. Children are immediately drawn into the book; explore the photos with them, discovering ways to express relationship ideas using the title words *more*, *fewer*, and *less*. Children often seem interested in more (because they want more), but thinking about fewer or less is not as much in their experience.

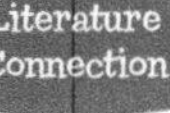

Three Bears Sort and Compare

This activity is based on ideas presented in "Transitive Relational Mappings in Three- and Four-Year-Olds: The Analogy of Goldilocks and the Three Bears," by U. Goswami in *Child Development* (1995). Read aloud *Goldilocks and the Three Bears* by Jan Brett several times. Now it's playtime! Choose a place in the classroom to transform into the house of the three bears (in our classroom we use the *casita*—home center). Gather the following props:

- three toy bears of three different sizes
- pots of three different sizes
- chairs of three different sizes
- towels in three different sizes to serve as the beds
- spoons, pillows, hats, backpacks, picnic items, aprons, and other objects that might be part of the bears' home and connect to the story

Support children in determining different ways to portray the three bears. Use the following chart to help children get into their roles as bears. Encourage children to compare and contrast the attributes.

Acting Out *The Three Bears*

Dimension Attribute	Baby Bear	Mommy Bear	Daddy Bear
Loudness of footsteps	quiet	steps can be heard okay	loud
Size of footsteps	tiny	medium-sized	huge
Pitch of voices	squeaky	normal sounding	thundering
Hardness of chairs	soft	a bit soft/a bit hard	hard
Temperature of porridge	warm	quite hot	boiling hot
Saltiness of porridge	not salty	a bit salty	very salty
Width of beds	narrow	medium-sized	wide
Position of mirrors on the wall	low	halfway up the wall	high up

Ask children questions to encourage the use of language like *bigger than* and *smaller than*. "How do you know that this spoon is for the baby bear? Which chair belongs to the Daddy bear? How do you know?" Change the story by increasing and decreasing the number of bears. "How can we make a house for five bears? What would we need?"

Using Attendance for Comparisons

Attendance provides a daily opportunity for children to develop number sense, to compare numbers, and to see how the number that describes the whole classroom community is broken into two parts: those who are present and those who are absent (Confer 2005).

Brenda uses a daily attendance chart consisting of a pocket chart with two sections; the lower section is labeled "Who is here today?" and the upper section, "Who is *not* here today?" Children have individual laminated photo cards featuring their name and photo. Each day before class we make sure each student's card is in the "Who is *not* here today?" section. When children enter the classroom, they move their photo card to the "Who is here today?" pocket.

An attendance chart in Brenda's classroom.

Later on, when we come to the circle for our morning gathering, we review our daily attendance chart and discuss our attendance data. You'll find that the use of a daily attendance chart has multiple benefits: it's a good way to teach the meaning of numerical symbols and the quantity they represent; it provides a real-life context that children understand (versus isolated drill and practice on a worksheet); it's used (and has a purpose!) on a daily basis; and the information (the photo cards) stays the same so there is less new information to process on a daily basis. Following are ideas for investigating the daily data gathered on an attendance chart.

How Many Are *Not* Here Today?

Direct children's attention to the daily attendance chart and ask, "How many are *not* here today?" Listen as children answer and explain their thinking. Make sure to point to the photo cards under "Who is not here today?" Sometimes a child who is present has forgotten to move his or her photo card and needs to quickly fix this bit of incorrect data.

See Reproducible F, Number Cards 1–20.

As children contribute answers to the question of how many, ask a child to come up and place the corresponding number card next to "Who is not here today?" (See Reproducible F for examples of number cards that could be used.)

At the beginning of the year children will likely need to be shown which numeral represents the number of classmates absent. As the year progresses, children are able to choose the numerals themselves. The activity can be varied by asking children to find a numeral that represents the number of absent girls and a numeral that represents the number of absent boys—then find how many are absent all together.

Brenda's Journal Page

Thinking About Zero

The other day Delicia counted 0 girls absent, 1 boy absent, and 1 child absent all together. "Hey," she said, "why are there two ones?" She seemed to be trying to make sense of what happens when one of the numbers is zero. I decided to wait until

continued

there were both boys and girls absent, as I realize that zero can be a challenging idea for children to grasp. I do want children to bump up against this notion of zero. Zero is not one of the counting numbers, so they won't see it when they count, but eventually they will need to use it to describe the quantity of the empty set. In our attendance situation, they will again need to deal with the idea of zero. This will take much more time to develop.

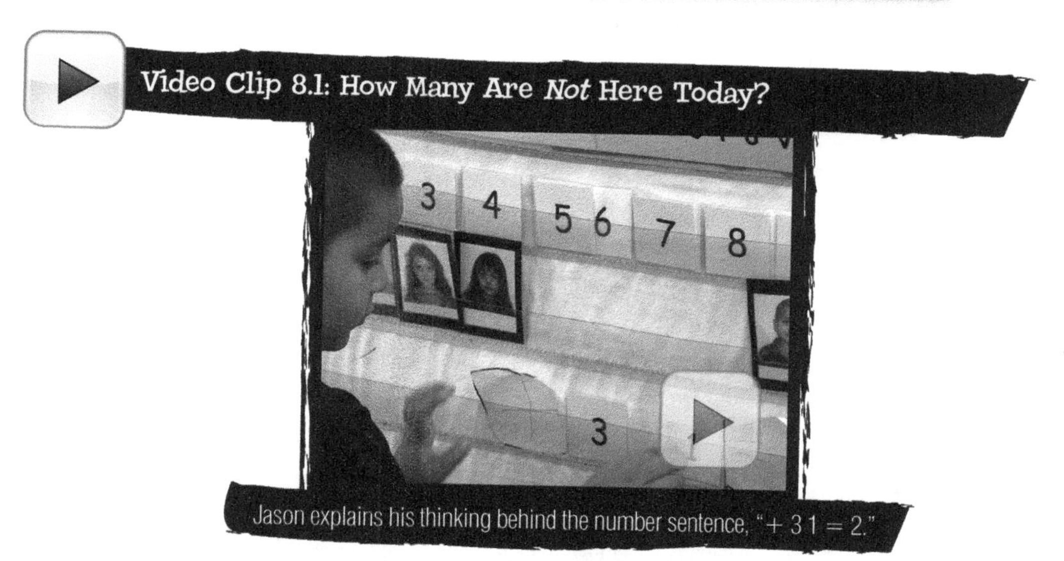

Video Clip 8.1: How Many Are *Not* Here Today?

Jason explains his thinking behind the number sentence, "+ 3 1 = 2."

To view the clip, scan the QR code or visit **mathsolutions.com/ TEACHPK81**

In Video Clip 8.1, Brenda encourages children to make their own number sentence to represent how many children are not here today. They are using an attendance chart to help them—on the attendance chart three girls are absent and two boys are absent. A child has placed number cards 3, 1, and 2 as well as some operation slips of paper in the pocket chart. First watch the video clip in its entirety. Reflect on the research insights in "The Big Ideas of Counting and Comparing," page 145. What connections come to mind?

Then watch the clip again, this time pausing at various intervals and thinking about the questions that follow.

Brenda notices that Jason has put up the number sentence on the attendance chart for the day. So she calls on Jason to come up and share his thinking about the number sentence, + 3 1 = 2. The clip starts with Brenda asking Jason to explain his thinking. Jason indicates that the 3 stands for the three girls who are absent and the 2 stands for the two boys. Stop the clip when the teacher asks Jason to sit down. What have you learned about Jason's understanding of the meaning of the numbers?

What We Learned: Jason has tried but cannot yet make sense of this number sentence. He does know that the 3 represents the three girls and the 2 represents the two boys. He is unsure of what to do with the number 1 that was also placed up on the pocket chart. The addition sign, equals sign, and sum of five are not yet correctly represented.

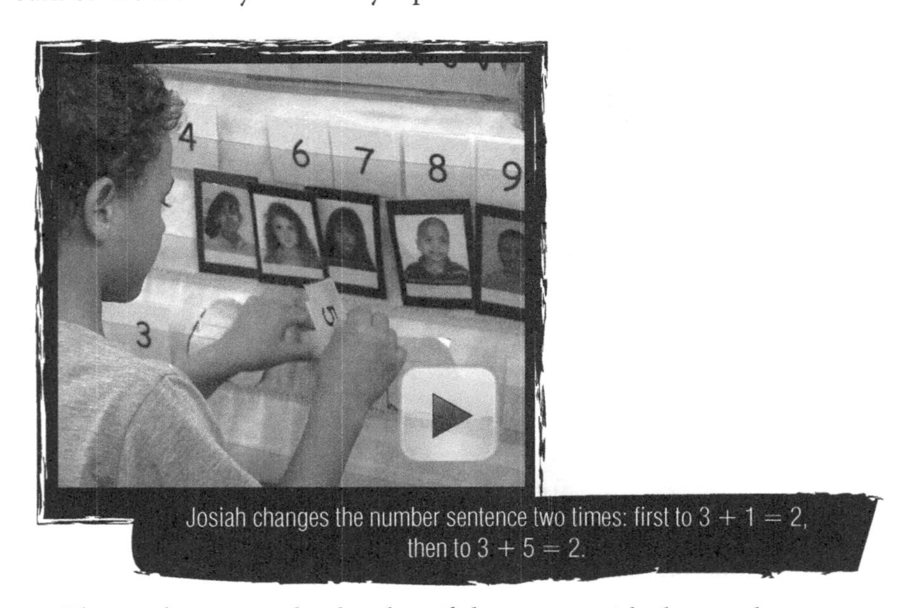

Josiah changes the number sentence two times: first to 3 + 1 = 2, then to 3 + 5 = 2.

The teacher now asks the class if they agree with the number sentence Jason created. The teacher asks Josiah, who disagrees, "How could we make this number sentence make sense?" Josiah changes the number sentence from + 3 1 = 2 to 3 + 1 = 2. The teacher asks Josiah to explain his thinking. He points out that the 3 is for the three girls and the 2 is for the two boys. The teacher asks Josiah what the 1 stands for. Josiah responds, "You put them all together and make . . ." The teacher asks, "How many is it altogether?" Josiah counts the photo cards, "1, 2, 3, 4, 5." The teacher asks, "Where's the five?" Josiah thinks for a moment and places the numeral 5 in the number sentence so it now reads 3 + 5 = 2. Stop the clip when the teacher asks Josiah to have a seat. What have you learned about Josiah's understanding of number? About the rest of the class's understanding? What do you notice about the questions the teacher asks Josiah?

What We Learned: The children are struggling to make sense of the abstract representation of the attendance data. Josiah represents the three girls and the two boys, but needs to revise the number for the total. When he needs to combine them to determine the total, he moves the pictures together and counts to obtain 5, and then changes 1 for 5. The number sentence is not in the correct order, but he does have the necessary number cards. We hear the children now agreeing with his incorrect number sentence.

Humberto changes the number sentence to read 3 + 2 = 5.

Continue watching the clip to the end. The teacher asks Humberto to help everyone make sense of the number sentence. She says, "I agree that the numbers are right, and the symbols are right, but I don't think that they are in the right order." Humberto silently changes the number sentence to read 3 + 2 = 5. The teacher asks, "What are you thinking, Humberto?" She wants to know why he moved the 5 and the 2. Humberto says, "Because it would make two." The teacher probes further, "What does this 5 right here stand for?" Humberto responds, "The five kids." The teacher continues, "What does this 2 right here stand for?" Humberto says, "The two boys." The teacher then asks, "And what does this 3 right here stand for?" Humberto says, "The three girls." The teacher then asks Liana to read the number sentence. She asks Liana if it makes sense to her and Liana responds affirmatively. What have you learned about Humberto's understanding of number? How does the teacher encourage Humberto to explain his thinking?

What We Learned: Humberto correctly arranges the number sentence to represent the absent children. He has a hard time explaining his thinking, but he can point to the pictures that go with the number cards. Throughout Video Clip 8.1 children struggle to find a way to arrange the numbers to make a number sentence that correctly shows how many children are absent. Through math talk, the teacher realizes that some children can put the number cards in the right place on the number frame, but they have little understanding of the numerical connection to the attendance chart. When she encourages the children to explain their thinking, it becomes apparent that they had placed numerals in the correct place, but were not making sense of the expression.

Math Talk

The Commutative Property of Addition

The commutative property of addition states that the order of the addends does not change the sum.

Conceptual vs. Social Knowledge

Ideas like the commutative property of addition are *conceptual* knowledge, which is different from *social* knowledge. Children can be told or shown *social* knowledge—for example, "When you cut with scissors, you should turn the paper, not the scissors." Conceptual knowledge, on the other hand, is developed within the child's mind (Burns 2007).

A Child's Mind

Order of Addends

In Brenda's class something interesting happened over time as children worked with creating number sentences to represent "How many are not here today?" Because one girl was absent for many days in a row, it became routine to always count how many girls were absent first (the same girl) and make that number the first addend in the number sentence; then count the boys for the second addend. One day Brenda asked her children how many boys were absent before she asked how many girls were absent. The children were confused when it came to creating the number sentence; they struggled with the idea that the order of the addends does not change the sum (commutative property of addition). Even though this is an important mathematical idea, Brenda had inadvertently created a procedural understanding of addition that was not conceptually meaningful. This was further complicated by the *social knowledge* of some children who insisted that to be polite, you needed to let girls go first. Brenda worked to find ways to help her children notice that in addition, the order of the addends can change and does not change the sum. Eventually she chose to approach this idea using a different context—that of red and white tokens. Children begin to grasp the idea that three red tokens plus two white tokens is the same total as two white tokens plus three red tokens.

How Many Are Here Today?

As an alternative to figuring out how many children are absent, have children count how many are present. In Brenda's class there are usually sixteen children; this provides a daily opportunity to practice saying the numbers 1–16. Considering that the irregular counting numbers in English are 11, 12, 13, 14, and 15, this is time well spent!

Brenda's Journal Page

The Number Stays the Same

Today when we worked with the attendance chart we counted the number of children present. I asked, "How many children are here today?" Together as a class we counted all the photo cards. Delicia was concerned about the total. She said, "Push Jackeline's picture in. We better count again!" Jackeline's photo card was farther away from the other children's cards. We moved it closer to the group, then we counted the pictures again and got the same number. Delicia seemed puzzled and uttered a "Huh." I think Delicia is trying to make sense of *conservation of number*—the idea that the total number stays the same even if the photo cards aren't spaced apart the same.

Math Talk

Conservation of Number

Conservation of number is the understanding that the number of objects remains the same even though they may have been rearranged. Children typically make sense of this idea around the age of six or seven, sometimes eight.

To view the clip, scan the QR code or visit **mathsolutions.com/TEACHPK82**

Video Clip 8.2: How Many Are Here Today?

Nate counts the number of children here today.

In Video Clip 8.2, Brenda focuses children's attention on the number of children present according to the attendance chart. The photo cards are arranged in the pocket chart in rows of five. The teacher first asks Gabi to tell her how many kids are on the first line (row). Gabi says four. The teacher asks her to count them. Gabi counts five. The teacher asks Gabi to count the next line; Gabi counts five. This continues for the third line (Gabi counts four), fourth line (Gabi counts two), and last line (Gabi counts one). The teacher asks Nate to count all the kids all together. Nate counts seventeen. The teacher asks, "How are we going to make a seventeen?" Nate chooses number cards 10 and 7. Watch the video clip in its entirety; what do you learn about Gabi's understanding of number? Nate's understanding of number? What do you think the teacher is trying to find out?

Math Talk

Tagging

Touching each of the objects while counting is called tagging.

What We Learned: Brenda is interested in finding out if Gabi will persist in counting each one, or if she can recognize that each row is the same. Notice that Gabi counts the pictures by tagging, even when there are only two pictures in the row. Nate counts and knows how to show 17 with a 10 and a 7.

How Many Are in Our Class?

In the previous activities we've explored using the attendance chart to figure out "How many are not here today?" and "How many are here today?" As children's mathematical knowledge progresses, take this activity a step further and encourage children to figure out, based on the attendance chart data, how many children in total are in their class. Children deal with part, part, whole relationships when they make a number sentence for *how many are here today + how many are absent = how many are in the class.*

Math Talk

The Equals sign

The equals sign is often misunderstood by children. They think of it as a punctuation sign signaling the end of the number sentence where the answer belongs. In order to help children think more about the equals sign as showing a relationship, change the placement of the equals sign. For example, instead of $12 + 4 = 16$, show $16 = 12 + 4$. Putting this in the context of an attendance chart, ask children to talk first about the total number of classmates in their class, and then to think about how many are here today and how many are absent. For example, say, "Sixteen children in our class is the same number as twelve children here and four who are absent today. $16 = 12 + 4$." In Brenda's class, on some days it is fun to write $16 = 16$ because everyone is present! On another day she writes $16 = 16 + 0 + 0$ when they think about how happy they are because everyone is present and zero people are absent!

Brenda's Journal Page

Number Sentences

Since we came back from Christmas break we have been writing daily number sentences that reflect the number of boys absent, the number of girls absent, and the number of children missing all together. It has been quite an up and down road as I listen to children try to explain their number sentences!

Isabella's mom asked me if I was teaching addition. She reported Isabella is asking

continued

her family to play school, and she is writing number sentences. Angelica writes number sentences on white boards after school while she waits for her nana to pick her up. So I know some of them are beginning to make sense of this daily challenge.

Attendance Data Represented by Cube Sticks

Consider using other ways to represent attendance data. Brenda likes to use a measurement model to think about the number of children in her class. She makes an attendance stick out of sixteen cubes, one cube for each child in her class. She arranges the cubes in this pattern: five red cubes, five white cubes, five red cubes, and one white cube. In the morning during circle time, Brenda passes a basket of blue cubes around and asks each child to take one. She then asks them to connect their blue cubes together to form a stick representing how many children are present in the class on that day. Children then compare their stick (how many children are in class today) to the length of the class attendance stick Brenda created (the total number of children in the class). Brenda then takes the stick of blue cubes and adds on yellow cubes for the total number of children *who are absent* (children actually name the yellow cubes with the names of the absent children!). Is the stick now the same length as the attendance stick? Sometimes it doesn't work out and everyone wonders why the two sticks are not the same length. Maybe someone left for speech class or is in the bathroom. The entire class is relieved when the stick with all the children present plus the ones that are absent is the same length as the class attendance stick.

A Child's Mind

Why the Red/White/Red Pattern for the Attendance Stick?

For the class attendance stick, Brenda arranges the cubes in this pattern: five red cubes, five white cubes, five red cubes, and one white cube. The reason Brenda uses groups of five red and five white cubes is to help children think about five as a unit as well as five individual cubes. This is called *unitizing* by fives. When children are able to *unitize*, they can think of the total (in this case, sixteen) as five and five and five and one more. They can also see sixteen as three hands of five and one more finger. This is part of a learning progression that will eventually lead to understanding place value, counting by fives and tens, and other ideas about how a number can be represented in different ways. This attendance stick also matches the arrangement of beads on the class rekenrek (see the next activity as well as activities in Chapter 7). Seeing a group of five red beads on the rekenrek and knowing that there are five allows a child to also see the next group of white beads as five more.

In contrast, when children *subitize*, they are able to instantly know how many objects are in a set *without counting*. This usually happens when they deal with two or three objects. Putting these ideas together is a way for children to have visual and mental constructions of quantities. Some may eventually instantly see *three* and *three* and be able to think *six*.

Having different models of the same kinds of ideas helps children begin to generalize about these ideas. Sometimes the arrangement of objects, such as the way dots are arranged on dice, makes subitizing much easier. Understanding these ideas takes time; eventually children will be able to explain their ideas and think about their own thinking—remember, young children are just beginning on this journey!

Math Talk

Unitizing

Unitizing is defined as being able to see a group as a *whole unit* and also know that it is *composed of parts.* Seeing a group of five red beads on the rekenrek and knowing that there are five allows a child to also see the next group of white beads as five more.

Math Talk

Subitizing

Subitizing is defined as seeing a small amount of objects and knowing how many there are *without* counting. Sometimes the arrangement of objects, such as the way dots are arranged on dice, makes subitizing much easier.

Brenda's Journal Page

Using Red and White Photo Frames

Today I wanted to make connections between the attendance stick and the attendance chart. To do so, I used red and white photo frames that fit behind each photo card in the chart. The attendance stick pattern (five red/five white/five red) can then be transferred to the rows of photo cards (envision five photo cards framed in red, then five framed in white, and so forth).

Children noticed lots of things about the complete rows of five framed photo cards, including how many paper frames have photos, and how many frames are empty because someone is absent. I think they are really bumping up against the notion of decomposing and composing five, and they are beginning to make sense of this. What I wonder about is, are they really unitizing? Nathaniel, for example, quickly notices the *fiveness* of the row, but never articulates this. The children notice that two rows of five are ten. When I show quantities on the bead boards, Nathaniel doesn't have to *count* to say seven, but he can't seem to explain how he is using five, and two more, to be able to say *seven*.

Attendance Data Represented by Rekenreks

Another way to represent attendance data is by using a rekenrek or bead board. Ask each child to move one of the wooden beads on the *rekenrek*. When everyone has had a turn, count the number of beads that have been moved.

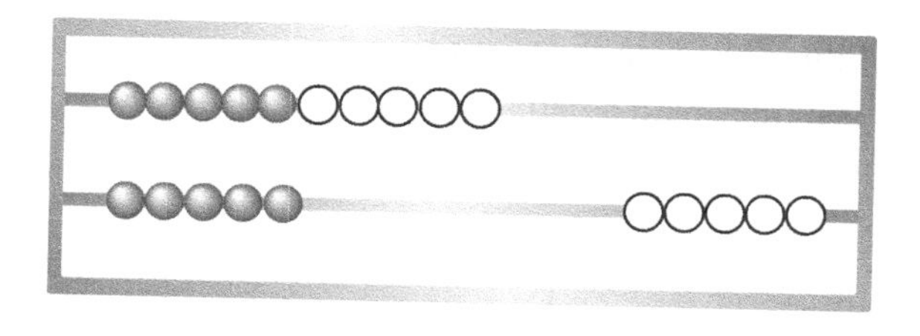

This rekenrek shows that fifteen beads have been moved; there are fifteen children in class today.

For more on using rekenreks, see Chapter 7, page 115.

The following math talk is used with the rekenrek in Brenda's classroom:

Let's count to see how many are here today. (15)

We should have 16. How many are absent? (1)

How many more do we need to show 16? (1)

If Carlos were here, he would push over this last one.

Who wants to pretend he is Carlos?

Oh Carlos, we're so glad you are here today. We missed you!

Using Real-World, Personalized Data Collection for Comparisons and Measurements

We want to find opportunities to count and compare things that matter to children in their own lives. We collect data regularly that can be easily compared so that children can see without counting which group has more. For example, we match data to grids or rows on pocket charts. Write each letter of a child's name in a one-inch square; then compare the length of each child's name. (See the next section, "How Long Is Your Name?") Counting and comparing the lengths of the data sets are only the first steps in making meaning from these experiences. When children generalize that more children like strawberries than apples, so the teacher should buy strawberries for a snack, they are beginning to use data to make decisions.

How Long Is Your Name?

In this activity children write their names on strips of paper, then compare the length of their name with their classmates' names. To start, prepare strips of squares mounted on cardstock. As children are settling in at the beginning of the school day, give each child a strip; using one square per letter, children write their names. Some children might not yet be proficient at writing; use a yellow highlighter to write these students' names on the strips, then have them trace their names with a pen. When children complete their names, cut any extra squares off of each strip.

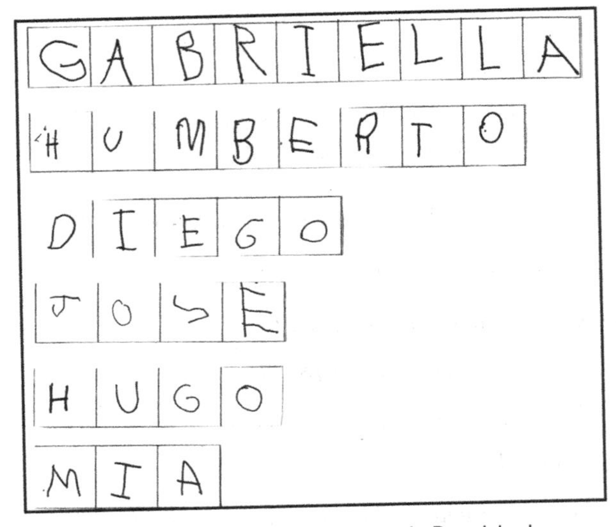

Name length strips made by children in Brenda's class.

We find that when children create name length strips, the project naturally leads them to compare their name lengths. Bring children's name length strips to circle time to further pursue the investigation. Tell students, "When you signed in today I heard you talk about the length of your name compared to the length of your friend's names." Ask children to count the letters in their names and sort their strips into groups by length on the carpet or on a pocket chart. Consider pairing up children to talk about what they notice in each of their names compared to the rest of the class. Use sentence frames to help students choose the words they want to say:

Sentence Frames for Comparing Name Length Strips

My name [name] is shorter than [name].

My name [name] is longer than [name].

My name [name] is the same length as [name].

In Brenda's class, students made many observations, including:

Gabriella *is longer than* Mia.

Mia *is shorter than* Gabriella.

Humberto is *longer* than Jose.

Diego is *shorter* than Humberto.

Jose *is the same length as* Hugo.

After children have had the opportunity to talk about their comparisons, create a class graph (use either poster board or a pocket chart) titled *How Many Letters in Your Name?* Children place their names on the graph accordingly.

A *How many letters in your name?* graph created by children in Brenda's class.

Math Talk

Words We Use When Measuring Length

The length of many items (for example, shoes, pants, tables, fabric, pencils, shoe laces, ribbon, and paper towels) can be measured in an early childhood classroom. Sometimes different words enter the picture when measuring; for example, we measure our *height*, and the *length* and *width* of a rectangular tabletop or two-dimensional objects. (In the "How Long is Your Name?" activity, the length is a horizontal measure of units; the width of each strip of paper is not measured.) For children, these words can be confusing. To clarify meaning, use gestures for words like *height* and *width*; this will help children see what part is being measured.

Now lead a class discussion focused on children's observations. This is an example of a conversation that transpired in Brenda's class around the graph:

Jackeline: *My name is the biggest.*

Brenda: *Yes, I notice that your name is the longest. Who notices something about the shorter names?*

Ricardo: *We don't have nobody in the twos.*

Delicia: *Lots of names are in the sevens. We should count 'em.*

Brenda: *What else do you notice? Who can find a name that is the same length as your own name? (*These kinds of open questions allow more children to notice things that are of interest.*)*

Teaching Insight

Name Strips

Name strips can be used for a variety of activities, from making class charts to sorting and playing games (their use is suggested where applicable in the activities throughout this resource). Name strips give children a purpose for writing their names. This increases student motivation, and children seem to take the task more seriously when they know their name strip is going to be put to use. Children can create a name strip every day as they sign in to class; as an alternative to the "name length strips" described in this activity, have children write their names on slips of paper that include their photo.

Name strips with photos created by children in Brenda's class.

Assessment Opportunity

Record your observations of children's thinking using Reproducible C3, Learning Progressions: Early Childhood/Measurement. Note which children can correctly determine lengths and tell which name strip is longer and which is shorter.

See Reproducible C3, Learning Progressions: Early Childhood/ Measurement.

The Letters in My Name

After children have learned to identify the letters in their names (this usually happens in November for Brenda's class), consider introducing this graphing activity, which also makes use of children's name strips. In this activity, focus on a specific letter—for example, the letter *O*. On a pocket chart, create a chart with the title, "Do you have an *O* in your name?" Label Yes and No columns. Ask students, "Do you have an *O* in your name?" Children place their name strips in the appropriate column on the graph. When we first start looking at name graphs this way, children tend to be surprised to see that other classmates have some of the same letters in their names. This is typical of egocentric preschoolers who mostly pay attention to their own names!

The *Do you have an O in your name?* graph created by children in Brenda's class.

Brenda's Journal Page

The Success of Letter Graphs

Today we created a graph for the question, "Do you have an *X* in your name?" The other day we graphed data for "Do You Have an *A* in Your Name?" The more letters we do, the more kids seem to be engaged. Today after talking about the graph, Delicia exclaimed, "Let's do *D*!" Nate chimed in with, "Let's do *N*." Nico (in his macho way) said,

continued

"Hey . . . Brenda . . . I have an *I*." (He was getting pretty grumpy because he didn't have an *A* or *E*.) During choice time Nico pulled me over to the graph and read all the names with *I's*. He counted eight names with *I's*. Humberto verified the count. Then they counted the names *without I's*. Nico then volunteered, "Let's count the names all together!" I was delighted that all this was happening during choice time—the children are really getting into it. Tomorrow I plan to ask Delicia and Nate why they want to choose a different letter for our graph.

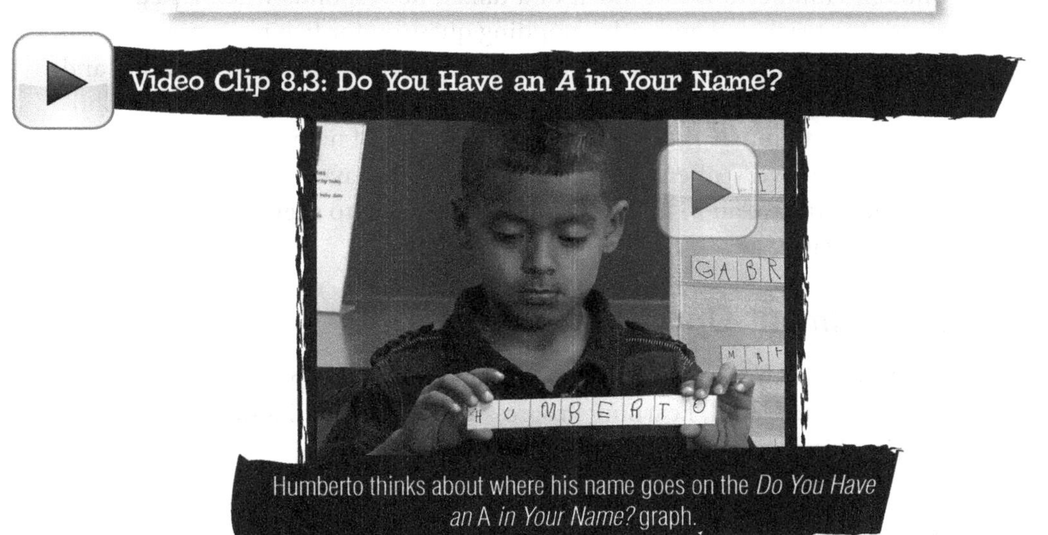

Humberto thinks about where his name goes on the *Do You Have an A in Your Name?* graph.

To view the clip, scan the QR code or visit **mathsolutions.com/TEACHPK83**

In Video Clip 8.3, Brenda works with children in completing and investigating letter graphs. They start with the graph "Do You Have an *A* in Your Name?" Alondra is the first child to respond to the graph. Liana, Gabriella, and others follow suit; all have *A*'s in their names. When it is Humberto's turn, he is the first to place his name in the No column. The teacher asks,

"Why did you put your name over on that side?" and "How many kids don't have A's so far?" Alondra starts to get children to respond to the graph. She asks Aaliyah, "Do you have an *A*?" She also asks Aracely the same thing in Spanish. The teacher then draws everyone's attention to the graph and asks, "Are there more people who have *A*'s or who do not have *A*'s?" After investigating, Brenda changes the graph's question to "Do You Have an *M* in Your Name?" Watch the clip in its entirety. What do you notice about children's engagement in the activity? Why does the teacher change the graphing question?

What We Learned: Alondra, who is the first to add data to the graph, takes on the role of the teacher in guiding other children to place their names on the graph; she seems highly engaged and interested in helping her peers contribute. Humberto is the only student participating who does not have an A in his name. The teacher encourages him to explore the data. Though Humberto is not much of a talker, he responds when asked questions. The teacher changes the graphing question for two main reasons: she wants to make sure Humberto's name is represented in the Yes column, and she wants to see how children will think about a different question. Children begin to notice that some letters are in lots of names, and some letters do not occur very often. Off camera, after they have investigated the data for "Do you have an *M* in your name?," they begin to suggest new questions to investigate.

Assessment Opportunity

See Reproducible C4 , Learning Progressions: Early Childhood/ Graphing Data.

Assess children as they discuss the data on their graphs. Use Reproducible C4, Learning Progressions: Early Childhood/ Graphing Data, to record your observations.

Name Comparison Books

Another comparison activity that makes great use of name strips is the creation of comparison books. Ideas for these books may be:

Ideas for Name Comparison Books

Longer Name Book

The sentence frame for each page in this book reads: *(blank) is longer than (blank).*

Shorter Name Book

The sentence frame for each page in this book reads: *(blank) is shorter than (blank).*

Same Length Name Book

The sentence frame for each page in this book reads: *(blank) is the same length as (blank).*

The More Letters Book

The sentence frame for each page in this book reads: *(blank) has more letters than (blank).*

The Less Letters Book

The sentence frame for each page in this book reads: *(blank) has less letters than (blank).*

Choose the title of your book. Make copies of the corresponding sentence frame for the book's pages (one for every two children). Ask children to complete the sentence frame on the page, using their name and that of a classmate's. Have them paste their name strips on the page accordingly. Have extra name strips available if children run out of names that can be used correctly.

Sample pages from name comparison books made in Brenda's class.

Assemble the books using a spiral binding machine, brads, or loose-leaf rings. These books are easy to put together and fun for children to read (it's captivating for children to see their name appear over and over in a book!). The books reinforce important academic language. Some children notice that their name is longer than one name, yet shorter than another name. In Brenda's class Marcos commented, "My name is longer than Sara's name, and my name is shorter than Ricardo's name. My name is long and short!" Also this project supports children in learning to read each other's names—thus meeting a literacy goal within a math project.

Home/School Connections

After the name comparison books have been in the class library for a while, let children check them out to take home and read to their families.

Circle Time

What Is the Weather Like Today?

Weather, like children's attendance, is data that can be collected daily. Have children go outside and make observations about the day's weather. Give them a card to record their observations (most children will draw a picture with a corresponding label). Collect the data daily throughout the month; at the end of the month, compile it in a bar graph. In Tucson and Santa Barbara, where we teach, the weather is not as interesting as in other parts of the country, but we do notice differences over time—for example, we have more cloudy days in January than we do in September!

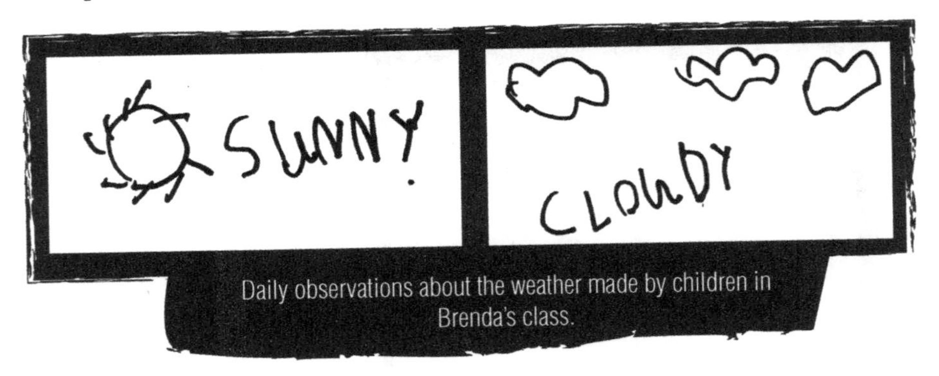

Daily observations about the weather made by children in Brenda's class.

Teaching Insight

Looking Back

Collecting data like the weather over time is a way to save information that may otherwise be forgotten. We post our weather graphs next to the monthly birthday graphs and any photos we've taken of that month's special events. This gives children a place to reflect on the past—they recount the first few days of school in September, a field trip to the pumpkin patch in October, our Thanksgiving Feast in November, and our winter gingerbread house project in December.

Do You Like Green Eggs and Ham?

Using Dr. Seuss books can develop children's interest in reading. (This data collection activity is especially great in preparation for NEA's Read Across America Day [www.nea.org/readacross].) Read *Green Eggs and Ham* by Dr. Seuss. Have children complete a Yes/No graph for the question "Have you ever tasted green eggs and ham?"

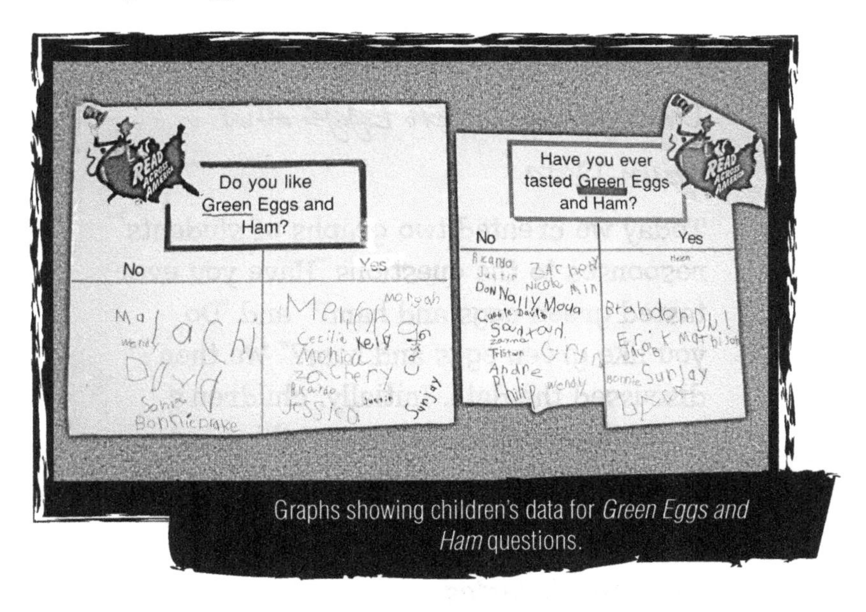

Graphs showing children's data for *Green Eggs and Ham* questions.

For added fun and as part of snack time, cook green eggs and ham and give everyone a chance to taste the concoction!

Have children write their names in the column that corresponds to their answer to the question, "Have you ever tasted green eggs and ham?" Then after tasting the concoction, have them complete a Yes/No graph for the question, "Do you like green eggs and ham?" and respond to the graph about whether they like green eggs and ham.

Encourage children to talk about the number of responses and how the two graphs are alike or different. Have them count the responses; which has more? Can they draw any conclusions from the graphs? Many children in our experience really enjoy the taste of the green eggs! We think the fun of the story and the cooking experience influence this opinion.

Assessment Opportunity

This is an interesting opportunity to assess children's understanding of the meaning of the graph. Use Reproducible C4, Learning Progressions: Early Childhood/Graphing Data to record your observations.

See Reproducible C4, Learning Progressions: Early Childhood/ Graphing Data.

Brenda's Journal Page

Discussing Green Eggs and Ham Data

Today we created two graphs of students' responses to the questions "Have you ever tasted green eggs and ham?" and "Do you like green eggs and ham?" We then discussed the data. Initially, children's observations dealt with everything but comparisons:

It's easy to make green eggs and ham.
I like how it tastes.

continued

We can make other green food.

Did Dr. Seuss eat this food, too?

I cook at my house.

I never breaked a egg before.

If you want you can break a egg in two parts.

Ham is like hot dogs.

What I wanted was for the children to talk about the number of responses and how the two graphs were alike or different. One child did say that you have to "taste green eggs and ham to know if you like the stuff."

I encouraged children to count the yes and no responses and tell which is more and which is less. They were able to do this. They found it challenging to draw any conclusions about the graphs; I think this will develop over time with more experience.

I'm planning to make a graph in which children choose which book they want to read—then we immediately read the book with the most names. I'm hoping this will show that we are making a graph to help make a decision.

How Many Pockets Do You Have Today?

In this activity children work in small groups to tally the number of pockets they have, connecting the number to a concrete model (interlocking cubes). First read *A Pocket for Corduroy* by Don Freeman, in which Corduroy the teddy bear gets a much-needed pocket. Children are naturally interested in knowing how many pockets they have after learning of Corduroy's adventure. Ask students, "How many pockets do we all have?" In order to facilitate finding out how many pockets are in the group, model placing one connecting cube in each of your pockets. Then take the cubes out and connect them, creating a train of cubes that represent your pockets. Place the train above your photo on a table (consider using photo name strips as explained in the activities presented earlier in this chapter—make sure every student has made a photo name strip). Support students as they put a cube in each of their pockets, count and connect the cubes, and place their cube train on display above their photo. When children have completed the activity, they will have created a graph showing all the data.

Children's graph in answer to the question, "How many pockets do we have today?"

Math Talk

One-to-One Correspondence

One-to-one correspondence means that there is one number for each item.

By using a cube for each pocket, children are practicing *one-to-one correspondence.* You could also rearrange the data in groups showing how many children have no pockets, one pocket, two pockets, three pockets, and so on. Discuss the data with children. Children are bound to make very broad observations such as, "Some people need more pockets so they can put stuff in them," whereas others may surprise you with their comparisons—one child in Brenda's class concluded, "If you are wearing jeans you have more pockets."

How Many People Live in Your Home?

Have each child draw his or her home and the people who live in it. Consider using index-sized cards for the drawings to make the graphing process easier. Ask children, "How many people live in your home?" Create a graph with numbers across the bottom. Have children place their drawings above the number that corresponds with the number of people in their home. Discuss the graph. In Brenda's class children made the following observations: "He has the same as me." "We both have six people." "Nobody gots one in their house."

Brenda asked the class why they thought there were no houses with only one person in them. One boy explained, "You gotta have someone to tuck you in at night!"

See Reproducible C2, Learning Progressions: Early Childhood/ Number.

Assessment Opportunity

Assess children as they think about who lives in their home with them and discuss the data. Use Reproducible C2, Learning Progressions: Early Childhood/Number to record your observations.

Circle Time

Which Juice Do You Prefer?

Sometimes young children think that the *winning* choice on a graph is better. They even cheer for one preference to be the most. This activity, which can be used with snack time, helps children realize that *less* might mean something very different. To start, write each student's name on a clear plastic cup (so children can visually compare the amounts) and place a one-pint container of juice (orange, grape, and apple juice work well) on each of three tables. Ask children to put their cup on the table that has the juice they prefer. Compare which table has more cups and which table has fewer. Which juice do most children prefer? Have children observe and discuss the data. In Brenda's class children made a broad range of observations: "There's more cups at the grape table." "Orange is only two." "I like apple juice the best." "We can make more orange juice by squeezing oranges."

Now have children sit down at the table on which they've placed their cup. Pour the corresponding juice into the cups at each table. See

Math Talk

Connecting to Fractions

In this "Which Juice Do You Prefer?" activity, even though children are not specifically learning about fractions, the teacher can begin to develop their foundational understanding that the larger the denominator, the smaller the part of the whole. When one pint of apple juice is shared equally by eight children, children notice that they don't get as much juice as the group that only has three children sharing the orange juice.

what children notice now—the tables with more cups have smaller portions, whereas the tables with fewer cups are full—in some cases, the children are even getting refills! In Brenda's class Nico was the first to comment. Nico said, "Hm, what's goin' on here? My table has more people but less juice!" Sarah said, "I wanted more grape juice, but we had too many cups."

Teaching Insight

Using Pint-Sized Containers

We've learned that it's important to use pint-sized juice containers for this activity. If you use a larger size (for example, quarts), the contrast between the portions is not as obvious to children.

Assessment Opportunity

See Reproducible C4, Learning Progressions: Early Childhood/ Graphing Data.

This is an interesting opportunity to assess children as they discuss the data. Use Reproducible C4, Learning Progressions: Early Childhood/Graphing Data to record your observations.

Circle Time

Which Apple Color Do You Like Best?

This activity reinforces the ideas in "Which Juice Do You Prefer?" For this activity gather two yellow, two green, and two red apples. Group the apples by color onto three different tables. Ask children to place their photo name strip (see earlier activities in this chapter) by the apples they like best. Count how many pictures are by each group of apples. Have children sit at the table with their photo name strip. Distribute shares of the apples accordingly (great for snack time!). Note what children observe. For example, if four children have chosen green apples as their favorite, each child will get half an apple. If eight children choose the two red apples, they each get one fourth of an apple. If two children choose the two yellow apples—wow, they each get to eat a whole apple! When everyone finishes eating their apples, distribute an outline drawing of an apple (see Reproducible I) and have each child color in the apple according to their choice. Place the apple drawings in a pocket chart to form a graph and further discuss the findings. In Brenda's class Delicia made the connection, "This is like the juice graph only it's with apples!"

See Reproducible I, Apple Template.

A Child's Mind

Dividing Up Quantities or Sharing Portions?

Both the juice and apple activities invite children to think about dividing up quantities. How can we help students with the idea of sharing a portion versus dividing up quantities? We've found the children's book *The Door Bell Rang* by Pat Hutchins, to be helpful. In this book children count out cookies and share them. Also try using small cups of red, green, and purple grapes instead of juice or apples in a graphing activity.

Assessment Opportunity

This is an interesting opportunity to assess children's thinking as they discuss the data on their graphs. Use Reproducible C4, Learning Progressions: Early Childhood/Graphing Data to record your observations.

See Reproducible C4, Learning Progressions: Early Childhood/ Graphing Data.

Circle Time

Which Cracker Shape Do You Like Best?

This introductory investigation focuses on the idea of attributes of shapes. Provide children with three different shapes of crackers: square, circle, and triangle. (Crackers in these shapes can easily be found in local grocery stores.) Place one of each cracker on a matching shape placemat for every child. Use Reproducible H to make placemats.

See Reproducible H, Shapes Placemat.

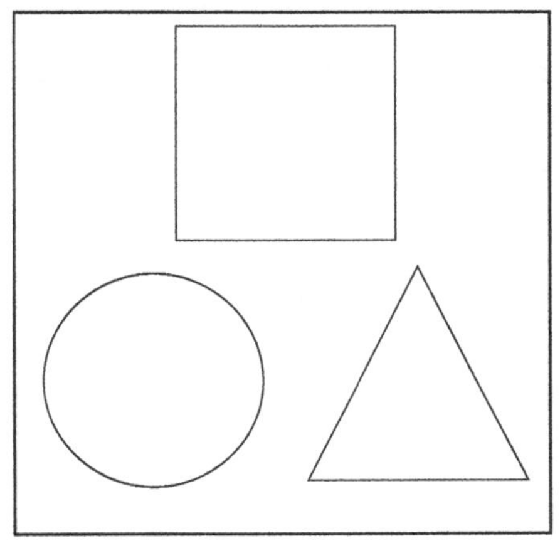

The shapes placemat.

Investigate each cracker and its shape with children. Have children investigate each cracker's flavor (nibble!). Once cracker shapes have been discussed and tasted, ask children which cracker they like best. Have children color in the corresponding cracker shape on their placemat, cut it out, and bring it up to a class graph. Count the shapes in each row. Which cracker do children like the most?

Assessment Opportunity

See Reproducible C4, Learning Progressions: Early Childhood/Graphing Data.

This is an interesting opportunity to assess children's thinking as they discuss the data on their graphs. Use Reproducible C4, Learning Progressions: Early Childhood/Graphing Data, to record your observations.

A Child's Mind

Attributes of Shapes

Children often learn the names of the shapes by remembering a mental picture of a shape, but do not identify the shape by how many corners or sides it has. We'll talk more about this in the geometry section, Chapter 9.

Brenda's Journal Page

A Cracker Conversation

This is the dialog I use for the cracker graph project. The suspense builds as we sample the different crackers!

Touch the square cracker. Touch the circle cracker. Touch the triangle cracker.

Now pick up the square cracker and let's count how many corners it has. Ready? One, two, three, four. Let's count how many sides it has. One, two, three, four.

Now put the square down and pick up the circle cracker. Let's count the corners. Ready? Oh, there are no corners! Put the circle cracker down.

continued

Pick up the triangle cracker. Let's count the corners. Ready? One, two, three. Let's count the sides. Ready? One, two, three.

We are going to decide which cracker we like best.

Let's take a tiny nibble on the corner of the triangle cracker. Yum. Put that cracker down and pick up the square cracker. Take a tiny nibble on one corner of the square cracker. Mm. That tastes good, too. Do you like it better than the triangle cracker? Let's taste the circle cracker now. Take a little bite. Mmm. Now go back to the triangle cracker and compare it to the other. Take another bite and think, is this the one I like best? Taste the crackers again until you have eaten them all up! Which cracker did you like best? Color in that cracker and write your name under the shape. Cut out your favorite cracker and bring it up to our class graph. We will find out which cracker is our favorite one.

Maybe we will have some different shapes next time for snack. What do you think?

For more number sense activities that can be used during snack time, see Chapter 3 (Pattern Snacks), Chapter 7 (Snack Time), Chapter 10 (Recipes That Build Important Mathematical Ideas), and Video Clips 5.4 and 7.2.

The activities suggested thus far present children with a question for gathering data and creating a graph. Once children are familiar with this process, give them the opportunity to form their own questions and gather the corresponding data. See the Surveys section of Chapter 7 for more insights.

See the Surveys section of Chapter 7 for more insights.

Using Real-World Small Group Investigations for Comparisons and Measurements

This section explores activities for comparisons and measurements that are best conducted with small groups to allow more teacher direction and support. Young children are really interested in comparing themselves to others and other things in their environment. Adults often pace off the length of a room, use their arm reach to measure lengths of cloth, and scoop flour to approximate a cup. Young children are beginning on this journey. They are beginning to learn more about their bodies:

I'm gonna stack the cylinders as high as me.

Am I as big as Anthony?

I gotta make this boat bigger so we both can fit in it.

How Tall Are We?

In this project we directly map the child's height to a strip of paper. We've found that paper from an adding machine or cash register roll works best. Find a wall space in the class that can be used to post the children's heights. First measure the height of a class teddy bear. Place the bear on the floor and mark the bear's feet and the top of its head on a strip of paper. Cut the length of the strip to match the bear's height. Post this strip on the wall and mark it with a teddy bear icon or the teddy bear's name. Then ask children, "Who is taller than our teddy? How can we find out?"

A Child's Mind

Height Sensitivities

Some young children are very sensitive about their height, especially if they are the shortest in the class. They don't want to be the baby. Therefore, start with something (the class teddy bear) that will be shorter than the shortest child.

Now it's the student's turn! Mark off each child's height on a strip of paper (this is easiest if each child is lying on the floor). Have children write their names and paste their photo at the top of the strip.

Markie measures Alexa's height.

Arrange the height strips on the wall and have children stand next to their strips. Encourage a conversation around the measurements. Review key vocabulary *height, tall, taller, short, shorter, measure* as necessary. Ask questions, such as "Who is tall? Who is taller than you? Who is the tallest?"

Key Questions

Who is tall?

Who is taller than you?

Who is the tallest?

Who is taller than teddy?

Who else can we measure?

Key Vocabulary

height	short
tall	shorter
taller	measure

On another day have children place their height strips in order from the shortest to the tallest. Some children benefit from finding two strips of paper that are the same length. Encourage them to find those two children and see

Math Talk

Talking About Length

Young children begin to think about measurement of lengths using direct comparisons. Later on they use nonstandard units such as craft sticks, toothpicks, or snap cubes to quantify and measure length. When they do not have enough of the units to measure the entire length, they begin to iterate the units while counting and moving them along the length they are measuring. We include rulers and other measurement tools in our centers as *grown up* props to suggest the idea of measurement, but mostly young children use direct comparisons when they talk about length. In time they will find the tools useful as they develop more understanding of the concepts of measurement.

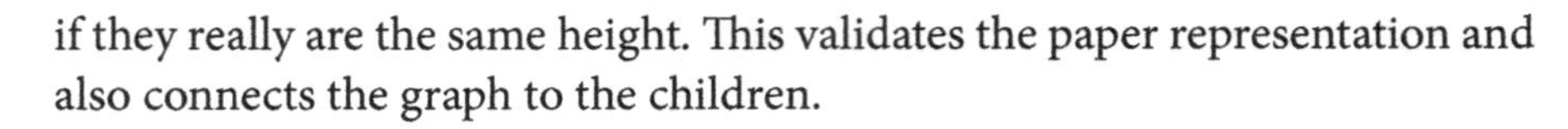

if they really are the same height. This validates the paper representation and also connects the graph to the children.

Small Group Time

How Many in a Handful?

In this small group investigation, each student works with a handful of objects. First children count what's in their handful and record the number on a tracing of their hand. After several experiences doing this, children are asked to predict how many might be in a handful before grabbing a handful; they then decide if their handful is more or less than their prediction.

To start this activity, choose the objects children will be using. At the beginning of the school year, choose large objects so the count is a more manageable quantity (between three and nine items per child). The following objects work especially well for children around the age of four:

Objects for Handfuls

- rocks
- walnuts
- wooden inch cubes
- grapes
- ceramic tiles
- magnetic letters
- binder clips
- felt-tip pens
- glue sticks

Organize the objects in wide-mouth containers (such as baskets) so children can easily grab the contents. First ask children to place one of their hands on a sheet of paper and trace around it. Then children grab a handful of objects, count how many they have, and record the total on the tracing. At the beginning of the year, children will likely draw the number of objects in their handful and the teacher will write the numeral. With practice, children will learn to write the numerals themselves. For children who need support counting, give them a five- or ten-frame (see Reproducibles J and K).

Once children have had several experiences with *handfuls*, ask them to predict first before they take a handful. They can then decide if their handful is more or less than their prediction. Five- and ten-frames are particularly useful in helping children see if their handful is more or less than what they predicted. These tools also help children see how many fives are in their handful. After children have completed their investigations and have represented their quantities in their hand drawings, put the pictures together in a class counting book. (For more on class counting books see Chapter 6).

Teaching Insight

Using Food as Counting Objects

Instead of using classroom objects for the handful, consider snack time items such as fish crackers, pretzels, strawberries, or grapes. After these items are counted and recorded, children can eat them! When they eat the objects one by one, have them count backwards to find the answer to "How many do you have now?"

See Reproducible J, Five-Frame and Reproducible K, Ten-Frame.

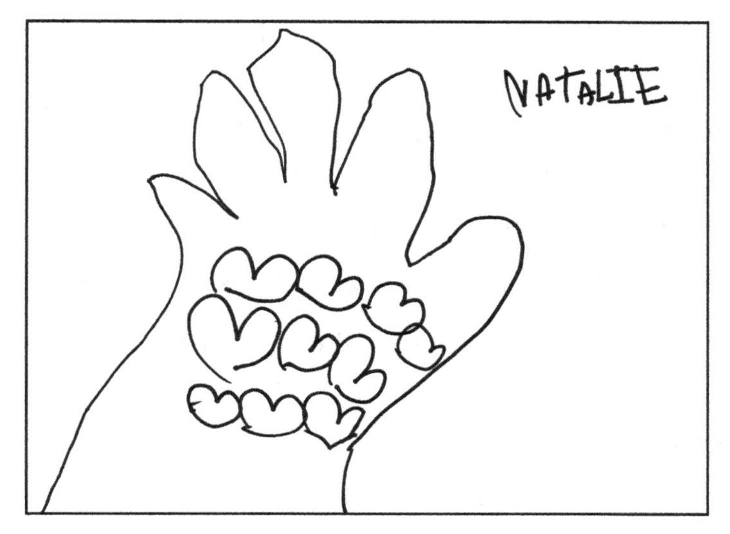

Natalie draws ten candy hearts to show what's in her handful.

See Chapter 6 for more on class counting books.

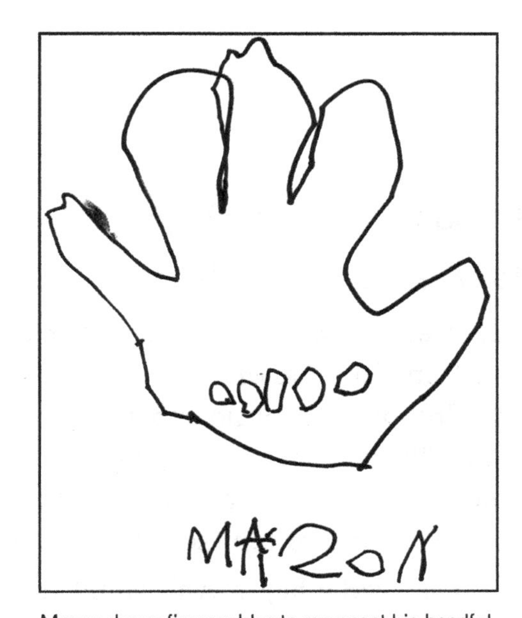

Mason draws five marbles to represent his handful.

This project can be repeated using different counting objects. Gradually the items can get smaller, allowing children to grab more items in their hands. Note if children observe that the size of the item is related to how much they can hold. Consider the following dialogue Brenda had with her student Humberto:

> **Brenda:** *Humberto, how come you could hold so many in your hand this time? Last time you only held five cubes.*
>
> **Humberto:** *My hands are bigger this time, 'cuz I'm bigger.*
>
> **Brenda:** *Oh, I see. I wonder how many cubes you could hold now?*

To further change the activity, instead of using a handful, see the ideas offered here.

Instead of a Handful, try . . .

- a scoop
- a pinch
- a spoonful
- tongs
- a spatula

See Reproducible L, Number Chart 1–20.

Math Talk

One-to-One Correspondence

One-to-one correspondence means that there is one number for each item.

Brenda's Journal Page

Using a Number Chart

This week at small group time we played "How Many in a Handful?" Children grabbed a handful of connecting cubes from a basket. To help them count, I gave each student a number chart consisting of two numbered rows of ten (see Reproducible L).

I observed a big growth spurt in children's ability to count. Many children now know the sequence of numbers and are showing *one-to-one correspondence.*

continued

Some children, after grabbing a handful of cubes, placed the cubes in the squares on the number chart. This strategy helped them organize the cubes; they were less likely to double-tag the cubes or forget which cubes had been counted. A nice strategy!

I was again reminded how young children are so playful. Santiago, a young child in age and academics, grabbed a handful of cubes and placed them in the squares of the number chart. He counted six cubes. I wanted to know more about his thinking, so I said, "Write the number six."

Santiago lifted the first cube. "Is that the number six?" I inquired.

Smiling from ear to ear, Santiago shook his head no. Then he lifted the second cube, revealing the numeral two. "Is that the number six?" I asked again.

Santiago shook his head no. We continued this game to the fifth cube. Beaming, Santiago said, "I wonder if that is the number six?"

Both of us knew where the real six was hidden and enjoyed the playful spirit of Santiago's newfound game!

Which Cup Holds More?

In this small group investigation children are presented with cups of various sizes and shapes. They predict which cup holds more and then test their thinking by filling a cup and pouring the contents from one cup to the next. This investigation often takes place at the multisensory table (see page 186). To start, carefully select the cups children will use for comparison. At the beginning of the year, choose two cups: one that is taller and narrow, and another that is shorter and wide. Later on in the year, choose a wider variety of containers to prompt especially interesting conversations and investigations.

Math Talk

Volume

When children first look at volume, they often think that the taller container will hold more. The volume of a container is determined by the area of the base multiplied by the height ($V = bh$). So, a container with a wide base will probably hold more than one with a narrow base. Sometimes our eyes trick us into thinking that the volume may be less.

Ideas for Cups

- olive jars
- salad dressing bottles
- jam jars
- honey bear containers
- sippy cups in interesting shapes
- salsa containers
- baby bottles
- various-sized spice jars

Ask children to predict which cup holds more. Have them test their thinking by filling one cup with water, birdseed, sand, or colored gravel (easily found in aquarium stores). Provide funnels and scoops to assist children in filling the cups. Ask children what they think will happen when they pour the full cup into another cup. Ask, “Does it overflow? What does that mean? What will happen if you try it again? What will happen if you fill the second cup and pour it into the first? What does this mean? So which cup holds more? What do we know now?”

Teaching Insight

What Should We Fill the Cups With?

The measurement media in this investigation can vary; consider water, birdseed, sand, or colored gravel (easily found in aquarium stores). Using different materials and different containers makes the activity seem fresh and new every time it’s done in class.

Children work at the sand table, pouring sand from one container to the next to determine which cup holds more.

Assessment Opportunity

After children have had sufficient exploratory time with a variety of containers, label the containers A, B, C. Have children draw the three containers, and mark with an X the container that they think holds the most.

In Michelle's drawing she's marked that container C holds more.

See Reproducible C3, Learning Progressions: Early Childhood/ Measurement.

Next, ask children to put three or four containers in order from the one holding the least to the one holding the most. Then reverse it (place containers in order from the one holding the most to the one holding the least). Collect children's drawings and record your observations using Reproducible C3, Learning Progressions: Early Childhood/Measurement.

Teaching Insight

There Might Be Spills!

When working with items that can spill, be prepared by teaching procedures to deal with this eventuality. Spread a shower curtain on the floor, and if you are dealing with liquids, have plenty of sponges and towels handy. Put a whiskbroom and dustpan in the bin that holds dry materials. At the conclusion of the activity, help children sweep up the dry materials.

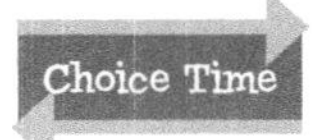

Comparing and Measuring at the Multisensory Table

A multisensory table is a valuable and important choice center for the early childhood classroom. Sometimes it is not used in preschool classrooms because it can be messy. We think that the positive aspects of freely exploring with a variety of media and measuring experiences are crucial for young children, so we work hard towards making this center manageable. Children also really enjoy the tactile stimulation of running their hands through various media! Each time the contents of the table are changed, it seems like we have created a new investigation, even though children are still measuring, filling, comparing, and experimenting with the same (various-sized) containers. Following are some of our favorite ideas for creating a multisensory table that invites children to freely compare and measure.

The table can be filled with water, birdseed, millet, flax seed, or very fine sand; coarse sand is problematic if there is a rug in the classroom. Glitter or jewels can be added to sand. When we use water, we sometimes add liquid detergent or blue food color to stimulate conversations and investigations. A water table is wonderful when the weather is warm and it can be placed outdoors. Washing various sized dishes is also something we've found children love to do (some children really enjoy washing dishes in warm soapy water after snack period).

Children working with water as a measurement media at the multisensory table.

Humberto investigating the size of a seed sprout planted at the multisensory table.

The Multisensory Table as a Garden

The table can be turned into a garden with the addition of potting soil. Provide opportunities for children to fill flower pots, peat moss cups, and egg cartons with potting soil and then plant seeds, such as fava beans (or lima beans), to see how they will grow. Then children can measure them!

The Multisensory Table as an Archeological Dig

The center can become an archeological investigative area with buried treasures. Provide a variety of scoops, funnels, and screens of different sizes to prompt counting and sorting. Change the shape and size of the containers to create new interest.

Which Measurement Tool?

This short measurement activity gives insight into how children choose tools (from toothpicks to paperclips) to measure something they've drawn. Do children notice the different length tools? Do they count how many fit on their drawing? Do they use the tools to keep track of their measure? It's important to note that the task gets students thinking about the tools, however this is not a means to solving a real-world problem requiring measurement. As teachers, we need to remember that the purpose for measuring something is to determine if we can use the data in some helpful way. In the real world, we measure so we can compare something. For example, *will this fit in that space?*

To start, assemble a collection of nonstandard tools—craft sticks, toothpicks, inch tiles, paperclips—that can be used to measure length. Give each child a large piece of paper (8 × 24 inches) and ask them to draw something tall. In Brenda's class one child drew a pirate flag, another drew a truck, and another made a tower for a prince. Then encourage each child to explore the measurement of their drawing. In this activity, Brenda queried Ali on his drawing of a tower:

Brenda: *That's a tall tower. Let's measure how tall it is. What should we use?* (Tito chooses the sticks and lays them out along the side of the tower.)

Tito: *It's six sticks tall.*

Brenda: *What if you use the toothpicks?* (Now Tito learns that his tower is fifteen toothpicks tall.)

Brenda: *What do you think, is it six sticks tall or fifteen toothpicks tall? You have two numbers.*

Tito: *I think it is fifteen tall, because that is taller.*

Next, give each child a small piece of paper (4 × 5 inches) and ask them to draw something small. Tito drew a house for a dog that lives near the tower. Prompt each child to measure the drawing.

Brenda: *Let's measure the doghouse. What should we use?* (Tito chooses paper clips and measures the doghouse.)

Brenda: *I noticed you didn't use the sticks. Why did you use the paper clips for this house?*

Tito: *You have to use the ones that fit. These are too big and this is too little.*

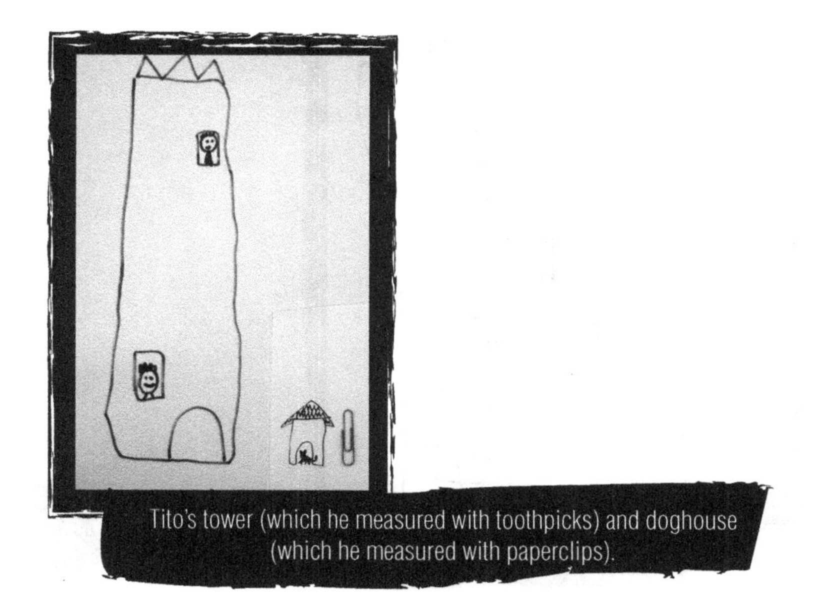

Tito's tower (which he measured with toothpicks) and doghouse (which he measured with paperclips).

Assessment Opportunity

The conversations that happen in this activity are valuable assessment opportunities. When children talk about the tools they want to use to measure, help them think about how people measure other things. Record your observations using Reproducible C3, Learning Progressions: Early Childhood/Measurement.

See Reproducible C3, Learning Progressions: Early Childhood/ Measurement.

Roberto's castle drawing, which shows that his castle is fifteen stories high.

Brenda's Journal Page

Roberto's Castle

Roberto drew a castle (*castillo*) that was as tall as the paper given him and he also drew some horizontal lines to show that his castle was fifteen stories tall. When he measured with the sticks he arrived at eight sticks, then he got twenty toothpicks for the height. I asked Roberto, "How tall is your tower? Is it eight sticks tall or twenty toothpicks tall?" He was perplexed for a while and then announced, "It's *fifteen stories* tall!" So, the measurement tool was not as meaningful to him as his own drawing!

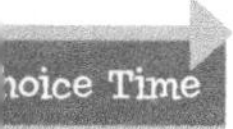

Which Is Heavier?

Young children find the pan balance to be an intriguing tool to investigate weight. At first children randomly pile things on either side and watch what happens. They do this over and over, intrigued. This kind of experimentation is crucial for them to begin to understand what happens when the pans are balanced.

Teaching Insight

Pan Balance

A pan balance is an absolutely essential tool that children use to compare weights. A pan balance can be ordered from education catalogs; the Internet has directions for making pan balances using margarine tubs and coat hangers. Have more than one pan balance in the classroom, because although pairs of children can share a pan balance, most children need to use one on their own. Pan balances can be placed in various parts of the room: in the block area, in the science area, and in the studio (see the Classroom Map on page 333).

Math Talk

Volume and Weight

Some children believe that bigger things weigh more than smaller things. We've thought about the story of a pound of feathers and a pound of gold, and believe it is important to find ways for students to explore how the size of an item might determine how much it weighs. These are ideas that will be explored again and again as children go through school.

There are many items that can be used to help children develop their understanding of balance and weight. We use objects that children are familiar with. We've found that young children are most interested in balancing items like cans of cat food, polished rocks, a snow globe, a miniature statue of liberty, ceramic tiles of various shapes and sizes, nuts and bolts of various sizes, wooden blocks, and toy pots and pans. When children work with these items, they keep coming back to the idea that these are *real* things. As Alondra used the pan balance she kept inquiring, almost in disbelief, "Brenda, is this a *real* can of cat food?"

Finding Items to Weigh: We ask children's families to walk around their homes and search out items that are small enough to fit in a hand, yet have some heft to them. These are exactly the items a child finds interesting to use with a pan balance investigation—after all, the items come from the real world! Families have donated an old (broken) pencil sharpener, a marble apple, a steel paperweight, a piece of petrified wood, a can of cat food, heavy magnets, door stops, and a small pipe wrench. Large objects that do not weigh very much, such as large pompoms, beach balls, and balloons, are also good choices.

Support children in explaining their thinking as they use the pan balance. In Brenda's class, as Hugo was comparing things on the pan balance, he was quick to tell Brenda each time which item weighed more. It was more challenging for him to talk about which item weighed less. Brenda wondered if this is because children are always wanting more, not less, and made a note to find ways to model thinking about *less* more often.

To help the children think more about weight, fill about eight half-cup-sized clear snack containers with a different item—nails, beans, cotton balls, lentils, sand, beads, paperclips, potting soil. Glue the lids on and also tape them closed, and using a permanent marker, write the contents of the container on each. Now you have a collection of containers with *a uniform volume size but a different weight.* Challenge children to investigate which container weighs the most or the least, and then try to order them by weight.

Five-Tower Game

See Reproducible J, Five-Frame.

In this investigative game students use five-frames (see Reproducible J—each student should have one five-frame) to keep track of their turns. Students take turns rolling a die, building a tower with their cubes that matches the roll of the die, and placing the tower in one cell of their five-frame. When they have each taken five turns, they connect their cubes to form a big tower. They then compare the lengths of the towers.

Since children are at various levels in being able to count out a quantity of cubes to match the number rolled on the die, model how to play this game first. If possible, use a giant foam die. Roll the die and place the corresponding number of cubes on the die's dots. For example, if a three is rolled, place three cubes over the three dots on the die. Then build a tower of three cubes and put this tower on one of the cells of the five-frame. This scaffolding makes the game more accessible for children who are still learning to count out accurately to six. Also, modeling encourages fair play; children see that the person whose turn it is only takes the number of cubes that matches the number she or he rolled. Since this game can move fairly quickly, play it consecutive times so most children have a chance to build the tallest, the shortest, and the middle-height tower. Encourage children to talk about equal lengths too; match up the towers and count the cubes in one of them. Do children know how many are in the other of equal length, or do they count it, too? What's the best way to think about this? In Brenda's classroom, when discussing the lengths of their towers, children made numerous comments including the following:

You don't have to count it, Brenda! It matches.

These are different, so you have more.

Mine is almost as long as yours.

If you had two more we would be the same.

This is way longer than that one.

We need more to make them the same.

Children compare their towers of five.

My Own Book: Numbers in My World

We talk about encouraging children to create their own books in Chapter 6, Using Counting Books and Songs. Here we introduce what we call a "Numbers in My World" book. There are many uses for numbers in daily life, and young children are just beginning to understand their purposes. Children find numbers in their world by building on what they already know and expanding their ideas about number. In small group time, over a three-week period, have children work on making their "Numbers in My World" book—one page at a time. Below is a suggested outline for an eleven-page book. After the books are created, have children read and share them. Specifically, have children compare the data in their books with data in their classmate's books. For example, model asking "How many people live in your home? How many cubes can you hold in your hand? Is your pet bigger or smaller than . . . ?"

Numbers in My World Pages

Page 1 My name is _______________. I have _______________ letters in my name. (Children can glue their daily photo name strip to this page.)

Page 2 I am _______________ years old. (Place a picture of a birthday cake and have children glue on the number of candles to represent their age.)

Page 3 There are _______________ people living in my house. (Encourage children to draw pictures of members of their family that live at their house.)

Page 4 My address is _______________. (Encourage children to draw a picture of their house.)

Page 5 My phone number is _______________. (Include an illustration of a phone with numbers at the bottom.)

Page 6 I can hold _______________ cubes in my hand. (Include an illustration of an open hand and have children write or draw the number on the hand.)

Page 7 I have _______________ friends. (Children may post photos of their friends on this page.)

Page 8 Today I counted to _______________.

Page 9 I can eat _______________ slices of pizza.

Page 10 I have _______________ brothers and _______________ sisters.

Page 11 I have _______________ pets. (Encourage children to draw their pets.)

Reflection Questions

1. How can children be engaged in comparing numbers and using terms such as *more, fewer,* or *same as*?
2. What real-world settings can be used to create a context for counting, comparing, and measuring?
3. What routines and everyday activities can be used to support children in counting and comparing?
4. How can instruction be differentiated so children are working at their own level of understanding about number?

5. How does the teacher know if the activities that the child is working on are appropriate and engaging?
6. How can children develop confidence and independence with counting, comparing and measurement?
7. How can families help their child with measuring things at home? What do they need to know?
8. What tools could be added to the physical environment to suggest measurement concepts and skill development?
9. What measurement experiences would be relevant to the culture, interests, or life experiences of children?

Grace: The giraffes live at the zoo and they come over here to eat their grass. All of 'em are going to sleep in this giraffe house.

Brenda: How do you know this is a good house for a giraffe?

Grace: Just look how tall the roof is! They need that roof when they're inside 'cuz they're tall too.

Chapter 9

Using Geometry and Spatial Skills to Build Number Sense

Overview

Preschool has traditionally been a time when young children learn about circles, squares, triangles, and rectangles. Also, early childhood teachers have long known how important block play is for young children. This chapter presents more robust and comprehensive ways to engage young children in learning about geometry and spatial skills that involve much more than just shapes and blocks. Recent research points to geometry as one of the most promising areas of study for young children. The ideas we share encourage children to develop and use their geometry skills in spatial orientation and spatial visualization; the ideas provide experiences that are integral to the work children do when solving problems, making projects, and describing mental maps. Children physically become involved in thinking about the position of their bodies in space, learn ways to describe physical locations, and *build, build, build* a wide variety of projects and constructions that are presented as visual and spatial problems to solve.

Continued

The Big Ideas of Geometry

Research supports the importance of geometry and spatial skills in early childhood. Read each research insight and reflect on it. Discuss with others what it means to you. How do these ideas match your own understanding of this topic?

Research Insights

1. For early childhood, the area of geometry is the second most important area of mathematics learning. One could argue that this area—including spatial thinking—is as important as number . . . Some research suggests that the very ability to represent magnitude is dependent on visuospatial systems in regions of the parietal cortex of the brain (Sarama and Clements 2009).
2. Blocks are considered the most useful and most used equipment in preschool and kindergarten programs (Bullock 1992).
3. Variations in shapes, sizes, and weight foster learning experiences from infancy through early childhood (Kinsman and Berk 1979).
4. *Geometry* means "earth measure," and geometry, spatial reasoning, and measurement are topics that connect with each other and with other mathematics as well as connect mathematics with real-world situations. For example, these core components are the foundations of number lines, arrays in multiplication, fractions, graphing, and topics beyond. They also lie at the heart of physics, chemistry, biology, geology and geography, art, and architecture (Fuson 2010).

Introducing Vocabulary for Geometry and Spatial Skills

Because young children are also learning English, it's especially important that we are mindful about finding ways to increase their receptive and productive vocabulary. Geometric tasks are well suited to this kind of language development because there is so much to talk about when children build things or move objects through space. Geometry is much more than naming shapes! Here are some key questions to think about in helping children foster language around the topic of geometry:

1. How do children talk about what they are doing when they move through space?
2. Can children talk about and describe imaginary or real maps of spaces that they have created?

3. When children put shapes together, what new shapes do they create? What do they notice about the shape and size of the parts?
4. When children decompose objects, what do they notice about the shape and size of the parts?
5. What happens when children view their projects or constructions from a different angle? Can they imagine what someone else sees from a different perspective?

Literature Connection

Rosie's Walk

In the delightfully humorous picture book, *Rosie's Walk* by Pat Hutchins, Rosie the hen walks *over, under, around,* and *through* various parts of the farmyard while a hungry fox tries (unsuccessfully) to pounce on her. Use this story to address the following directional words:

Key Vocabulary

- in and out
- top and bottom
- over and under
- up and down
- forward and backward
- around and through
- in front and behind
- above and below

(Note that we don't spend too much time on the terms *left* and *right* because children will find these particular ideas confusing for several more years.)

After reading aloud the story, draw a map of Rosie's walk and review it with children. Then have children act it out and invent new walks for Rosie. Set up an obstacle course using chairs, tables, boxes and other classroom items. Support children in mapping their actions. Attach children's photos to their maps and label their paths. Consider putting all the maps together in a class book. Maps from Brenda's classroom included:

Jose walked around the box.

Natalie tiptoed near the chair.

Sara crawled under the table.

Vivi hopped away from the blocks.

Juan stepped on the square.

Manuel fell off the chair.

Simon stood beside the table.

Nico walked between Manuel and Juan.

Maps of Natalie's and Jose's walks in Brenda's classroom.

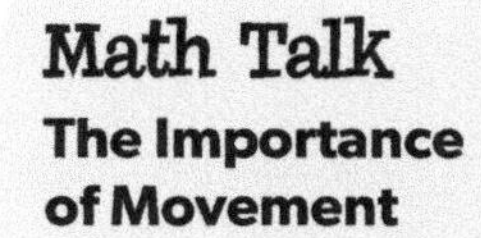

Math Talk

The Importance of Movement

If children do not have an opportunity to move their bodies through, around, and under various objects, they will have difficulty with the meaning of these kinds of relational terms. In geometry, when they turn or rotate shapes and/or flip them over, they often think these are new or different shapes. Planning time for children to playfully learn these ideas will support them later on when they will need to interpret such things as drawings on a flat page of three-dimensional objects in order to determine how they look from a different perspective (Boehm 2000).

terature nnection

Exactly the Opposite

In *Exactly the Opposite* by Tana Hoban, pairs of opposites are presented in full-color photos on a two-page spread; the wordless photos allow readers to interpret the photos as they understand them. You'll find open-ended images for *empty and full, open and closed, large and small, front and back, near and far, up and down,* and more. Read and explore the photos with children; we have found that the more we change the order of the relationship words (front and back, back and front), the more focused young children are on using the corresponding language to talk about the meaning of the relationships.

Using Total Physical Response (TPR)

Total Physical Response (TPR) was originally developed to aid the learning of second languages (Asher 1965). It involves acting out physical movements as part of learning. TPR is also very effective in early childhood classrooms to support children in developing the language of location, speed, and direction. Children need many opportunities to dance and to use all sorts of patterns and physical movements to describe themselves in space.

Mia moves *through* a hula hoop during a TPR activity in Brenda's classroom.

Following are a few of our favorite rhymes and songs that get children physically involved with such language, specifically key vocabulary.

Key Vocabulary

- high, low
- fast, slow
- near, far
- over, under
- loud, quiet
- open, closed
- round, corner
- bend, straight, curved
- around

Teddy Bear

Teddy Bear, Teddy Bear, turn around.

Teddy Bear, Teddy Bear, touch the ground.

Teddy Bear, Teddy Bear, touch your heart.

Teddy Bear, Teddy Bear, legs apart.

Teddy Bear, Teddy Bear, touch your toe.

Teddy Bear, Teddy Bear, hands down low.

Teddy Bear, Teddy Bear, touch your eye.

Teddy Bear, Teddy Bear, hands up high.

Teddy Bear, Teddy Bear, stand so tall.

Teddy Bear, Teddy Bear, down you fall!

Teddy Bear, Teddy Bear, jump up high.

Teddy Bear, Teddy Bear, wave good-bye.

Step, Step, Step

We step, step, step, and tap, tap, tap, and then we turn around.

We step, step, step, and tap, tap, tap, and bow without a sound.

We clap down low, we clap up high.

We clap the ground, we clap the sky.

We step, step, step and tap, tap, tap, and then we sit right down.

Opposites

Big, bigger, biggest, more than all the rest,

(gesture with hands farther and farther apart)

Small, smaller, smallest, less and less and less,

(gesture with hands closer and closer together)

High, low, fast, slow,

(hands high, hands low, roll them fast, roll them slowly)

There's more than all the rest. (gesture with wide hands for more)

Head, Shoulders, Knees, and Toes

Head, Shoulders, Knees, and Toes

Head, Shoulders, Knees, and Toes

Eyes and Ears and Mouth and Nose

Head, Shoulders, Knees, and Toes

Sing this familiar preschool song with the regular lyrics, and then find ways to change it. Encourage children to contribute their ideas and suggestions for what to sing and do; once they realize how the lyrics can be modified, they are eager to call out their ideas (of course, they always remember to sing the song loud and fast!). Some ideas to consider are:

- First sing the song slowly, then sing it fast.
- Sing it with a sad face, then make it a happy song.

- Sing it starting at the toes and reverse the order.
- Sing it quietly, then sing it loudly.

The Hokey Pokey

Put your one foot in, put your one foot out, put your one foot in, and shake it all about.

Do the Hokey Pokey, and turn yourself around.

That's what it's all about!

Repeat with other body parts and variations, using suggestions from children.

For more on using rhymes and songs in the classroom, see Chapter 6, Using Counting Books, Rhymes, and Songs.

Exploring Shapes

In this section we share activities that get students started in exploring shapes. Children need practice in manipulating various shapes made out of plastic, wood, glass, metal, fabric, and foam and arranging them in different orientations. They begin to notice where shapes are in their environment. Because work with shapes is important in later years, children's learning about shapes goes beyond just knowing the names. They need to be able to describe the shapes and know how they go together with other shapes. The activities in this section emphasize the importance of giving children opportunities to explore a wide variety of shapes, think about three-dimensional figures, and understand congruency.

A Shape Museum

Consider creating a Shape Museum for exploring shapes. Recall the creation and use of a Collection Museum (Chapter 2) and a Pattern Museum (Chapter 3). Use pattern blocks and other shapes for this new museum that focuses on geometrical shapes. Add to the Shape Museum by collecting different objects that are interesting and familiar. Packages of crackers in different shapes, beach balls, and cans of soup are interesting things to begin with. Tana Hoban's book *Shapes, Shapes, Shapes* has photos of objects that can be collected for the Shape Museum.

Simon Says Shapes!

This classic game, which traditionally uses commands such as *touch your shoulders* and *touch your elbows*, can be changed up to practice children's understanding of shapes by having children act out commands such as

"Make a shape that has corners. Make a shape with a partner that has four sides. Make a shape with three people that is a letter of the alphabet." Here are some examples:

Simon says, "Make a shape that has corners."

Simon says, "Make a shape that is round."

Simon says, "Make a shape that is as tall as you can be."

Simon says, "Make a shape that is very flat and low."

Simon says, "Make a shape with a partner that has four sides."

Simon says, "Make a shape with a partner that has curves."

Simon says, "Make a shape with a partner that has sharp angles."

Simon says, "Make a shape with three people that is a letter of the alphabet."

The Shape of Things

Of all the shape books available, one of our favorites is *The Shape of Things* by Dayle Ann Dodds, which uses clever paper-collage art to show children how circles, squares, and triangles are parts of things they see every day. We keep this book near the flannel board and felt shapes area to help suggest ideas for collages and arrangements that children can make with their own variety of shapes.

A shape collage made by Ali in Brenda's class, described by the child as being a "a cool spaceship and a truck."

Sorting with Felt Shapes

In this activity children use the magical tool, a flannel board, to sort a collection of felt shapes. To start, cut out a variety of shapes from various colors of felt (see Reproducible M for ideas).

See Reproducible M, Shape Templates.

Because children usually think about sorting shapes by color first, provide a wide variety of shapes and colors for sorting. Stick the shapes on the flannel board in all orientations, some with a horizontal base and others in different orientations. Then have children decide which shapes should go together. Eventually we want to try to name or label these groups. *These have corners*, for example. Examples of felt shapes and the ways they might be sorted are shown here.

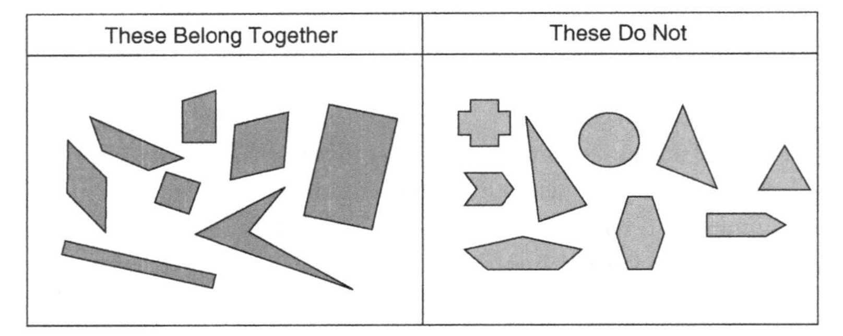

Felt shape sort. (All the quadrilaterals are on the left. Non quadrilaterals are on the right.)

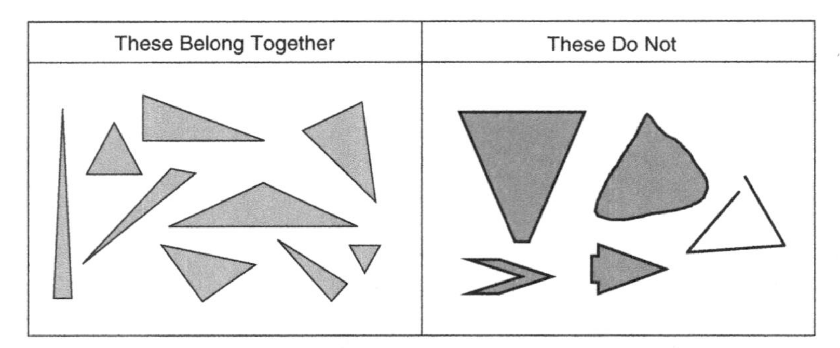

Triangles and nontriangles sort.

Teaching Insight

The "Magic" Flannel Board

To make a flannel board cover a piece of half-inch-thick foam board or wood fiberboard with a solid color square yard of cotton flannel. Staple the flannel to the back of the board. Flannel boards are also available in educational supply catalogs. Children are fascinated with the idea that the felt pieces stick to the flannel board. They also will stick to their shirts! Children may enjoy marching around the classroom, showing off the shapes while they are affixed to their shirts.

It is true that children often start with sorting shapes by color—for example, putting all green shapes together. To help children sort by thinking about other attributes besides color, give children some shapes that are all made from the same color of felt. The shapes will determine the possible categories. If all shapes are red, but some have curves and the rest have straight sides, the conversation will center around looking at the sides of the shapes. If some of the shapes have three sides and others have four sides, then counting the number of sides will emerge as the sorting strategy. These activities will probably take place initially during Circle Time, but also can be incorporated in Small Group Time if children are struggling to grasp how to sort. During Choice Time, children also enjoy arranging the shapes on the flannel board to make pictures of houses, cars, toys, animals, and so forth.

A Child's Mind

Understanding a Wide Variety of Shapes

Children form visual templates or models of shapes they have seen in their experience. When they see triangles, if they have only been presented with equilateral triangles (all sides equal) or isosceles triangles (at least two sides equal), always with a horizontal base, then their informal notions of triangles are limited to that kind of presentation of *triangle*.

Moreover, young children may think about rectangles as a *door* shape if they have not been exposed to other rectangles, including the *square rectangles* that have the necessary four sides and four right angles, and additionally have four equal length sides. They also may not have been exposed to very narrow rectangles that do not look like a door. Further, if children have not been exposed to trapezoids, or irregular shapes, they may not think these are *real* shapes. It is important to share a wide variety of shapes with children. They need to manipulate them and see that they can be used to create different arrangements and patterns.

For more activities focused on developing children's sorting skills, see Chapter 2, Collecting, Sorting, and Classifying.

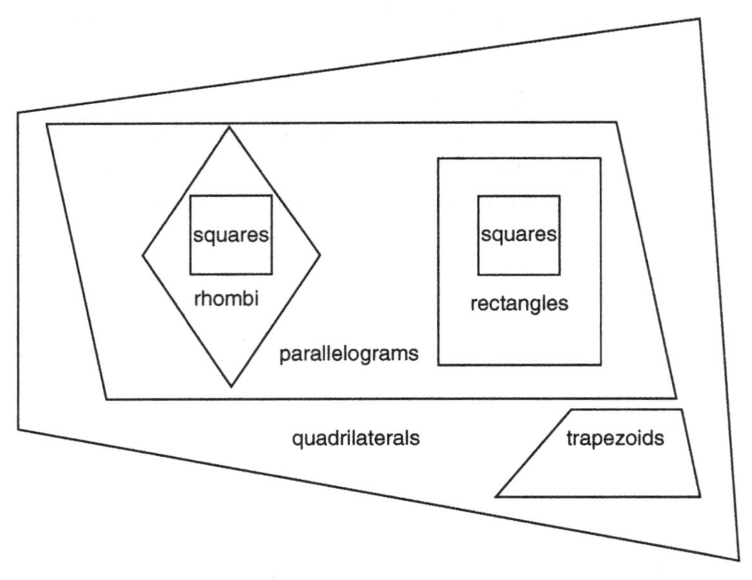

This diagram helps demonstrate the relationships between quadrilaterals. (Source: *Teaching Children Mathematics*, February 1999).

Exploring Shapes Using a Light Table

Choice Time

In our classroom we designate space for the light table and refer to this as our Light Table Center (see the Classroom Map, page 333). This is a very engaging center. A light table provides opportunities to explore how colors can be mixed, how shadows and transparent objects can be manipulated, and how overlapping various objects can create new shapes. If teachers do not have a light table, an overhead projector will also work. We stock our light table with a slew of useful tools: a collection of transparent shapes, including rulers, picnic plates, bottles, and pattern blocks, as well as some opaque shapes.

Suggested Tools for the Light Table

transparent shapes

transparent rulers

transparent colorful picnic plates, cups, and flatware

transparent plastic cosmetic bottles

transparent plastic compartmentalized boxes

transparent plastic shapes (pattern blocks and tangrams)

colorful silk fabric scraps

some opaque shapes as well as transparent ones

For children's shape explorations on the light table, we prepare a collection of transparent blue and yellow shapes using cut up acetate sheets from an art store or colorful transparent folders from an office supply store. See Reproducible M, Shapes Templates for shapes. Give children various tasks such as matching *congruent* shapes or making a green shape. Make sure there are regular and irregular shapes. Children need to rotate and flip these shapes in order for them to match up the edges.

Math Talk

Congruency

In geometry, two figures are *congruent* when they have the same shape and size. If one shape is placed on top of another shape, they match perfectly.

See Reproducible M, Shape Templates.

Math Talk

Regular and Irregular Shapes

A regular shape like a square or an equilateral triangle has all equal length sides. In the pattern block shape set, all the pattern blocks are regular except the trapezoid, which is irregular. There are many irregular triangles in the real world, but only the equilateral triangle has equal interior angles and equal side lengths. So a square is a regular rectangle because it has equal length sides. A rhombus is a regular parallelogram. See the diagram on page 208 for a visual of this relationship.

Liana and Humberto working with transparent shapes at the light table in Brenda's classroom.

Shapes on the light table, created from the Shapes Templates.

See Reproducible C7, Learning Progressions: Early Childhood/Geometric and Spatial Thinking.

Assessment Opportunity

Assess children's work at a light table. Use Reproducible C7, Learning Progressions: Early Childhood/Geometric and Spatial Thinking to record your observations.

Video Clip 9.1: Exploring Shapes Using a Light Table

To view the clip, scan the QR code or visit **mathsolutions.com/ TEACHPK91**

Children match blue and yellow shapes at the light table to make green.

In Video Clip 9.1, Brenda works with children to explore shapes at the light table. First children work with two-dimensional shapes, then move to three-dimensional projects. Watch how the children manipulate the shapes and know when they have been successful. Pause the clip at the intervals indicated below and think about the questions that follow.

In the first part of this clip children take turns matching blue and yellow shapes to make green. Children think ahead to which shapes they will choose when it is their turn. Brenda uses the term congruent in the context of matching their shapes. Stop the clip after viewing this activity. What observations can you make about children's understanding of shapes? How do they go about the task of matching shapes?

What We Learned: Although they did not identify the shapes by name, the children were very engaged and interested in making green shapes by matching up the yellow and blue shapes and superimposing them upon one another. In most cases they needed to rotate the shapes and in some cases they needed to flip the shapes in order to make them match. They also determined that some shapes were missing because they could not match them up with a partner. Some children seemed very excited about the idea that they could make green by mixing yellow and blue (something to be explored later).

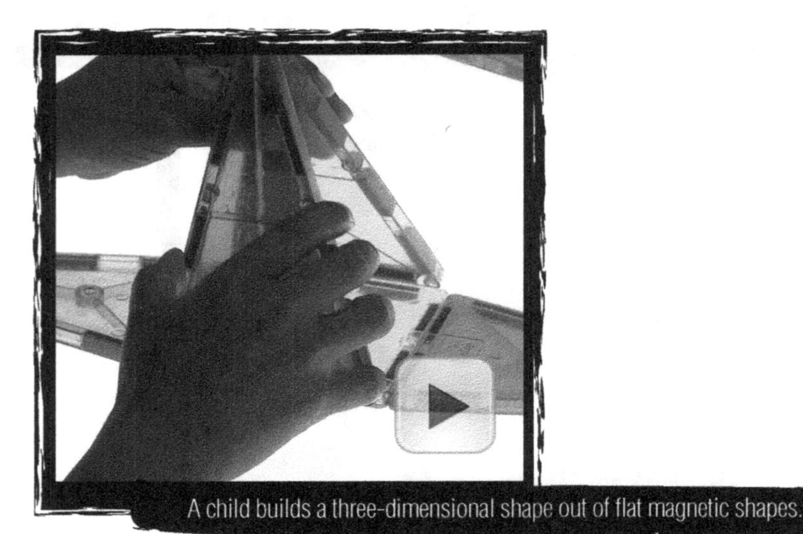

A child builds a three-dimensional shape out of flat magnetic shapes.

In the second part of this clip children explore two-dimensional and three-dimensional shapes by manipulating magnetic flat shapes. Brenda challenges children to build nets. Watch the clip to the end. What observations can you make about children's exploration of two- and three-dimensional shapes?

What We Learned: Sometimes it is very difficult to figure out how to do this work. The magnets allow the student to put together a collection of different shapes easily, but figuring out how the net should be formed is challenging. Adrian tries to keep the shape upright in order to make a three-dimensional figure.

Light Table Twister

We couldn't resist mentioning one of our favorite light table games for encouraging the exploration of shapes. This is a hands-only version of the classic game Twister. Place a set of transparent dots and a spinner on the light table. Challenge children to try to touch each color dot in succession. They make interesting shapes with their bodies and hands and get lots of practice using sequence ideas of first, second, third, and so on.

Teaching Insight

Tracing on the Light Table

In addition to using the light table to develop mathematical concepts, the light table is a great tool for supporting children's fine motor skills in tracing. Children enjoy tracing letters on the light table—tape lightweight paper over transparent patterns on the light table and give children markers to trace the letters that come through. Children can also trace transparent digital pictures of classmates, friends, familiar adults, and storybook characters; stories naturally emerge from this task, and sometimes children include shapes with the characters as well. When we are investigating a science unit, we put images of snails and tarantulas on the light table, place parchment paper over them, and have children trace around the images. Children then have the option to color in their drawings.

Michelle's snail drawing was made by tracing a snail image on the light table.

Sorting with Geoboards

This activity is like other sorting activities, only here the children have the opportunity to create their own shapes using geoboards. It's important that children first have many opportunities to explore making various shapes and pictures with geoboards.

Teaching Insight

Geoboards

A geoboard is a plastic or wooden board with half-driven nails or pegs on a square in typically a 5 × 5 array. Children place rubber bands around the pegs to create shapes and geometric designs. We call the rubber bands "geobands" to make clear that they are used to make geometric shapes. Teach children how to put the geobands on and take them off by putting their finger on the peg so no one gets hurt. Children usually work on their own geoboard, so having enough boards for the size of the group is highly recommended. If teachers do not have enough geoboards for the whole class then they can do these sorting activities with a small group.

Imanol shows the shapes he created in his explorations of the geoboard.

Angelica shows the shape she made on her geoboard.

After children are familiar with using geoboards, challenge them to make one shape that touches only three, four, or five nails or pegs on the geoboard. Once students have made their shapes, put all the geoboards together on the rug and explain that the shapes now need to be sorted; for example, move geoboard shapes that have shapes with four sides into a circle on the rug. (A hula hoop can be used to designate a *special* group.) Children then find other geoboard shapes that go with the ones in the circle. Note, if we only use four nails or pegs, all the figures may have four sides and there won't be as much to sort.

On another day sort geoboards according to different shaped triangles to help the children notice that all of these triangles have three straight sides.

Sometimes teachers can copy the shapes onto pieces of paper (it is typically too difficult for young children to accurately copy their geoboard shapes to a paper representation, so this is likely an adult task). Children want to save their shapes, but they also want to make new shapes, so a paper copy preserves their creation. These paper copies can be sorted as well. Children can also color these and put them together to make their own shape books. Encourage children to talk about their shapes as they do any of these activities.

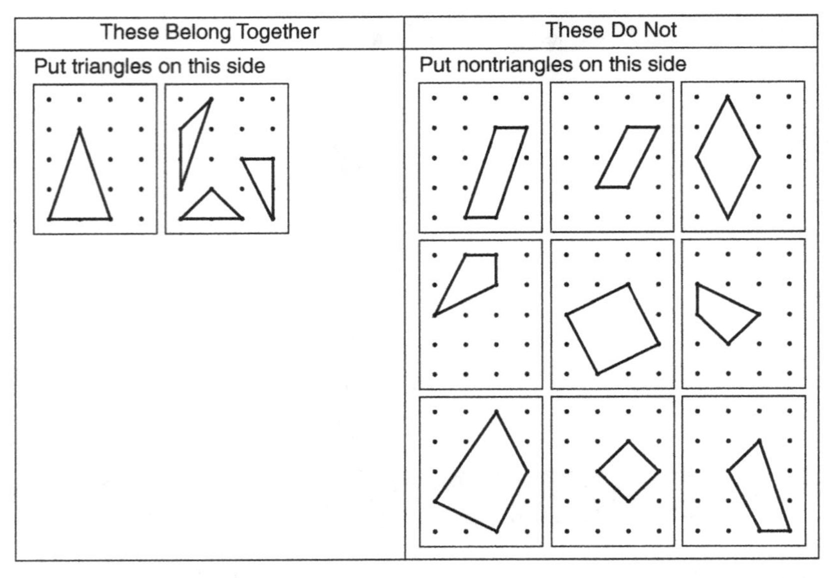

A geoboard sort with the categories "triangles" and "nontriangles."

Literature Connection

Cubes, Cones, Cylinders, and Spheres

When the topic of three-dimensional shapes is introduced, use *Cubes, Cones, Cylinders, & Spheres* by Tana Hoban. The stunning book features full-color photos that lead readers on a treasure hunt to find shapes. The wordless pages leave the search entirely up to the reader, evoking powerful opportunities for understanding how these shapes infiltrate daily life. After sharing the book and talking about the photos, take children on their own treasure hunt; walk around the school or neighborhood looking for and identifying three-dimensional shapes. Some found items (or photos of found items) might even be contributions to the class Shape Museum (see the activity on page 205 in this chapter).

Valentine Boxes

To celebrate Valentine's Day we have children create valentine boxes in the studio. These boxes are ultimately used to store their valentines. The mathematical problem is that children must take a three-dimensional box and figure out a way to cover the surface area neatly with paper. Collect shoeboxes and other boxes of various shapes and sizes. Give children scissors, tape, and a choice of paper. Explain to children that they need to cover their valentine box so that it is no longer a shoebox but a valentine box. Implicit in these instructions is that the box must be completely covered. Call children's attention to the different faces of the box, but mostly leave the task open-ended. When children have finished covering their boxes, give them time to decorate them.

It is interesting to see how children go about this task. Some of their strategies involve wrapping the paper around and around the box, like a blanket, and then finding a way to tape or glue all this paper on to the box. Other children trace the shape of a face of the box onto their paper, cut this out, and glue it on the matching face. Some children seem to appreciate the special paper and find ways to conserve it, creating less waste. Others crumple it in large sheets to fit around their boxes. After children have completed their boxes, make sure their names (and possibly photos) are on the boxes as well as a slit cut in the top for mail delivery, so valentines can be delivered to the rightful child!

The *studio* is a place in the classroom for children to make projects and express themselves using a variety of materials. For more insights on using the studio, see Chapter 2. See also the Classroom Map on page 333.

Isabella's strategy for covering her valentine box is to first wrap paper around the box.

Maya chose to decorate her valentine box with an interesting shape.

Imanol's finished valentine box.

Math Talk

Three-Dimensional Figures

Thinking about the distinction between a three-dimensional figure and the shapes found on the faces of the rectangular prism box is a big idea for young children. Children are able to identify *circle*, and often say *circle* when trying to describe a sphere. Similarly, they say *square* or *rectangle* when trying to describe a rectangular prism. They are able to see and use the term *face* when describing the shapes they see on their rectangular prism box. In this project they become familiar with the number of faces on the box and the idea that some of the faces match each other.

Assessment Opportunity

Once children have created their valentine boxes, consider providing ribbons for the boxes. You can make this an interesting assessment opportunity by posing the question, "Which ribbon is longer?" Present several lengths of ribbon to a child. In addition to length, make sure each ribbon is a different color and width. Ask key questions, such as, *Which ribbon is longer? How do you know? Can you put the ribbons in order according to length?*

Observe how the child approaches this task. Then cut the ribbon the child has chosen to decorate the box. Record your observations of her or his thinking using Reproducible C3, Learning Progressions: Early Childhood/Measurement.

See Reproducible C3, Learning Progressions: Early Childhood/ Measurement.

Finding Congruent Shapes

In this activity the idea of *congruency* is introduced and explored while simultaneously helping children understand shapes. We will be matching congruent two-dimensional and three-dimensional shapes. To start, collect a set of matching pairs of shapes and blocks. Make sure that no two matching shapes share the same color. Present children with the collection; ask them to take turns matching the shapes. To do this, they need to test for congruency by placing one shape on top of the other—do they match? Model matching a pair of shapes. Tell children, "See if you can find a pair of shapes that are congruent like these two." Sometimes children will need to flip or rotate a shape in order to make it match.

Math Talk

Congruency

In geometry, two figures are *congruent* when they have the same shape and size. If one shape is placed on top of another shape, they match perfectly.

Assessment Opportunity

A variation of this activity becomes a valuable assessment opportunity. Put a collection of a few block shapes in a large, thick sock. Then put a collection of matching shapes on the table. Ask the child to reach into the sock, touch the shapes, and find one of the shapes that is congruent to a shape on the table. Can she or he find the matching shape? The child can use the shape on the table to aid in finding its match; however, he or she can only touch (not see!) the shapes in the sock. Later on, do this assessment again, only put all the shapes in the sock (leave none on the table). The child now has to name the shape he is feeling just before he takes it out of the sock.

Observe how children match the shapes. Record your observations of children's thinking using Reproducible C7, Learning Progressions: Early Childhood/ Geometric and Spatial Thinking.

See Reproducible C7, Learning Progressions: Early Childhood/Geometric and Spatial Thinking.

Exploring Spatial Relationships

Imagine the challenge of teaching a robot how to do a relatively simple task like setting the table. We would need to teach the robot about not only how to recognize what knives, forks, and spoons were, but also how to place them in the correct orientation and space them with the fork on the left and the knife and spoon on the right. The distance between these utensils would have to be a little more than the diameter of the plate. Learning about spatial relationships is very complex work.

When children are learning about their place in the world they begin to learn where they are in relation to their homes (as they travel to school), their school (as they navigate to their classroom), and their classroom (as they find their place in the circle on the rug). Spatial activities in the early childhood classroom help children to begin to see how they relate to the things in the world around them.

Where Is It?

This activity gives children the opportunity to demonstrate their understanding of spatial/relational language. Instead of being asked to describe a set of directions, they can show they know the meaning of the directional language by following the directions. Children show their understanding of the spatial/relational language, and the activity feels like a buried treasure game.

In this activity place a collection of treasures in plain sight and also hide some from view. The adults as well as children help each volunteer child find one of the treasures by describing its location. To introduce the activity we use a model town consisting of small toys such as cars, houses, trees, and blocks. Our treasures are all sorts of small items—little shapes, play cookies, gold stars, a shell fossil, valentine cards, and more.

Find the treasure that is under the doll.

Find the treasure that is next to the small car.

On another day we can move from the model town to the entire classroom, and hide treasures throughout the classroom. To help students find the treasures, we describe their locations (the square block is *near* the sandbox, the toy car is *beside* the couch, the fossil shell is *on top of* the studio table). Then it's the children's turn. They hide a treasure of their choice and challenge the teacher to find it (as the teacher, playfully hide your eyes as students set up their challenges). In order for the teacher to successfully find it, students must describe the location. This also gives children a chance to feel that they are in charge of the thinking.

Is There a Shorter Route?

As part of spatial relations, provide opportunities for children to grapple with the concept of distance—specifically the idea that a straight line is the shortest distance between two points. Create a model town from small toy houses, cars, and trees. Tell children they're going on a drive around town. Drive a toy car from one spot to another, and then challenge children to find a shorter route. Develop the idea that a straight line is the shortest distance between two points again and again using other objects (slowly moving turtles, hopping bunnies, and even walking across the model town with your fingers). On another day, show the shortest route from the classroom to the playground and ask children to find a longer route. Encourage them to explain their thinking. Ask, "How do you know that this way is longer? How do you know that that way is shorter?"

Not a Box

This activity provides plenty of opportunities to support children's use of language in describing spatial relations. First read *Not a Box* by Antoinette Portis. In this simple book, a little rabbit is shown sitting in a box, but the rabbit insists *it is not a box!* Using a little imagination, the box becomes a boat, a house, a mountain, a burning building, and even a robot. After reading the book, give children cardboard boxes and encourage them to use their imagination to build something. Stand back and watch what they come up with. Provide tape, cutting tools, and other items upon request. Ask key questions like the following to engage children in conversation about their creations when they're done.

- What do you want to make with your box?
- Does your box remind you of something?
- What will you put inside your box?
- Where is the bottom of your box?
- Which sides are the same size?
- How can you make sure your box will hold your [car]?
- How will you put the two boxes together?

Gabi became a pirate in a ship made by the class out of a box.

Puzzle Challenges

When children put together puzzles, they practice hand-to-eye coordination, solve spatial problems, and practice decision-making skills. They learn persistence and patience. When there are multiple solutions to puzzles, children learn to appreciate their own efforts as well as the efforts of others. The following collection of puzzles deals with manipulating geometric shapes to create an appealing design or picture.

Math Talk

Is It a Rectangle?

The shapes on Reproducible N are all rectangles because they have four sides and right angles. Some are *regular* rectangles with equal length sides.

Rectangle Puzzles

In this puzzle activity children fill in the area of rectangles, thus developing their concept of area. First give children a paper rectangle (see Reproducible N) and a collection of one-inch tiles. Ask children, "Can you cover the rectangle with some of these square tiles?" Some children may fill in the shapes with stripes or a repeating pattern. Once children have completed their puzzle, ask, "How many square tiles did you use?" When children report how many of each *color* tile they use, they are responding to a part/whole question. This can be another opportunity to reinforce the concept of area or parts of the whole.

See Reproducible N, Rectangle Puzzle Templates.

Teaching Insight

Making Puzzles

To prevent the tiles from sliding off the card, apply a bead of white glue around the perimeter of each shape, and then sprinkle fine sand onto the glue. This forms a barrier around the shape.

Flag Puzzles

ll Group Time

In this activity children create their own flags by fitting colored rectangles onto an 8-by-10–inch canvas (black paper, a chance to make a flag for the pirate ship). Give each student an 8-by-10–inch piece of black paper and ten each of 2-by-4–inch red, white, and blue rectangles (use the 2-by-4–inch rectangle from Reproducible N).

See Reproducible N, Rectangle Puzzle Templates.

Explain to children that they are in charge of creating a flag. To do so, their rectangles need to fit together and completely cover their entire black paper without overlapping. After children have created their flags, they can glue the rectangles down. Ask children to count how many rectangles of each color they used and how many rectangles in all.

Gabi's flag puzzle has 3 red + 4 white + 3 blue rectangles.

Record children's answers in a number sentence representing the three different colors—for example, 3 red + 4 white + 3 blue = 10 rectangles in all.

Encourage further thinking by asking children key questions such as "How many horizontal rectangles are in your flag? How many vertical rectangles?"

Display the flags for everyone to see. Ask, "Which flags match? Which flags are almost the same?" Since there are many ways for children to complete this puzzle, seeing all the flags on display is compelling. Children enjoy noticing their own contribution as well as seeing other flags that may be similar.

Hexagon Puzzles

Small Group Time

This activity is similar to the previous rectangle puzzles activity, but children cover a hexagon shape instead of a rectangle. Use the hexagon shape in Reproducible O to create the puzzles for this activity. Transfer the shape to card stock, using the copy machine to enlarge the shape 102% so the blocks will fit more easily within its outline. Give each student a paper hexagon and a collection of pattern blocks that includes the red trapezoids, the yellow hexagons, the green triangles, and the blue rhombi. The orange squares and the tan rhombi won't work in this puzzle. (For more on pattern blocks, see "Using Pattern Blocks," page 226.) Ask, "Can you cover the hexagon with some of these shapes?" There are many ways to complete this puzzle—for example, the hexagon can be filled with twenty-four green triangle pattern blocks. This activity can lead to ideas of equivalence. It is interesting for students to notice how different people can try the same puzzle and come up with a different solution.

See Reproducible O, Hexagon Puzzle Template.

These pattern blocks are used for the hexagon puzzle.

Math Talk

Equivalence

The yellow hexagon is equivalent to six of the green triangles, three of the blue rhombi, or two of the red trapezoids. Children can discover this when they put the green, blue, and red blocks on top of the yellow hexagon. If two trapezoids equal the area of the yellow hexagon (i.e., cover it completely), we can say that each trapezoid is one-half of the yellow hexagon, and two halves are equivalent to the one whole hexagon. Similarly, since three blue rhombi cover the yellow hexagon, we can say that each rhombus is one-third of the hexagon and three-thirds are equivalent to one whole. When children explore with these fractional equivalent relationships, they are forming a foundation of understanding about the meaning of fractions, but from their perspective, they are just making them the same shapes. We do not introduce the language of equivalence with them, but for now talk about how the shapes are the same size.

Tangram Puzzles

As students solve these puzzles they are building their spatial visualization and spatial reasoning skills. Tangram puzzles are made from a square divided into seven pieces. The seven pieces can be arranged to form many different shapes and pictures (see Reproducible Q).

See Reproducible Q, Tangram Puzzle Shapes.

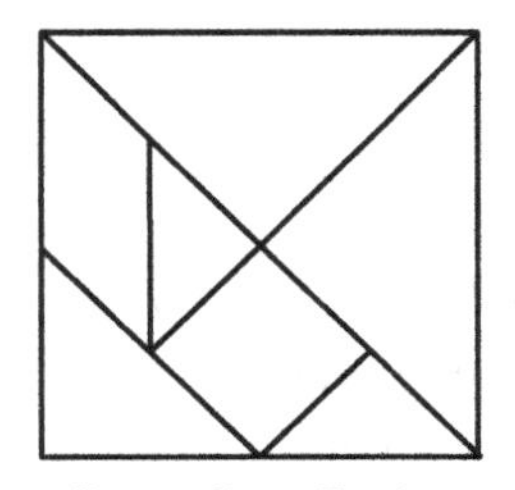

Tangram Shapes Template

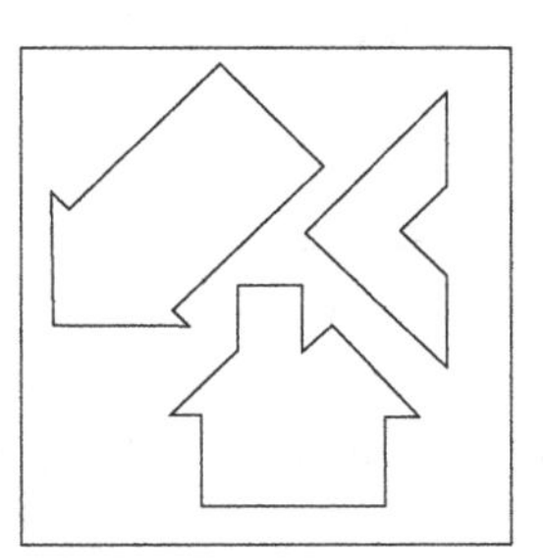

Tangram Puzzle Shapes

See Reproducible P, Tangram Shapes Puzzle.

See Reproducible Q, Tangram Puzzle Shapes.

See Reproducible C7, Learning Progressions: Early Childhood/Geometric and Spatial Thinking.

To solve a tangram puzzle, children need to rotate and flip their pieces in order to fit them in the outline shape. To start, give each student multiple sets of the seven tangram pieces (Reproducible P) and at least one of the outline shapes (Reproducible Q). Explain to children that they need to fit their pieces into the shape to fill it and "solve the puzzle." There are many ways for children to build congruent shapes using these tangram pieces. All of the tangram puzzles can be solved using only the smallest right triangles, and each of the other pieces may also be formed by two, four, or eight of the smallest triangles. Older children and adults can be challenged to solve the puzzles using only one complete set of the seven tangram shapes.

Assessment Opportunity

All of the puzzle activities presented in this section provide valuable assessment opportunities. Record your observations as children complete their puzzles; use Reproducible C7: Learning Progressions/ Early Childhood Geometric and Spatial Thinking.

Math Talk

Congruency

In geometry, two figures are congruent when they have the same shape and size. If we put one shape on top of another shape, they match perfectly.

Turning Shapes

Turning a shape in space is called a *rotation*. Flipping a shape is called a *reflection*. When children employ these *transformations* they develop geometric ideas about how the shape may look different, but still has the same size, area, angles, and side lengths. Young children do not need to know these terms, but they do learn a great deal about these geometric ideas.

Teaching Insight

Making Puzzles

Use the shapes in Reproducible S to create the puzzles for this activity. Transfer the shapes to card stock, using the copy machine to enlarge the shape 102% so the blocks will fit more easily within its outline. Now apply a bead of white glue around the perimeter of the shape, and then sprinkle fine sand onto the glue. This forms a barrier around the shape to prevent the blocks from sliding off the card. Reproducible R: Pattern Block Triangle Template can also be used to create more original pattern block puzzles.

Using Pattern Blocks

Pattern blocks are beautiful math manipulatives. They allow children to see how shapes can be decomposed into other shapes. When children have a chance to become familiar with the properties and relationships inherent in these blocks, creative designs and pictures seem to naturally evolve.

When introducing pattern blocks to the classroom, give children an opportunity to freely explore using them. We find that children purposefully choose the blocks they want to use in their designs. The designs they create include animals, flowers, boats and ships, rockets and planes, cars, trains, and many other subjects.

See Reproducible S, Pattern Block Puzzle Shapes.

Alexa and Isabella created symmetrical flowers during their pattern block exploration.

A basket of pattern blocks in Brenda's class.

Teaching Insight

Pattern Blocks

Pattern blocks are colorful plastic and wood blocks available in sets of about 250 blocks. We have found that we use several sets, some for the Choice Time area, others in the block area or in the Pattern Museum. The pattern blocks in our classrooms are all constructed using the same dimensions (one inch) for the sides with the exception of the red trapezoid, which has one side two inches long. By placing the yellow, red, blue, and green blocks on a pattern block triangle template (see Reproducible R), we can see how they are related. The green equilateral triangle is one unit, the blue rhombus measures two units, the red trapezoid measures three units, and the yellow hexagon measures six units. The internal angles of all of the pattern block shapes are 30 degrees, 60 degrees, 90 degrees, 120 degrees or 150 degrees, so the blocks can be put together to form appealing shapes. The orange square and the tan rhombus cannot be superimposed on this template to create a shape puzzle, but they do have the same side length and related angles as the other blocks.

See Reproducible R, Pattern Block Triangle Template.

Danella makes a paper replication of her pattern block design.

Children can save their pattern block creations by replicating them with paper. Use colored paper pattern block shapes, glue, and sturdy black paper for the background.

Small Group Time

Pattern Block Puzzles

Like the rectangle, hexagon, and tangram shape puzzles introduced earlier in this chapter, pattern blocks can be used to complete puzzles. Give children pattern blocks and a copy of one of the shapes (puzzles) in Reproducible S: Pattern Block Puzzle Shapes. Transfer the shapes to card stock, using the copy machine to enlarge the shape 102% so the blocks will fit more easily within its outline. Challenge children to fit the red, blue, green, and yellow pattern blocks into the shape.

See Reproducible S, Pattern Block Puzzle Shapes.

Children informally learn about fractional relationships and equivalence when they work with pattern block puzzles. Because there is more than one solution for each of the puzzles, children who are sitting side by side and working on the same task can compare solutions and note the similarities and differences.

Assessment Opportunity

Observe children as they work; ask the child to tell you the number of yellow, red, blue and green blocks she uses to solve her puzzle. Use Reproducible C7: Learning Progressions/Early Childhood Geometric and Spatial Thinking.

See Reproducible C7, Learning Progressions: Early Childhood/Geometric and Spatial Thinking.

Pattern Block Mosaics

Another pattern block activity that immediately invites children to explore spatial relations is the creation of mosaics. Show children mosaic tile designs and point out how much surface area a mosaic covers—from floors to tables. Give children pattern blocks and challenge them to cover a table with blocks so that no part of the surface shows through.

An example of a pattern block mosaic.

Jose works on his pattern block mosaic, the goal being to cover the whole table!

Connecting Cube Puzzles

In this activity children create pictures out of connecting cubes; their pictures then become puzzles for their classmates to complete. To start, give each child a set of connecting cubes and a piece of paper as the "canvas." Allow children to freely explore creating their cube pictures—they'll create everything from giraffes and trees to slides and teeter-totters! When a child is done with his picture, trace around it onto the paper, thus creating a puzzle outline. Now another classmate tries to solve the puzzle by filling the outline with cubes. Classmates can ask the author of the puzzle for help as needed. Children appreciate making their own pictures and enjoy being the author of the puzzle task.

Teaching Insight

Connecting Cubes

In previous classroom activities, connecting cubes were used to make repeating and growing patterns. In this section they are used to make different shapes and pictures. Children can count the number of cubes they used to make their picture as well as name their constructions. These cubes also can be used for measurement activities as a nonstandard unit. Snap Cubes, Linker Cubes, Unifix Cubes, and Multilink Cubes are some of the ones most often used in the classroom.

Camron checks out connecting cube pictures.

Manuel calls his interlocking cube puzzle the stair step.

Exploring Parts and Wholes

Activities in this section focus on learning about parts and the whole. From a mathematical perspective, children need to know that they can take apart quantities and make sense of them by thinking, for example, of how many tens and ones are in a number like 24 (2 tens and 4 ones), what factors are in 12 (1, 2, 3, 4, 6, and 12), or what do we get when we cut something in half and then cut it in half again (fourths). There are many ways that we can look at the whole and then see how the parts relate to the whole. With our youngest children we try to provide some physical opportunities for them to literally take things apart.

Santiago takes an appliance apart.

Xavier and Diego connect plumbing pipes to create their imaginary machine.

Putting Together/Taking Apart

One of the most powerful ways to reinforce the big idea of parts and wholes for young children is to give them opportunities to put things together—and take them apart! We collect appliances, circuit boards, and small machines from thrift stores and garage sales and keep them in our classroom center called the "Take Apart Center." The items they gather and extract from this center will eventually find their way to the studio where they will be used to make all sorts of constructions. In the spirit of putting together and taking apart, children undo wires and screws, create their own transformers, match nuts and bolts, use hand drills to make places for screws, washers, and nuts, and wind copper wire around bolts to make their own springs. We've also observed them using measurement to determine how they can fit things together! In the process of creating and disassembling their imaginary machines, children learn the language of tools: wire cutter, wrench, Phillip's head screwdriver, pliers, and vise grip.

As children work on these projects, observe and listen. See the key questions provided to guide observations.

Key Questions While Observing Children's Constructions

- How would you describe and characterize the constructions children are making? Are they more horizontal than vertical? Is there symmetry in their building? Does the project contain balancing parts?
- Are there recognizable elements in the project that children name and share with others?
- Does the child make revisions or continue to work with the same topic or project over a period of time?
- Do stories, songs, or games that occur elsewhere in the classroom inspire the work?
- Does the child work collaboratively with other children on these projects?
- How does the size and shape of the materials children choose to work with determine the final construction?

Iliana has made a spring from a piece of wire in the take apart center.

Teaching Insight

Follow the Child's Lead

There are times when it may be appropriate to show children how to do something, such as using scissors or a hand drill. For other kinds of learning, arrange the environment in such a way that children are in charge of it. Listen and respond when they ask for details, information, or help. Follow their leads and build on their ideas. This can be a challenge for the teacher; however, it's important to remember that children are powerful constructors of their own learning.

A teacher helps hold an appliance while children take the lead in cutting wires.

Constructing with Blocks

Tinkertoys, LEGOS, Erector, Lincoln Logs, and the like support children's play in putting things together. However, we've found that it's usually the simplest toys that lend themselves to the most imaginative play and construction—and hence this focus on blocks. Place wooden blocks sorted by shape on low shelves that children can easily access. These are called unit blocks and they have been a staple for early childhood classrooms since the early 1900s. There are numerous resources available online and in books about the use of these blocks, as well as many articles in journals on their effective use. The beauty of these blocks involves their aesthetic character because they are carefully made of maple, birch, or beech wood. They all are related to one another; there are doubles, quadruples, and various fractions of the standard unit. Children reach for the block they need when they are making a construction. When the blocks are all arranged on the shelves in a logical and systematic way, children just seem to know how to find the length they are looking for to create the construction they envision.

Myreyah holds the tower she created with various colored transparent blocks in Brenda's class.

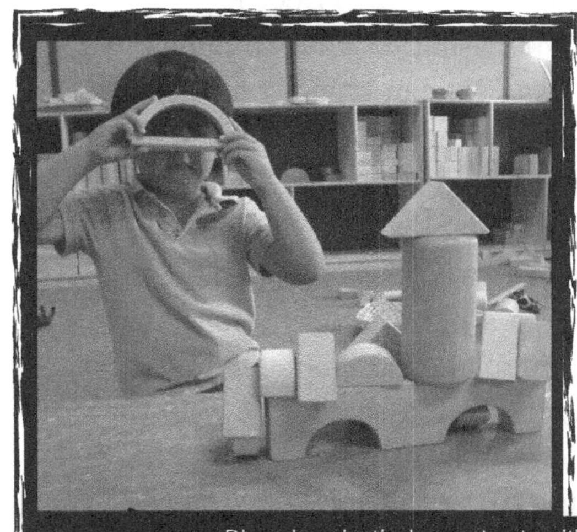

Diego imaginatively constructs with blocks in Brenda's class.

Blocks are sorted on open low shelves according to shape in Brenda's classroom.

Brenda's Journal Page

Scottie's Transformations

Every day during Choice Time Scottie first heads for the basket of what he calls "transforming toys." He can transform them from cars into robots and back into cars. Then Scottie goes into the block center. I've noticed that Scottie tends to pick a type of block and make new things from it. Today he picked right triangles and made a pizza. It was interesting to watch him manipulate the triangles to get all the right angles facing the same way. With the same type of blocks, he then discovered how to make space ships that don't fall over (he put the right angles together). The other boys try

continued

to make space ships but have not discovered the secret of the right angles. Then Scottie used triangle prism blocks to form a complete "circle" that he declared was a launching pad for his transforming toys.

When we were putting the blocks away Scottie discovered the right triangles could be put together to form a rectangle. He said, "Hey, how about that!" He made a couple of rectangles, then put the blocks away.

Scottie's triangle launch pad for his "transforming toys."

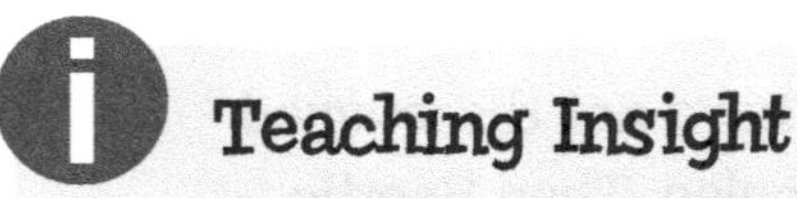

Teaching Insight

Interacting During Block Construction

It's our role as adults to observe and listen as children freely make their block constructions. The questions we ask ourselves as we observe children taking things apart are the same questions we ask with blocks. The answers we obtain tell us about their developing abilities and interests. We can make note of their geometric and spatial skills such as creating balance and symmetry. When appropriate, we provide a narration of what we are noticing, using academic language that we want our children to hear. We might make comments such as: Your building is as tall as your waist. Those long blocks are holding up the short ones. Those people are as long as their beds. You had to be careful so your towers would balance and not fall over.

In seeing Natalie's construction, Brenda comments, "Your puzzle is symmetrical; both sides match each other."

Sometimes we put vehicles or figures of animals and people in baskets near the blocks to prompt children to make different constructions. Children tend to be captivated by miniature items and quickly incorporate them into their play and stories. When they work with miniatures, they not only develop their fine motor skills, they also create stories about the items.

Continued

Similarly, when children have giant blocks, they create projects that allow them to get inside their construction. Once there, they may pretend to steer their vehicle, hide from imagined danger, or cuddle with a soft toy and picture book for a cozy story time session.

Anthony makes a project involving making one bed for each of his people figures.

Xavier steers a truck through his block construction.

As we observe, we ask ourselves, how does the size and shape of the materials children choose to work with determine the final construction?

We think it is important to have a few props to suggest a scenario, but young children have such good imaginations that it takes very little to get them interested in the construction tasks.

Jackeline makes a "train with passengers" involving blocks shaped like people.

Brenda's Journal Page

Perspective and the Size of Blocks

I've noticed that the size of the blocks children choose influences their perspective. When they play with small blocks at a table, they tend to look into their constructions from the side.

When they play with big blocks, usually on the floor, they tend to look down at their work from above and build from the floor to waist or eye level.

Assessment Opportunity

Record your observations of children during block construction time using Reproducible C7, Learning Progressions: Early Childhood/Geometric and Spatial Thinking.

See Reproducible C7, Learning Progressions: Early Childhood/Geometric and Spatial Thinking.

Teaching Insight

Stages of Block Play

According to Johnson, children move through various stages when building with blocks. Review the following stages and think about the mathematical ideas connected to each stage.

Stage 1: Blocks are carried around but are not used for construction (very young children).

Stage 2: Building begins. Children mostly make rows, either horizontal (on the floor) or vertical (stacked). There is much repetition in this early building pattern, which is basic functional play with blocks.

Stage 3: Children create bridges (or portals) by using two blocks to support a third. In architecture this is known as the *post-and-lintel system.*

Stage 4: Children create enclosures, placing blocks in such a way that they enclose a space. Bridging and enclosures are among the earliest technical problems children solve when playing with blocks; these occur soon after a child begins to use blocks regularly.

Stage 5: With age, children become steadily more imaginative in their block building. They use more blocks, create more elaborate designs, and incorporate patterns and balance into their constructions.

Stage 6: Naming of structures for dramatic play begins. Before this stage, children may have named their structures, but not necessarily based on the function of the building. Now children build a ship and name it a pirate's ship, for example (see Video Clip 9.2). This stage of block building corresponds to the "realistic" stage in art development.

Stage 7: Children use blocks to represent things they know, like cities, cars, airplanes, and houses. They also use blocks to stimulate dramatic play activities: blocks become a zoo, farm, shopping center, and other locations (Johnson, 1933).

Math Talk

Equivalent Lengths

Children find ways to make equivalent lengths when they build with unit blocks. This kind of exploration will help them later as they work with fractional representations and more specific measurement relationships.

Brenda's Journal Page

Fair Trades

Marcos and Ricardo were sitting side-by-side, building separate block constructions. Marcos ran out of the kind of block he wanted so he reached over and took one block from Ricardo's building.

> Ricardo: Hey, that's my block. You can't take that.
>
> Marcos: But I need it. Look at this. (He shows how it fits in the structure he is building.)
>
> Ricardo: You can use two of these for that one. (He shows Marcos how to match up equivalent lengths.)
>
> Marcos: Yeah, but I need the long ones for my roof.
>
> Ricardo: Give me all of your short ones and you can have these.

Apparently this is a fair trade and both boys continued to build their structures.

These boys are finding a way to not only resolve a conflict; they also are coming up with what they considered a fair trade.

Video Clip 9.2: Building with Blocks

To view the clip, scan the QR code or visit **mathsolutions.com/ TEACHPK92**

Angel and Scottie working together in the block play area.

In Video Clip 9.2, children are involved in building various construction projects with blocks. Watch the video clip in its entirety several times. Make note of your observations. Consider the seven stages of block play listed on page 241. What stage do you think each child or group of children is at? Also consider the key questions, which were introduced in the previous activity, "Putting Together/Taking Apart."

Key Questions While Observing Children's Constructions

- How can we describe and characterize the constructions children are making? Are they more horizontal than vertical? Is there symmetry in their building? Does the project contain balancing parts?
- Are there recognizable elements in the project that children name and share with others?
- Does the child make revisions or continue to work with the same topic or project over a period of time?
- Do stories, songs, or games that occur elsewhere in the classroom inspire the work?
- Does the child work collaboratively with other children on these projects?
- How does the size and shape of the materials children choose to work with determine the final construction?

What We Learned: This clip opens with an overview of the block play area.

Notice that the blocks are sorted by shape and stored on low shelves for easy access.

Angel's building play involves using a measurement tape.

There is a measurement tape in the block area and the children use it to measure their construction. They also have hard hats for their construction site and some protective goggles. These items seem to make their play more authentic.

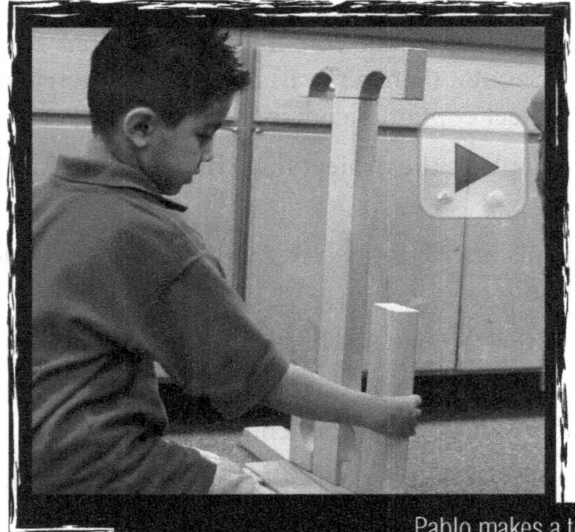

Pablo makes a tower

Two five-year-old boys are working more or less together, building a structure with symmetry. They are learning about gravity, stability, weight, and balance when they build with blocks. From what they are building, they are most likely at stages 3 and 4.

The boys are purposefully choosing the blocks they need to make their structures. They occasionally use the measurement tape to "measure" their building, which is part of their dramatic play. The structures have symmetry and are built up rather than on the plane of the floor. There is little conversation as they are building.

Angel has some cars to use as props. Mason notices this and is interested in what he is doing.

One of these boys decides to add small cars to his project; we see another boy observing this and the camera switches to this boy's construction.

Mason stacks towers.

This boy, Mason, is three years old. Now we see a younger child with the blocks. We find it fascinating to think about the stages that children pass through when working with blocks; as opposed to the two older boys, Mason is working alone, yet notices what the other boys are working on. He builds by stacking towers that are next to each other. He is learning how to balance the blocks and match up blocks that can be stacked. It is interesting to note that the youngest children usually carry blocks around and move them from place to place, watching the activities of older children. Older children often build with a purpose and tell stories about their constructions.

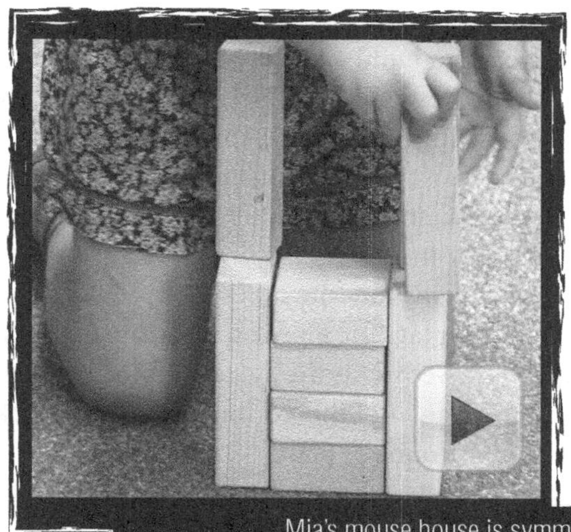

Mia's mouse house is symmetrical and vertical.

In the next construction project a young girl nearby is working by herself on a project. Mia is in costume. She is making a window for a little mouse castle. Notice the symmetry in her construction. We think Mia is at stage 5 in her block building because she is using her imagination to create this environment for the mouse.

Hugo, in pirate costume, is making pirate notes.

In the last segment children have dressed up to play the parts of pirates building a ship. These four- and five-year-old boys are working together with an end product in mind. They are wearing the costumes they will need for their dramatic play. The boys are going to build a pirate boat; they are planning to build a specific kind of structure. They have done this project day after day, refining their skills and exhibiting persistence. The pirates have outlined their big boat with blocks. They are making a platform for the bridge of the boat. They place matching blocks around the perimeter. The pirate boat has extra details and is big enough to sit inside. It has some windows. Once they have established the boat, Hugo begins to write notes on his tablet. The boys are fully involved in their dramatic play (for more on dress up and play, see the next section of this chapter). If we revisit the stages of block play, it seems like these pirates are working at stage 7 of this continuum. Their block structure is crucial as a setting for their dramatic play.

Choice Time

Documenting Block Construction Projects

See Video Clip 9.2.

After children have completed a construction project, challenge them to document their work by making a map of it. The maps they make help them learn how to represent their constructions with drawings. We saw in Video Clip 9.2 how the boys building their pirate ship started to take notes and record their project. Here are more examples of children's documentations.

Aaliah is drawing a picture of her construction project to document it.

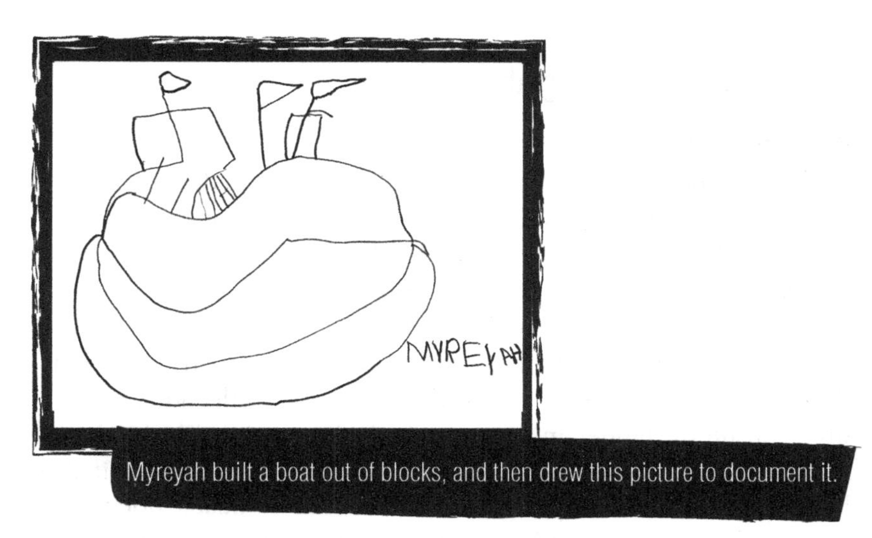

Myreyah built a boat out of blocks, and then drew this picture to document it.

It is important to remember that young children are just beginning to learn how to use drawings, words, letters, and numbers to represent their thinking. Children are trying to show us what they know, and we are challenged to find the message and meaning in their work. The challenge for the preschool teacher is to interpret this documentation with respect and thoughtfulness.

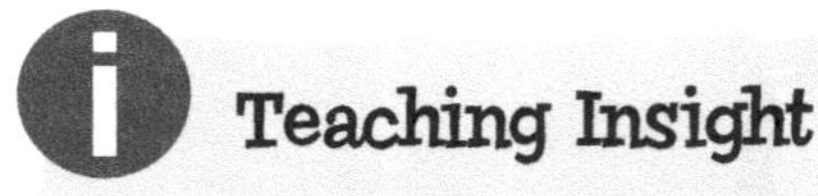

Teaching Insight

Block Construction Binders

In our classrooms we are continually taking photos to document the complexity of children's constructions. We print out the photos and place them in a binder near the block area. This binder serves as a reference for children during their construction time; they often consult these pages when they plan what they want to build. When some children have developed an interesting feature such as tiling the floors of their structure, or building a turret for a castle, other children consult the binder and try to copy the innovation. The binder encourages children's block building to become more complex. It also helps us record children's progress and serves as a valuable document to showcase children's work for classmates, families, and school program evaluators.

A block construction binder, titled "Developing Learning Relationships Through Block Building: Our Research and Our Stories," is kept with the blocks in Brenda's classroom.

Teaching Insight

Addressing Gender Issues in Block Construction

We've noticed in our classrooms that boys typically spend more time in the block area while girls tend to gravitate to the home center. The preferences that children make about visiting the block area seem to evolve from the children's home experiences more than their school experiences. We value the contribution that block building gives in the development of young children's geometric thinking and must ensure that all children have equal access to these tools. In order to deal with this potential inequity, the following ideas can be used to encourage access.

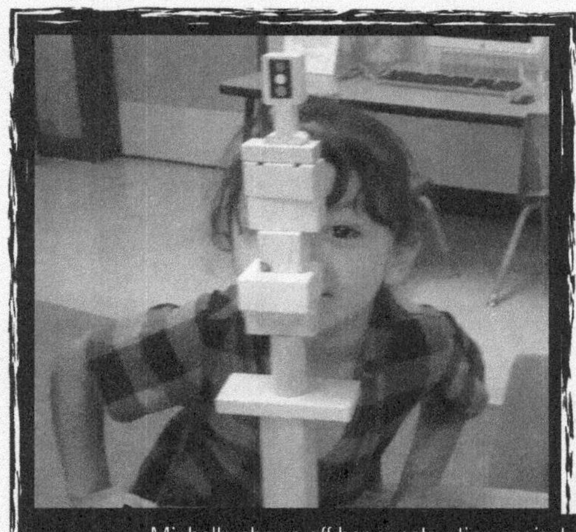

Michelle shows off her construction project, which she calls "fancy traffic sign."

Literature Connection

Louise Builds a House Read aloud *Louise Builds a House* by Louise Planner. In this book the main character, Louise, makes creative, deliberate choices about how she wants to build a house—the roof must be flat in order to fly kites from it, a life-sized chessboard is a must, a garden of vegetables will be out back, and of course—there has to be a moat. The strong female character with lots of tools and lots of imagination encourages girls to engage in block building for themselves.

Continued

Choice Time

Girls' Day in the Block Area To further encourage girls, we declare one day a week as *Girl's Day* in the block area. Making explicit this expectation helps girls feel more comfortable invading the domain that the boys seem to have set up. In turn, on these days the boys may be more comfortable going to the home center and playing with the kitchen and dress-up clothes.

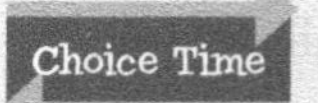

Princess Props Another strategy to encourage girls to build with blocks is to put princess-type toys, tiny baby dolls, and horses in a variety of sizes and colors in the block construction area. These items seem to be very attractive for girls. Encourage female architect/builders to build furniture, stables, and the like for the toys (just like Louise does for her house!).

Brenda's Journal Page

A Castle for Ponies

Marissa and Luisa were engaged in block play today. Marissa was making a castle for the ponies. She instructed Luisa, "Do it like me. You need a square one." Marissa motioned to a cube, which Luisa took and placed in the castle. Marissa promptly exclaimed, "No, not that way, you need to turn it over."

continued

Luisa defended her placement of the cube, explaining, "You can put it like this, 'cuz it's the same."

Marissa thought about it, commenting, "Now it looks right."

I was excited to see that both Marissa and Luisa are embracing new ideas, specifically thinking about rotation of geometric solids.

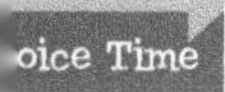

Constructing with Rods

The rods (Cuisenaire Rods) that the children are using in these activities are really like color-coded line segments of different lengths from one centimeter to ten centimeters in length. They are different from the unit blocks and the pattern blocks because they are designed to model length, whereas the pattern blocks show angle and area equivalence, and the unit blocks measure relationships in volume. Some children are drawn to the rods because they are so simple and easy to manipulate. As they continue to use the rods, children will begin to notice that the orange rods are all the longest, and all the other rods are one or more white cubes shorter than the orange rods. Length is the critical attribute in all these rods.

Alexa and Isabella create shapes out of rods in Brenda's class.

Brenda's Journal Page

A Rod Bridge Over Hot Lava

Today Pablo and Sergio sorted rods by length and put them together to make a bridge. I said to them, "I see you matched the lengths of the rods to make your bridge. Tell me the story of this bridge." They explained that their bridge was for "different-sized animals to cross over hot lava." They wanted to make the bridge longer, so they kept changing the width when they ran out of one color rod.

To make their story fit the materials, they added "The elephants can go across, but when they get to this part (pointing to the yellow rods) they hafta be careful." They addressed the crossing of little creatures too—"The mice can run all the way across 'cuz they're small."

Pablo and Sergio's rod bridge for "different-sized animals to cross over hot lava."

continued

I find it interesting that the words they used to describe what they were doing emerged from the physical attributes of the construction they were making. They began with a sorting activity, collecting all the orange 10-centimeter rods. Then they found another length and incorporated all those rods into their construction. Their story emerged as they worked with the rods, and they naturally narrated and justified their work.

hoice Time

Studio Collages and Assemblages

The studio can be used for more explorations of geometric and spatial relations. Place shapes of various materials in containers and encourage children to create collages and assemblages from the materials. They then describe their creations using their own words.

Gabi and Jackeline choose paper shapes in the studio for their collages.

> The *studio* is a place in the classroom for children to make projects and express themselves using a variety of materials. For more insights on using the studio, see Chapter 2. See also the Classroom Map, page 333.

Teaching Insight

Collages and Assemblages

A *collage* is an artistic collection of mostly two-dimensional shapes and images. The images may be drawings, paper shapes, or magazine photos. An *assemblage* is an artistic process. It consists of making a three-dimensional artistic composition by assembling various objects.

When we ask children about their creations we learn much about their interests and skills. For example, Gabi made a collage using small shapes of colorful giftwrap and patterned paper. She explained how she cut some of the pieces into triangles and arranged them so they fit together on her rectangular sheet of paper. She also superimposed some shapes on top of other shapes to create layers and depth. Last but not least, the pen lines between the shapes are, per Gabi, "the names of her friends." Here's what Gabi told us (in her words): "This is my puzzle. I put the shapes together. Here's a triangle. I wrote the names."

Gabi's puzzle collage.

Self-Portraits

In the studio center children draw portraits of themselves. When our class study unit was identity, we gave children mirrors to study their own facial features. We then asked them to draw self-portraits. In doing so, children show their ability to compose drawings with symmetry and use details to make their self-portraits as complete as they can.

In their self-portraits Mia and Jose captured the details of their faces.

Reflection Questions

1. How can teachers extend children's activities and problem solving with the introduction of new materials?
2. In 1957, Dutch educators Dina van Hiele-Geldof and Pierre van Hiele wrote about the development of a student's understanding of geometric reasoning and proof that progresses through five distinct levels. How can the teacher help the child towards the next level of development? (See www.keypress.com/x6772.xml)
3. How does the teacher extend the children's thinking by making suggestions without interrupting the play?
4. Some children seem to spend more time with one or two familiar activities. How does the teacher encourage all children to participate in a wide variety of activities?
5. How should the teacher introduce important mathematical vocabulary to the children? How important is mathematical vocabulary in early childhood settings?

6. How can the teacher document student growth in activities such as block building when some observers might think children are *just playing*?
7. What are some materials that engage children in exploring and manipulating shapes?
8. How can families help their children with spatial relationships at home? What do they need to know?
9. What are some songs or games that are useful in involving children in movement in space? How can you use these songs and games to increase student use of words in describing spatial relationships?
10. How can children use blocks and other geometric tools to compare, measure, order, count, and classify?

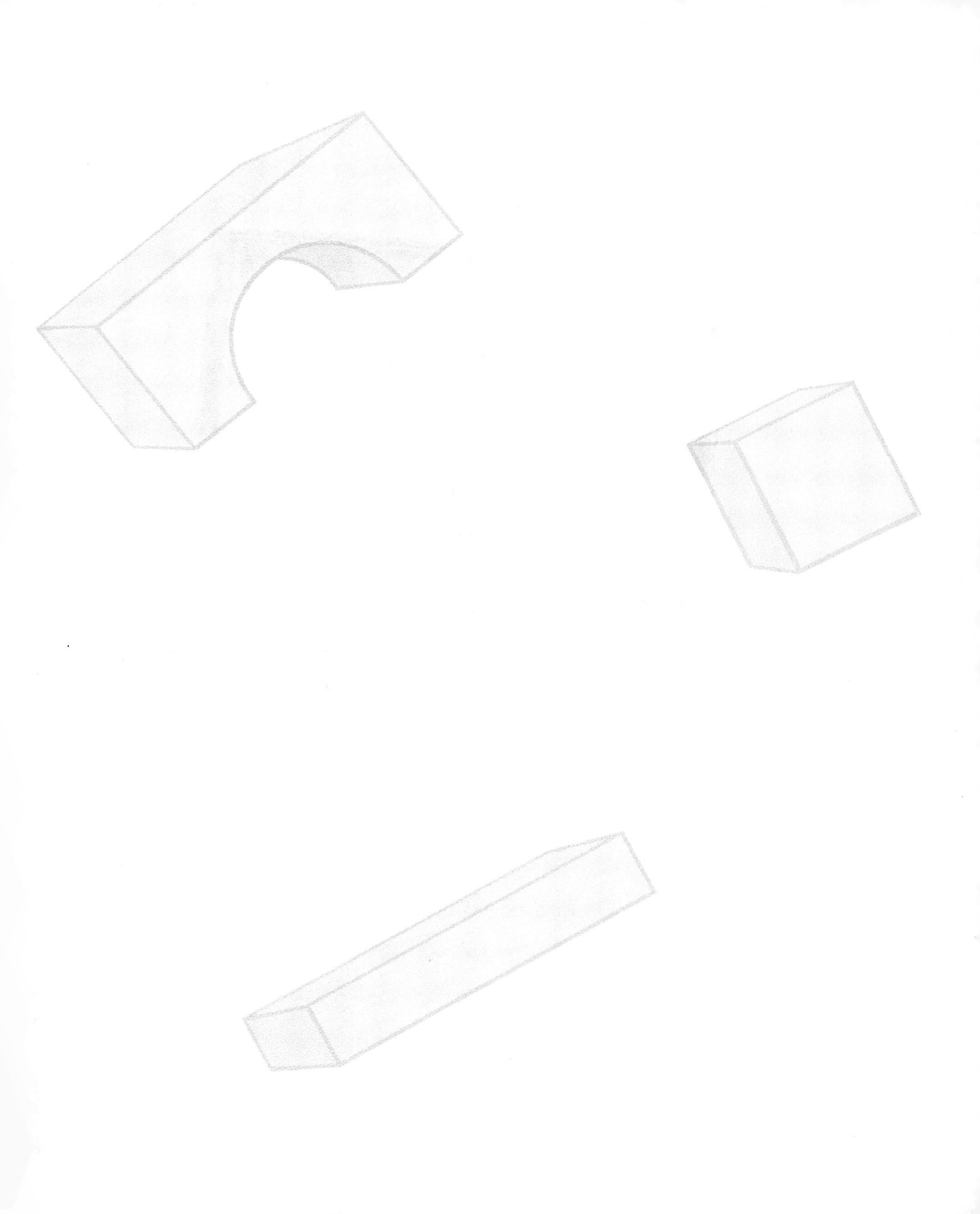

Grrr, this dinosaur can eat you. He has five spikes. He eats meat.

—Ali

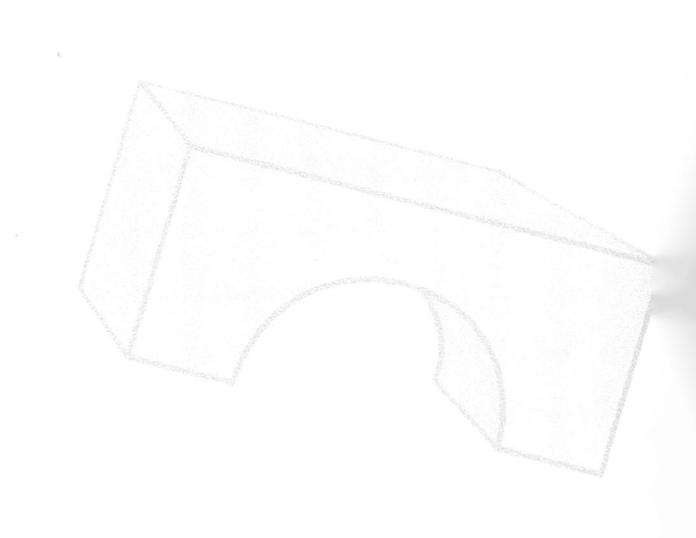

Chapter 10

Using Foundational Projects to Build Number Sense

Overview

At the end of each school year it is always bittersweet to see our little group of children move on into the big world of elementary school. These children come into our class as *babies* and walk out as *students.* They exhibit so many strong, new skills. They feel comfortable picking up a pen and writing or drawing; they know how to go about building marvelous complex constructions; they eagerly portray characters in familiar stories; and they can carry on conversations about all sorts of things from snails to symmetry.

As teachers, we have a list of basic content that we want our students to experience before the school year finishes. This chapter describes a selection of open-ended foundational investigations that focus on specific mathematics and oral language objectives, but can be extended to other content areas when children show interest. We encourage teachers to not only try these activities but also use them as templates for other projects that will meet the special interests of their own students.

Continued

Brenda's Journal Page

Building the Foundation

I had Damian as a student in kindergarten. He often chose to work in the block area. I remember talking with him about the perimeter of his constructions and how he could tile the inside of his corrals. When he was in middle school he came back to my classroom and said he remembered tiling the floors, recalling the area and the perimeter of his corrals. He was appreciative of the support I gave him in building this foundation for his middle-school math class. I felt so good knowing this.

Using Recipes to Build Important Mathematical Ideas

Recipes can be used to facilitate children's growth in mathematics. Embedded in the following recipes are informal operations, division, and fair shares. Recipes are written so that each child prepares an individual portion.

For more ideas on using food, see the following snack time activities throughout this resource: Chapter 3 "Pattern Snacks," Chapter 7 "Snack Time," Chapter 8 "Do You Like Green Eggs and Ham?, Which Juice Do You Prefer?, Which Apple Color Do You Like Best?, Which Cracker Shape Do You Like Best?," and Video Clips 5.4 and 7.2.

What Is Half?

mall Group Time

In this activity children make lemonade using a recipe that requires half a lemon—and encourages twice the exploration!

Tell students, "Today we are making lemonade. We need one-half of a lemon to make one serving." To introduce the idea of *half*, cut a lemon into unequal parts. Ask, "Is this half? Is this fair? Why or why not?" Encourage children to explain their thinking, then revisit what needs to be done. "We want to make sure each person has one-half of a lemon for our recipe. Show me where to cut this lemon so that there are two equal parts." Then cut the lemon in half.

Introduce the recipe for making lemonade. Read aloud the ingredients in the recipe for lemonade. Stop when you get to $\frac{1}{2}$ cup of water. Talk about the idea of half again. This time, show a clear plastic measuring cup with a permanent marker line drawn around the circumference to indicate the half-cup amount. Ask, "How do we know this is half of a cup?" Encourage children to explain their thinking.

Key Vocabulary

half	equal parts
same size	next
cup	fair share
first	then

The Lemonade Recipe

Serving size: one

$\frac{1}{2}$ lemon (squeezed to make juice)

2 spoons of sugar

$\frac{1}{2}$ cup of water

2 ice cubes

Mix, stir, and taste.

After you have read through the recipe with children, check their comprehension by asking key questions, "Who can tell us the recipe for lemonade? What do we do first? What do we do next?"

Listen as students share their understanding of the recipe directions. Now it's time to make lemonade!

Each child squeezes half of a lemon and pours the juice into a cup (sometimes there are seeds that should be removed). They then scoop out two spoons of sugar and stir this into the lemon juice until the sugar is dissolved. Then they add the half-cup of water, the two ice cubes, and drink their lemonade. Once they are done, ask them if they think they could remember how to make lemonade if they wanted to make it again at home. Look back over the recipe and review the ingredients and the steps. Use key vocabulary *half, cup, equal share, same size*, and sequence words *first, next, then*. Encourage further explorations by posing questions such as, "If each person needs one-half of a lemon, how many lemons will we need for two children? I have two lemons now; how many glasses of lemonade can we make with these two lemons?"

More Ideas for Understanding Halves: Children need many experiences to understand that fractional parts need to be of equal size. When they deal with the idea of half, it is important to talk about the idea of a "fair share" in the conversation—when they cut a sandwich in half, there is no such thing as the larger half. However, if the sandwich is cut into different-sized pieces, it has unequal parts and thus there is likely a larger piece. Once "half" has been introduced to students using the lemonade recipe, find other ways to incorporate halves into your daily activities. Following are a few of our favorites.

Folding Paper Have students fold a paper in half so the corners match and both sides are *congruent* or match up perfectly. We can also fold paper into fourths and then open it up and check to see if all four of the spaces are the same size. Halves can be cut on diagonals, too.

Boiled Eggs Boil eggs and then shell them with students. Cut each egg in half. Serve half of an egg to each child during snack time. This is a very engaging snack preparation activity; many children have not had the opportunity to take the shell off of a hardboiled egg and will be fascinated with this task.

Peanut Butter or Cheese Sandwiches Cut peanut butter or cheese sandwiches in half for snack time. Cut some on the diagonal and some into rectangular shapes. Talk about each being "one half" of a sandwich.

Pizza Snacks For each individual pizza snack, spread tomato sauce over half of an English muffin, top with grated cheese, and toast in a toaster oven. Serve during snack time.

Apples Cut apples in half for snack time. (This might be used in conjunction with the activity, "Which Apple Color Do You Like Best?" in Chapter 8.)

Congruent Blocks Though not as tasty as the previous ideas, this naturally fits into children's block play. Find two congruent blocks that go together to make a new shape. Explore with students how each is "half" of the new shape.

Half the Class Many other activities address the concept of half naturally; for example, sometimes an activity will require that half of the class come up to the front of the room. Take the time to discuss the concept of half during these opportunities.

Gabi and Daniela build horse race tracks using blocks of equivalent sizes.

Oobleck and Twice as Much

Centered around a classic Dr. Seuss story, this project involves students with making *oobleck* and exploring its sticky characteristics. To start, read *Bartholomew and the Oobleck* by Dr. Seuss. In this story, the king is bored with rain, fog, sun, and snow. He wants something new to come out of the sky and orders that sticky *oobleck* cover everything. Bartholomew realizes that this is not a good idea and struggles to save the kingdom.

Explain to children that they will make *oobleck*; but to do so, there's a bit of math talk involved. Introduce the recipe.

Teaching Insight

Adjust the Recipe!

You can make small batches with smaller cups, larger batches with larger cups, or double the batch using the original *oobleck* recipe; simply adhere to one part water and two parts cornstarch (twice as much). Use any kind of measurement tools.

Recipe for *Oobleck*

1 cup water

2 cups cornstarch

a few drops of food coloring (in the story *oobleck* is green)

Mix the ingredients together well.

Key Vocabulary

twice as many	solid
double	liquid
measure	

Math Talk

Ratio and Proportion

Ratio and proportion become very important when students learn more about algebraic topics in the upper grades. Recipes, however, are familiar contexts where ratio and proportions can be informally explored.

Adjust the quantities in the recipe depending on the number that children need to practice counting; for example, if your children are working with counting to eight, use four tablespoons of water and eight tablespoons of cornstarch. Simply adhere to the one part water and two parts cornstarch ratio. Have children count out the measurements with you. Explain, "Twice means two times. This recipe uses twice as much cornstarch as water."

After you have made *oobleck*, have children use scoops, spoons, take handfuls, and squeeze the substance to decide whether it is a liquid or a solid (consider doing this outside!).

***Oobleck:* Is It a Liquid or a Solid?**

- Can it be poured? (liquid)
- Can it be molded? (solid)
- When gently touched, can you poke through it? (liquid)
- Can you press a scoop of it together? (solid)
- Tap on it with your palm flat; does it feel hard? (solid)
- Can you scoop it into another container using your hands? (if it drains out, it's a liquid!)

Peanut Butter Dough Shapes

Children really enjoy cooking and measurement experiences. They also like playing with dough. This project responds to all of these interests, and has one other important attribute: children can eat their creation!

Give each child a small bowl, spoon, and piece of wax paper. Follow the recipe's directions. After the dough is made, have children mold it into shapes, using their hands, palms, and fingers, and then eat the shapes. (Note that this recipe calls for peanut butter; do not use if any children have a peanut allergy.)

Teaching Insight

More Dough

Many other dough recipes can be discovered at the following site: www.playdoughrecipe.com.

Key Vocabulary

measure	flat
half	shapes
fourth	

Recipe for Peanut Butter Dough

$\frac{1}{2}$ cup powdered milk

$\frac{1}{4}$ cup peanut butter

1 Tb. honey or corn syrup

Add the powdered milk, peanut butter, and honey or corn syrup to a bowl and stir to mix. Roll the mixture flat and cut into shapes using sticks or plastic knives. Place each shape on wax paper until you are ready to eat them. Makes enough dough for one child.

Teaching Insight

Measuring Cups

The peanut butter play dough recipe requires the use of a half-cup measure and one-fourth cup measure. These same cup measures can be included in other class measurement exploration projects so children become familiar with them. Children can scoop up sand or water and notice that one of the measures is twice as big as the other, or that it takes two of one cup to fill the other cup.

Using Science to Build Important Mathematical Ideas

Children have very positive attitudes toward mathematics and science during the preschool years, and opportunities to use mathematics and logical thinking to solve problems help children develop dispositions such as curiosity, imagination, flexibility, inventiveness, and persistence. These positive attitudes toward learning contribute to future success in and out of school and should be preserved by providing appropriate materials and instruction in the preschool years (Brenneman 2009).

Science learning in the preschool classroom should be hands on and meaningful. By connecting science and mathematics, teachers are building the foundational understanding that is needed to measure and explain phenomena in the real world. In the following activities, children explore things in the natural world that are around them every day but often go unnoticed. By looking more carefully and making observations, children can begin to find ways to talk about the world as they explore it.

Brenda's Journal Page

Lilian Katz's Ideas

Foundational investigations connect to the emerging curriculum and support the Reggio Emilia approach. Children are really interested in math and science ideas! Projects can help children delve more into a curriculum of their interests.

Foundational projects:

1. provide children with opportunities to apply skills;
2. address children's proficiencies;
3. stress intrinsic motivation; and
4. encourage children to determine what to work on and accepts them as experts about their needs (Katz and Chard 1989).

My class has been involved with several really interesting projects this year: The Horse Project, The Pirate Project, The Rock Project, The Dinosaur Project, and The Machine Project. I feel confident that my students will always fondly remember their preschool year because of their involvement in these projects.

Shapes and Shadows

This activity has two parts to it; in the first part (the "inside" part is done in the classroom) children explore shadows using shadow puppets and other items. In the second ("outside") part children go outside and trace their own shadows, then try to fit back into them. Make sure children are familiar with key vocabulary.

Key Vocabulary

light	outline
shadow	shapes
length	change over time
height	

Inside: Shadow Puppets: To introduce this project, tell a story using shadows. Take turns with children holding up various puppets, shapes, or materials to a light source (such as an overhead projector) to make shadows on a wall or screen. To develop ideas about how shadows are formed, ask some of the key questions.

Key Questions

What happens when you move the puppet close to the light?

What happens when you move the puppet far from the light?

What happens if you have two light sources?

Teaching Insight

Making Shadow Puppets and Other Shadow Items

To make shadow puppets, duplicate animal shapes onto cardstock and cut them out, then staple each figure to a craft stick. The following items can also be used to create shadows and stimulate conversation: clear water bottles, transparent and opaque shapes, colored water in a glass, transparent buttons and marbles, and die-cut cardstock shapes.

Sample shadow puppets made with cut card stock and craft sticks.

Outside: Your Shadow: Take children outside on a clear, sunny day. Each child should have a partner and a stick of chalk. The first child strikes and holds a pose, staying as still as possible while the partner traces around the outline of the shadow on the pavement or on black butcher paper. The partner labels the shadow by writing the child's name inside the shadow outline. Then partners switch roles. After the shadow shapes are traced, children try to fit back into their own shadow shape; they can also try to fit inside their partner's shadow shape and even the teacher's shadow shape for a playful challenge! Encourage children to describe their shadows.

Note the time of day that the shadow shapes were originally traced. Bring the class outside again when the sun is higher in the sky. Tell children to again try to fit into their shape. They will notice that now there is a different shadow shape. If possible, trace the new shape next to the original shape. Encourage children to think about how the position of the sun can change the shadow.

Puddle Perimeters and the Sun

This project, ideal for a rainy day, encourages children to explore the concepts of perimeter and evaporation. Children should be familiar with the key vocabulary.

Key Vocabulary

outline

perimeter

change over time

A Child's Mind

Shadows

Children are fascinated by shadows. Most children know that when the sun is clearly visible, shadows are created. They usually do not know what will happen if there is more than one light source. They also do not necessarily know about how transparent or opaque items can create different types of shadows.

Math Talk

Shadow Lengths and Height

Later in upper grades, children learn that measurement of shadow lengths is one way to calculate the height of tall objects like flagpoles or trees. This informal introduction in preschool is a foundational idea about how shadows are used to measure things.

Math Talk

Perimeter

Perimeter is the measure of the path that surrounds an area. The perimeter of a circle is called the *circumference.*

After it rains, take children outside and count the puddles. Have children use chalk to trace around the perimeter of some of the puddles. Later on in the day, go outside again and look at the puddles. Are they still the same size? Trace around the new perimeters. (If there is no rainfall where the school is located, use a sprinkler to make puddles.)

Choose one large puddle and have everyone march through it. Then use chalk to mark the new perimeter of this puddle. (In marching through the puddle, children extend the puddle size by moving the water across a larger area.)

Visit the puddles again in the afternoon to see how they may have changed. Compare the puddle tracings and ask children, "What is happening? Where do you think the water went?"

A Child's Mind

Rain Clouds

Children learn about evaporation and the water cycle later on in school. At this age, they notice heavy rain clouds and see how water comes down from the clouds when it rains. When there is fog, point out how the clouds are low to the ground—"we are walking through the clouds." Explain that the big, white, puffy clouds are wet, too, but they are high in the sky.

Water to Steam

In this project children compare the amount of water in a cup before it is boiled to the amount of water left after boiling. Then they share their ideas about what's happening. Children should be familiar with the key vocabulary:

Key Vocabulary

half of a cup

less

measure

Mark a measuring cup at the half-cup measure with a permanent marker. Measure half a cup of water into a saucepan and put the pan on a burner. Ask children, "What do you think will happen to the water when we heat it?" Turn the burner on, stand back, and watch. Ask children, "What do you notice?" You'll likely get observations such as "The water is boiling." "It is hot." "Steam is coming out of the pot."

Boil the water until it is significantly reduced in volume. Turn off the heat and pour the water back into the same measurement cup. Ask the key questions.

Key Questions

What happened to the water?

Why do we have less water now?

Where did it go?

How much water boiled away?

How do we know?"

A Child's Mind

Understanding Steam

Children draw some logical conclusions that the water went *somewhere*. (They saw it in the form of steam as it went up.) Maybe some of the water collected on a cold surface nearby to form droplets. Using a dry paper towel, it is possible to collect some of this water. Finding ways to help children explain that the water is somewhere, but it is not visible right now, will help them think about how rain sometimes comes down out of the sky.

Does It Sink or Float?

Small Group Time

In this "splash" of a project, children explore the concepts of sinking and floating, comparing various objects and predicting what might happen when they are placed in water. They will be introduced to a *prediction graph* and a *results graph*. Plan to do this outside if the weather is nice, or use a shower curtain to protect the floor. Children should be familiar with the key vocabulary:

Key Vocabulary

actual results	less
compare	more
graph	prediction

Collect objects from around the classroom (and from home) that will make for a compelling "Does it sink or float?" investigation. Try to find a variety of items in various colors and shapes, and composed of plastic, glass, metal, wood, plant and vegetable parts, fruit, and fabric.

Fill a large basin with water (a baby bathtub works well) and have plenty of towels available. Model what is meant by *sink* and *float*. Choose one item that will float and another that will sink (a cork and a marble, for example) and test them out in the basin of water. What happens?

Then have children draw and label the collection of objects that will be used in the investigation. Explain that these drawings will be used on a *prediction graph* to keep track of items they predict will sink or float.

Teaching Insight

Children's Drawings

Children's work is important and useful. Children's work should be visible, so take opportunities for children to create their own drawings and labels when possible. Making observational drawings also helps children look at details carefully—a necessary skill in reading.

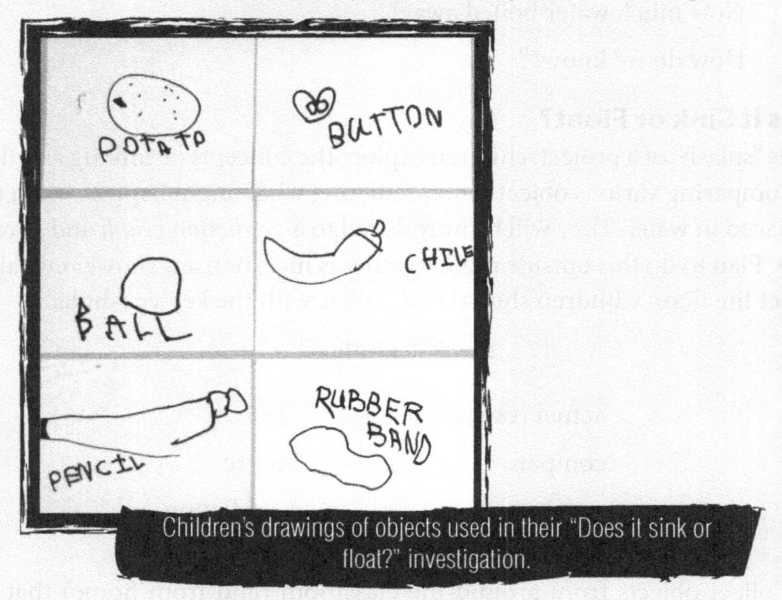

Children's drawings of objects used in their "Does it sink or float?" investigation.

Math Talk

Comparing Prediction Data to Actual Results

Later on in school, children will be comparing theoretical data to empirical data, when they investigate such things as tossing coins or rolling for two dice sums. It's important to find ways to talk about how predictions are what we think might happen, but we are not sure. The results are what actually happened.

Create a *prediction graph* titled "What We Think: Will It Sink or Float?" Label one column *These Will Sink* and the other column *These Will Float*. Use visuals as needed to help children differentiate between the two.

Children first predict which objects will sink or float and place their corresponding drawings on the *prediction graph*. Encourage children to explain why they think the item will sink or float.

Then create a *results graph* similar to the prediction graph, but which instead reflects the actual results. As children take turns testing each object in the water basin, they place the items on the results graph. Children then compare the two graphs. Prompt children to talk about why the numbers of items on the two graphs may be different. Describe what is known for sure.

Pose questions about what might happen with different items that may have similar attributes—for example, "If the potato floats, what do you think will happen with a carrot?"

Brenda's Journal Page

Do Pumpkins Sink or Float?

It's October and today we went to the pumpkin patch. Yesterday I took the opportunity to revisit the topic of sink and float. My students have had multiple experiences sinking and floating objects. When we got back from the pumpkin patch, I asked everyone about their pumpkins, specifically, "Will your pumpkin sink or float?" Because their pumpkins are so big and heavy, the children thought they would sink. They were in for a delightful surprise!

Extension: Who Sank the Boat? As a follow-up to "Does it Sink or Float?" read *Who Sank the Boat?* by Pamela Allen. In this book a cow, a donkey, a sheep, a pig, and a tiny little mouse all try to take a ride in a boat—but uh oh! It's too full. We are told the outcome upfront, but who's the culprit?

Does a Magnet Pick It Up?

This activity follows that same format as the investigation "Does It Sink or Float?" What can a magnet pick up? What things does a magnet attract? In this investigation children explore answers to these questions and create a prediction graph and a results graph. Make sure they are familiar with the key vocabulary.

Key Vocabulary

actual results

compare

graph

less

more

prediction

Collect objects that will make for a compelling investigation with magnets. Try to find a variety of items in various colors and shapes, and made of plastic, rubber, glass, different kinds of metals (aluminum, copper, steel, and iron), wood, plant and vegetable parts, fruit, and fabric.

To introduce this task, model how a magnet can pick up some items and not others. Choose two items (a paperclip and a rubber band, for example) and test them out with the magnet. What happens?

Then have children draw and label the collection of objects that will be used in the investigation. Have students create drawings of the objects and label them. Explain that these drawings will be used on a *prediction graph* to keep track of which items we think the magnet picks up and which items we think won't be picked up.

Teaching Insight

Children's Drawings

Children's work is important and useful. We want children's work to be visible, so we take opportunities for students to create their own drawings and labels when possible. Making observational drawings also helps children look at details carefully—a necessary skill in reading.

Children's drawings of objects used in their magnet investigation.

Create a *prediction graph* titled "What We Think a Magnet Will Pick Up." Label one column *What a Magnet Will Pick Up* and the other column *What a Magnet Will Not Pick Up*. Use visuals as needed to help children differentiate between the two.

Children first predict which objects they think the magnet will pick up and place their corresponding drawings on the prediction graph. Encourage children to explain why they think the magnet will or will not pick up the item.

Then create a *results graph,* which is similar to the prediction graph but it instead reflects the actual results. As children take turns testing each object with the magnet, they place the items on the results graph. Children then compare the two graphs. Prompt children to talk about why the numbers of items on the two graphs may be different. Describe what is known for sure. Ask children to explain why they think the item is attracted to the magnet. Students may say:

I think the magnet will pick up the candy 'cuz it's got a silver wrapper.

I think the magnet will pick up the marble because it's hard.

Pose questions about what might happen with different items that may have some similar attributes, for example, "If the magnet doesn't pick up the crayon, what do you think will happen with a pencil?"

Math Talk

Comparing Prediction Data to Actual Results

Later on in school, children will be comparing theoretical data to empirical data, when they investigate such things as tossing coins or rolling for two dice sums. It's important to find ways to talk about how predictions are what we think might happen, but we are not sure. The results are what actually happened.

Extension: What Magnets Can Do: As a follow-up to the magnets project, read *What Magnets Can Do* by Allan Fowler. This book uses bright photographs of everyday objects to explore the subject.

Daniela creates her clay dinosaur in Brenda's classroom.

Creating Clay Dinosaurs

Clay projects allow children to look at three-dimensional objects and try to copy them. (We like to use earth clay, rather than prefabricated modeling clay.) We find that our study of dinosaurs is especially conducive to clay creations; as children learn about different kinds of dinosaurs, they want to make their own dinosaurs with clay.

Our clay creations happen in the studio (for more on the use of a studio in classrooms, see Chapter 2). Provide dinosaur models for children to look at as they create them in clay. Children sometimes assemble their clay constructions by making parts of the body and putting them together. Encourage children to talk about their creations. Use these conversations to document children's language development and counting skills. Children also develop their fine motor skills when they use a stylus or other tools to scribe details on their clay projects.

Ali's clay dinosaur, which he points out has "five spikes."

Small Group Time

The Balance Game

The Balance Game was designed to promote number concepts using physical tasks (Kamii 2008). To play it, children put a paper plate on an empty plastic beverage bottle and take turns carefully adding one connecting cube at a time to the plate without making it fall. Children become engaged in finding a way to balance more cubes on top of the plate. When they play, they know immediately if their strategy works. They keep trying and employ several interesting strategies.

Ali reaches for his falling plate as he plays the Balance Game.

A Child's Mind

Exploring Balance

Some children notice that if they put more cubes in the center of the plate, the plate does not tip over. They try to use logical thinking to reason why the plate tips. Children test to see if their thinking is a productive way to continue. Some try to connect all the cubes into train sticks and/or put the sticks on the plate before they put it up on top of the bottle. These children are finding their own way to ensure that more cubes will balance on the plate instead of waiting for their turn to add one cube at a time.

Grace tries a handful of cubes, but they knock the plate off balance.

Because children are developing physical understandings of ways to keep the plate from tipping, they are physically and actively engaged in the game. An implicit aspect of the game becomes the need to quantify the cubes on the plate. In order to compare which strategy works best, children need to count the cubes! This game was designed to promote number concepts using physical tasks (Kamii 2008).

Teaching Insight

Other Balance Games

Other games in this genre are *Pick Up Sticks* and *Jenga*. These games involve a pile of randomly arranged thin sticks or a tower stack of small blocks of wood. The players take turns removing the sticks or blocks without causing any movement of the remaining pieces. Children are compelled to count to determine how many they can remove.

Using Dramatic Play to Build Important Mathematical Ideas

Who hasn't heard a child say, "Let's pretend"? It is natural and an easy way for the child to approach almost any situation with convincing efforts to dramatically reenact a compelling or familiar situation. In dramatic play children show how they understand the real world. Young children benefit from playfully exploring the idea of a store. They have had a great deal of experience going to the store with their families, and they are keen observers. In the dramatic play store, they learn about different jobs, how money is used, and think about the business of a store from a new perspective. They see that numbers are part of the real world.

oice Time

The Grocery Store

After children have been in school for about one month, set up a grocery store center in the classroom. Children love to play store. They select items, pay for them, bag the groceries, and receive change from the cashier. Challenge children to explore the math involved in grocery store transactions and help them understand the key vocabulary.

Exploring the Math in a Grocery Store

- Give children small stickers and marking pens and encourage them to "price" items.
- Ask children to buy three items for breakfast, five items for dinner, and so forth.
- Have children sort the coins.
- Have children stack the boxes so they fit on the shelves.

Key Vocabulary

price

money

cash

customer

cashier

buy

sell

The grocery store in Brenda's classroom is a space with low shelves, a small table and chair, a cash register with play money, and an assortment of grocery items (empty food boxes, food cans, cartons, and plastic fruits and vegetables). These items can be sorted by shapes and also by food categories: fruits, vegetables, dairy, meat, canned goods, and packages. Brenda displays illustrated signs to encourage sorting.

Diego and Hugo playing store.

Teaching Insight

Collecting Items for the Grocery Store

Before the grocery store is launched in the classroom, the teacher (and families) can begin to save containers from home. Open cans on the bottom and rinse them out. Stuff empty cereal and cracker boxes with tissue paper or newsprint and glue them closed. Collect milk cartons and yogurt containers, and rinse them well! (This is important.) If you do not have plastic fruit and vegetables, you can make them out of papier-mâché. A head of lettuce can be made from crumpled green paper wrapped in plastic wrap.

The Shoe Store

A little later on in the school year, change the grocery store to a shoe store. Request donations of old shoes from families or visit thrift stores. Children role-play the actions of the customer and the salesperson; they arrange the shoes by size, match pairs, and try them on to see how they look. Challenge children to explore the math involved in shoe store transactions.

Exploring the Math in a Shoe Store

- Have students measure their feet.
- Arrange shoe displays (by size and matching pairs).
- Use small stickers and marking pens to "price" shoes.
- Fill out receipt books (these can be purchased from office supply stores).

Teaching Insight

Making a Foot Measure

To make a foot measure, glue two rulers on either side of a foot outline on heavy cardboard. Children enjoy putting their foot on the measure to see how long their foot is!

Shoes are really interesting to young children, and there are many different attributes to talk about. Encourage conversations about who wears ballet slippers, cowboy boots, flip flops, tap dance shoes, rain boots, silver or gold pumps, moccasins, running trainers, soccer cleats, work boots, wooden clogs, shiny patent leather shoes, roller skates, dress shoes, high heels, bedroom slippers, snow boots, steel toed boots, and so forth.

Math Talk

Talking About Twos

Things that come in pairs help children think about counting by twos. Children can talk about the idea that one pair of shoes is two shoes and two pairs of shoes are four shoes. Mittens, socks, chopsticks, twins, and earrings also come in pairs. Later on in first grade, children learn about adding doubles (2 + 2, 3 + 3, 4 + 4) and use those known facts to think about near doubles (2 + 3, 3 + 4, 4 + 5). This foundational work also supports the idea of even numbers because each shoe has a partner.

Teaching Insight

Collecting Shoes

To have enough shoes for the shoe store, request donations from friends and families and go to thrift stores for special finds. Children are especially interested in dress up shoes and baby shoes. Since babies grow out of their shoe sizes so quickly, it's not hard to find these.

Gabi in the shoe store in Brenda's classroom.

Shoes sorted, matched, and displayed in the classroom shoe store.

Nico with the cash register in the shoe store.

Teaching Insight

Even More Stores!

Create even more kinds of stores in the classroom to encourage sorting and classification as well as practicing role-playing with money. Consider creating The Toy Store, The Art Materials Store, The Dress Up Store, and The Rock Store (gem and minerals). We have had success with all of these stores in engaging children in conversations and play.

Video Clip 10.1: Dramatic Play in the Hospital

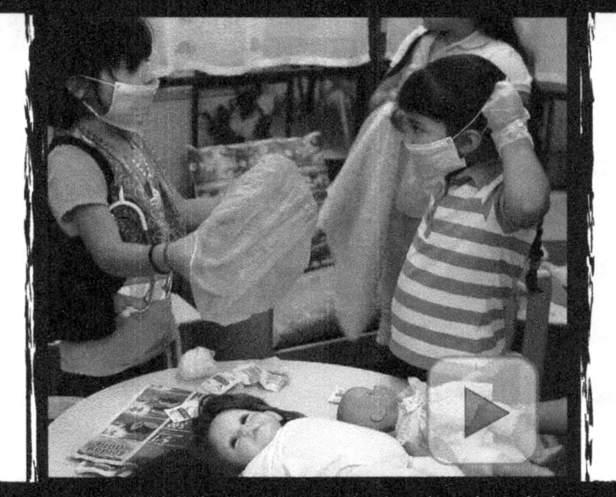

Iesha and Michelle dress up in the class hospital.

To view the clip, scan the QR code or visit **mathsolutions.com/TEACHPK101**

To help children learn about how to be healthy and take good care of themselves, we transform classroom space into a hospital, and provide props to support the dramatic play—bandages, stethoscope, mask, rubber gloves, mirrors, flashlights, magnifying glasses, gauze, tape, eye charts, growth charts, stop watches, measuring tapes, different size medicine bottles, a scale for weighing, and so forth.

In Video Clip 10.1 children are at play in the hospital center in Brenda's classroom. Watch the video clip in its entirety. Record your observations. How do you think such play supports the development of mathematical ideas?

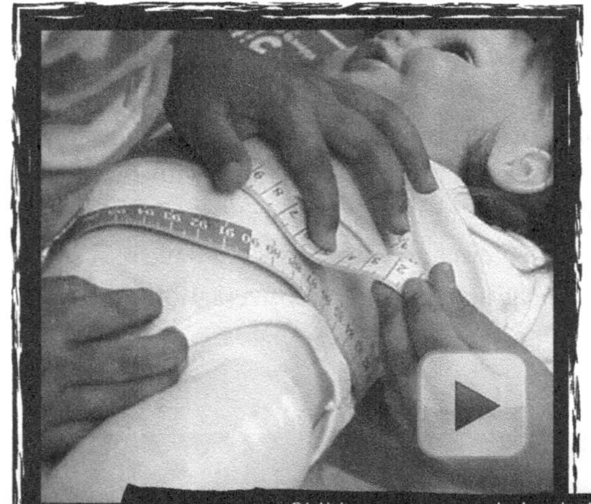

Children measure a baby during hospital play.

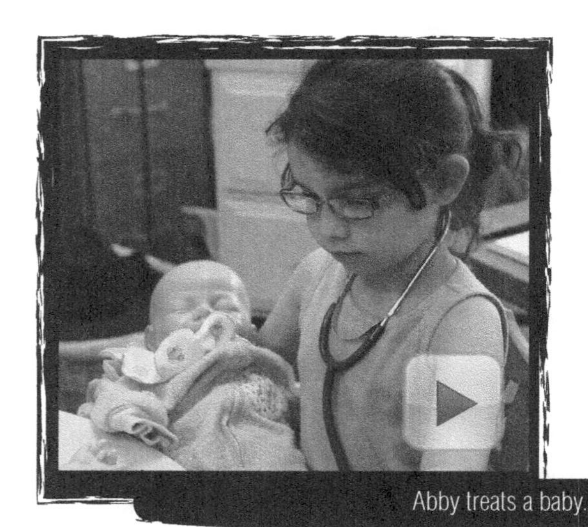

Abby treats a baby.

Alexa takes doctor notes and surveys patients' health.

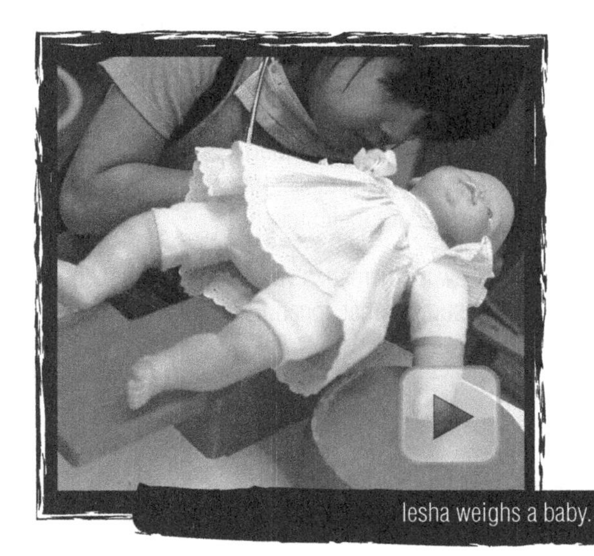

Iesha weighs a baby.

What We Learned: These children are very engaged in taking care of a new baby in the class hospital. They make sure the baby is clean. They listen to the baby's heart and lungs. With a few props, young children become fully immersed in acting out scenarios that are very interesting to them. The teacher uses this interest to bring out the mathematical ideas. They measure the baby. They listen and count the baby's heartbeats. They measure medicine and give the baby shots. They take the baby's temperature. When children wrap up the baby, they make sure the blanket fits around it. They write down numbers and notes to remember what they found out on the clipboards. They make appointments and write down times for appointments.

Reflection Questions

1. How can teachers challenge different children in the class to reason mathematically according to their individual levels of understanding?
2. How can some of the activities in this chapter be made progressively more challenging?
3. What is the value of integrating mathematics learning with science, beginning reading, physical education, or dramatic arts?
4. How can families help their children develop mathematical ideas at home when they do chores, projects, or homework? How can families learn about the mathematical ideas in activities they may already be doing with their child?
5. If teachers have specific interests in dancing, music, camping or science, for example, how can they bring those interests into the classroom and create a meaningful mathematical learning experience for their students?
6. Think about how young children learn new mathematics vocabulary. What is the value in having concrete experiences to support that vocabulary development?
7. What characteristics do you find in projects such as these? How do these characteristics connect to student learning?

Reproducibles

A. Observation Questions: Mathematics in an Early Childhood Classroom

B. Letter to Families for Support in Creating Collections of Stuff

C. Assessment Opportunities: Learning Progressions
   - C1 Learning Progressions: Materials
   - C2 Learning Progressions: Early Childhood/Number
   - C3 Learning Progressions: Early Childhood/Measurement
   - C4 Learning Progressions: Early Childhood/Graphing Data
   - C5 Learning Progressions: Early Childhood/Sorting and Classification
   - C6 Learning Progressions: Early Childhood/Pattern
   - C7 Learning Progressions: Early Childhood/Geometric and Spatial Thinking

D. Selected Bibliography of Children's Books for Supporting Mathematical Ideas

E. Quick Images: Dot Cards

F. Number Cards 1–20

G. Matching Picture Cards

H. Shapes Placemat

I. Apple Template

J. Five-Frame

K. Ten-Frame

L. Number Chart 1–20

M. Shapes Templates

N. Rectangle Puzzle Templates

O. Hexagon Puzzle Template

P. Tangram Shapes Template

Q. Tangram Puzzle Shapes

R. Pattern Block Triangle Template

S. Pattern Block Puzzle Shapes

T. Hundreds Chart

All reproducibles are also available as downloadable, printable versions at www.mathsolutions.com/teachingpreschoolreproducibles.

Observation Questions

Mathematics in an Early Childhood Classroom

Observe mathematics in a preschool classroom. Use the following questions to guide you in recording your observations. If you are a teacher, think about these questions as they apply to your own classroom.

1. Do the children hear the words *mathematics* or *math* during the day? Is there explicit attention to this topic in the daily schedule?

2. What mathematics do you see the children doing?

3. Does the teacher extend children's dramatic play by joining in?

4. Are the questions that are posed open-ended and thought provoking? In what ways?

5. Are children encouraged to make choices? How?

6. Does the teacher show interest in what the children are doing? How?

7. Does the teacher make specific comments that extend children's thinking and language and focus on key experiences? How?

8. Is there a balance between teacher talk and child talk throughout the day? In what ways?

Reproducible B

Letter to Families for Support in Creating Collections of Stuff

Dear Families,

In math class we are learning about counting and sorting collections. Please help us by contributing interesting small items to our classroom collections. We are happy to receive any items that children may use to count, sort, and make projects with. Ideas include the following

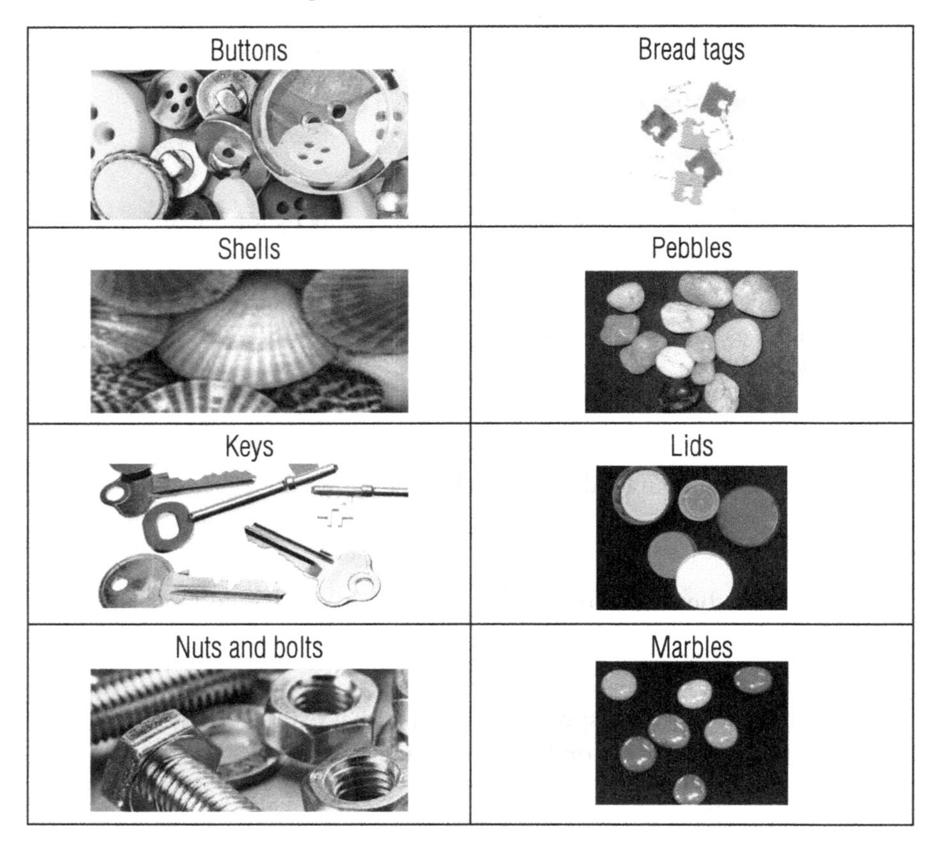

Buttons	Bread tags
Shells	Pebbles
Keys	Lids
Nuts and bolts	Marbles

Thank you so much!

Sincerely,

[Your Child's Teacher]

Learning Progressions: Materials

Use this list to create a kit of materials for use with the Learning Progressions assessment documents (Reproducibles C2–C7).

Number Tasks

1. Set of dot cards in various arrangements 1–5 and 6–10 (see Reproducible E)
2. Two sets of 10 lima beans or wooden cubes in a sandwich bag
3. Cube train of 3 red, 2 blue
4. Cube train of 3 green, 2 yellow
5. Cards with some capital letters and some numerals
6. Strip of numerals out of order: 6 2 3 1 9 7 8 4 0 5
7. Cube train lengths in various lengths using different colors: 4 red, 5 blue, 6 green, 7 yellow
8. Five cube train 3 yellow + 2 blue and another 2 yellow + 3 blue
9. Cube train of 5 yellow + 2 blue

Measurement Tasks

1. Cube trains in various lengths using different colors: 4 red, 5 blue, 6 green, 7 yellow, 5 green
2. Five ribbon or yarn lengths in various colors: 6 inches, 7 inches, 9 inches, 10 inches, 11 inches
3. Same size snack containers filled with different items
4. Pan balance
5. Four or five clear containers of different shapes and sizes
6. Birdseed or sand for measurement
7. Scoops
8. Sequence drawings for a familiar activity (getting up in AM, planting a seed, etc.)

Graphing Data

1. Class graph with two columns (Yes/No)
2. Class cracker graph data on preferences

(continued)

Reproducible C1 (Materials, *continued*)

Sorting and Classification

1. Objects to sort:
   - ☐ buttons
   - ☐ lids
   - ☐ keys
   - ☐ bread tags
   - ☐ attribute blocks, geometric shapes
   - ☐ shells
   - ☐ wooden objects (sticks, cubes, etc.)
   - ☐ metal objects (washers, screws, nuts and bolts, etc.)
   - ☐ plastic objects (small toys, game pieces, LEGOS, etc.)
   - ☐ rocks

Pattern

1. Unsorted single snap cubes in various colors
2. Pattern blocks
3. Sorting objects (above)
4. Wooden or plastic beads in various attributes

Geometry/Spatial Thinking

1. Collection of unit blocks
2. Collection of transparent shapes
3. Light table or overhead projector
4. Pattern block puzzles
5. Tangram puzzles
6. Other shape puzzles
7. Paper shapes, glue sticks, background paper
8. Blue and yellow acetate rectangles

Learning Progressions: Early Childhood/Number

Name of Student:

Dates Noted: (Use different color pen for each observation.)

Number	Details/Prompt	Examples	Notes
Counting	Counts orally *Please count as high as you can go, I want to hear what you say.*	One, two, three, four, five. . . . Record what the child says. Note which numbers are skipped and the order the child uses.	How high? Counts to ten? ☐ Yes ☐ No Counts to 20? ☐ Yes ☐ No Beyond 20? ☐ Yes ☐ No Counting backwards from 10? ☐ Yes ☐ No
	Instant identification of small set of dots or objects—subitizing. *What do you see here? How many?*	Use dot cards such as these:	Up to 3? ☐ Yes ☐ No Up to 5? ☐ Yes ☐ No When does the child count the dots instead of saying the number?
	Counting objects Spread out a collection of about ten beans or cubes. *Please count these.* *So how many are there?*	Counts correctly in sequence, tagging each object. Counts correctly in sequence, but does not tag each object, so counting is not accurate. Knows that the last number counted is the amount of the set.	Accurate to which number? ☐ Does not tag objects. (If accurate to ten, try fifteen or twenty items.)
	Count out a target amount *Please give me five beans.* *Now make sure I have seven beans.*	Counts out accurately. Remembers to stop at 5. Counts out accurately. Remembers to stop at 7.	Or does the child add two more to 5?
Estimating	*How many do you think are in the jar?* (Start with about eight or nine things.)	Number is way off or a non-number (eleventeen). Number is their age or friendly number, but not correct. Number seems reasonable	(see table below)

Number in Jar	Estimate Given
8	
12	
5	

(continued)

Reproducible C2 (Early Childhood/Number, *continued*)

Number	Details/Prompt	Examples	Notes
Comparing	Recognizes when shown two different dot cards: *Which is more?* *Which is less?*	Use dot cards such as those above. Then show cube train of three red and two blue. *Are there more red or blue?* Show cube train of three green and two yellow. *Are there less green or yellow?*	Instant response for more? ☐ Yes ☐ No Instant response for less? ☐ Yes ☐ No Counts to determine more or less? ☐ Yes ☐ No Does the child need clarification for the meaning of more and less?
Recognizing or Reading Numerals	*Point to the numbers.* Show a collection of numbers and letters. Show numerals 0–10 (out of order). *What's this?*	Use capitals and handwritten numbers: A D 3 6 2 T 8 6 2 3 1 9 7 8 4 0 5	Identifies numbers? ☐ Yes ☐ No Circles those that are recognized?
Order	*Put dot cards in order from least to most.* *Put these numbers in order from least to most.*	Show dot cards. Record what the child does. Show cube trains of four, five, six, and seven cube lengths and record what the child does. Show numeral cards. Record what the child does.	Does the child need clarification for the meaning of *order*, *least* or *most*? ☐ Yes ☐ No
Operations	*How many blue? How many yellow? How many blue and yellow?*	Show cube train of three yellow and two blue.	How does the child determine the amount?
	Are there more blue or yellow? How do you know?	Show a train of three blue + two yellow + two blue + five yellow.	How does the child determine the amount?
	One more: *How many now?*	Show and confirm a group of five cubes and then add one more. How does the child determine how many now?	☐ Counts all to find out. ☐ Knows one more without counting.
Notes:			

Learning Progressions: Early Childhood/Measurement

Name of Student:

Dates Noted: (Use different color pen for each observation.)

Measurement	Details/Prompt	Examples	Notes
Length	*Which is longer?* *Which is shorter?* *Which are the same?*	Show a collection of four, same color/different length cube trains or lengths of ribbon or yarn.	How does the child determine the lengths?
Weight	*Which weighs more?* *Which weighs less?* *Which are the same weight?*	Show three objects that are all about the same size but different weights (e.g., bean bags filled with gravel, beans and styrofoam). Have a pan balance available for comparison.	What does the child do with the pan balance to check for weight?
Volume	*Which holds more?* *Which holds less?* *Which ones hold the same amount?*	Show four or five clear glass or plastic containers such as jam jars, drinking glass and food storage containers. Have scoops and birdseed or rice for measurements. Challenge the child to consider the volume of a tall thin container (salad dressing bottle, pitcher for iced tea mix) if the first task is too easy.	What does the child do with the objects to check for volume?
Time	*What happens first?* *What happens next?* *What happens last?*	Show sequence pictures for a familiar activity such as getting up in the morning or planting a seed and taking care of a plant.	How does the child arrange the pictures? (left to right?)
Notes:			

Learning Progressions: Early Childhood/Graphing Data

Name of Student:

Dates Noted: (Use different color pen for each observation.)

Graphing, Data	Details/Prompt	Examples	Notes
	Comparing two columns *Which has more?* *Which has less?* *How do you know?* Comparing three columns *Which has the most?* *Which has the least?* *How do you know?*	Use data from a Yes/No class graph: Do you like green eggs and ham? Use data from a preference/choice class graph: Which cracker shape do you like best? Square Circle Triangle	How does the child respond to the data? Comments from the child about the graph:
Notes:			

Learning Progressions: Early Childhood/Sorting and Classification

Name of Student:

Dates Noted: (Use different color pen for each observation.)

Sorting and Classification	Details/Prompt	Examples	Notes
	Sorts objects by given attribute: *Sort the blocks by color.* Sorts objects by self-chosen attribute. *Tell how you sorted these.* Sorts objects by attribute other than color (shape or size, for example).	Present a variety of objects that have multiple attributes on different days: ☐ buttons ☐ lids ☐ keys ☐ bread tag fasteners ☐ attribute blocks, geometric shapes ☐ shells ☐ wooden objects (sticks, cubes, etc.) ☐ metal objects (washers, screws, nuts and bolts, etc.) ☐ plastic objects (small toys, game pieces, LEGOS, etc.) ☐ rocks (polished, rough, various colors and shapes) ☐ other ______	Record how the child sorts the objects. How does the child name the groups? To move a child beyond sorting by color, present a set of objects that are all red, yellow, or blue.
Notes:			

Learning Progressions: Early Childhood/Pattern

Name of Student:

Dates Noted:

Pattern	Details/Prompt	Examples	Notes
Copy cube train pattern with colors	*Can you make this pattern with these cubes?* ☐ AB ☐ ABC ☐ ABB ☐ Other ________	Record what the student does. How does the student read the pattern? Record the words chosen.	Break the pattern into three sections. *Can you fix it?*
Make own cube train pattern with colors	☐ AB ☐ ABC ☐ ABB ☐ Other ________	Record what the student does. How does the student read the pattern? Record the words chosen.	Break the pattern into three sections. *Can you fix it?*
Pattern block patterns	☐ AB ☐ ABC ☐ ABB ☐ Other ________	☐ Linear ☐ Two-dimensional ☐ Symmetrical	How does the student describe the pattern?
Using found objects	☐ AB ☐ ABC ☐ ABB ☐ Other ________	Record what the child says about the pattern. Use beads, shells, metal objects, keys, color cubes, Cuisenaire rods, etc.	
Bead patterns	☐ AB ☐ ABC ☐ ABB ☐ Other ________		

Learning Progressions: Early Childhood/Geometric and Spatial Thinking

Name of Student:

Dates Noted: (Use different color pen for each observation.)

Geometric and Spatial Thinking	Details/Prompt	Examples	Notes
	Sorts shapes by matching up congruent shapes *What can you do with these blocks?* *Which ones go together?*	Present a variety of blocks. Present a variety of transparent shapes on the light table.	Record how the child sorts the shapes.
	Makes equivalent shapes *Which are the same?*	Present a variety of blocks. Present a variety of transparent shapes on the light table.	Record how the child matches the shapes.
Puzzles	Present shape puzzles, tangram puzzles, and other mosaic-type resources.	Rotates shapes to fit in the frames. Enjoys working with puzzles.	
Geometric Pictures	Present cut-paper shapes, background paper and glue sticks.	Child makes original pictures with the pieces.	Record what the child says about the shapes. ☐ names some shapes ☐ uses language such as *over, under, near, above*
Creating Shapes	*Can you make a green triangle?* *Can you make a green square?* *Can you make a green rectangle?*	On the light table, present blue and yellow rectangular acetate sheets of various shapes and sizes.	Record what the child does.

Reproducible D

Selected Bibliography of Children's Books for Supporting Mathematical Ideas

Aardema,Verna. 1975. *Why Mosquitoes Buzz in People's Ears: A West African Tale.* New York: Puffin Pied Piper.

Allen, Pamela. 1996. *Who Sank the Boat?* London: Puffin.

Barton, Byron. 1989. *Dinosaurs, Dinosaurs*. New York: Thomas Y. Crowell.

Brett, Jan. 1992. *Goldilocks and the Three Bears.* New York: Putnam Publishing Group.

Carle, Eric. 1979. *The Very Busy Spider*. New York: Philomel Books.

———. 1979. *The Very Hungry Caterpillar*. New York: Philomel Books.

Carter, David A. 1992. *Over in the Meadow*. New York: Scholastic.

Christelow, Ellen. 1993. *Five Little Monkeys Sitting in a Tree*. New York: Clarion Books.

———. 1996. *Five Little Monkeys Jumping on the Bed*. New York: Clarion Books.

Crews, Donald. 2010. *Ten Black Dots.* New York: Greenwillow Books.

Dodds, Dale Ann. 2002. *The Shape of Things.* New York: Houghton Mifflin.

Dwight, Laura. 1991. *We Are All Alike . . . We Are All Different.* New York: Scholastic.

Falwell, Cathryn. 1993. *Feast for Ten*. New York: Clarion Books.

Fowler, Allan. 1995. *What Magnets Can Do*. New York: Scholastic.

Freeman, Don. 1980. *A Pocket for Corduroy*. London: Puffin.

Galdone, Paul. 1973. *The Three Billy Goats Gruff.* Boston: Seabury Press.

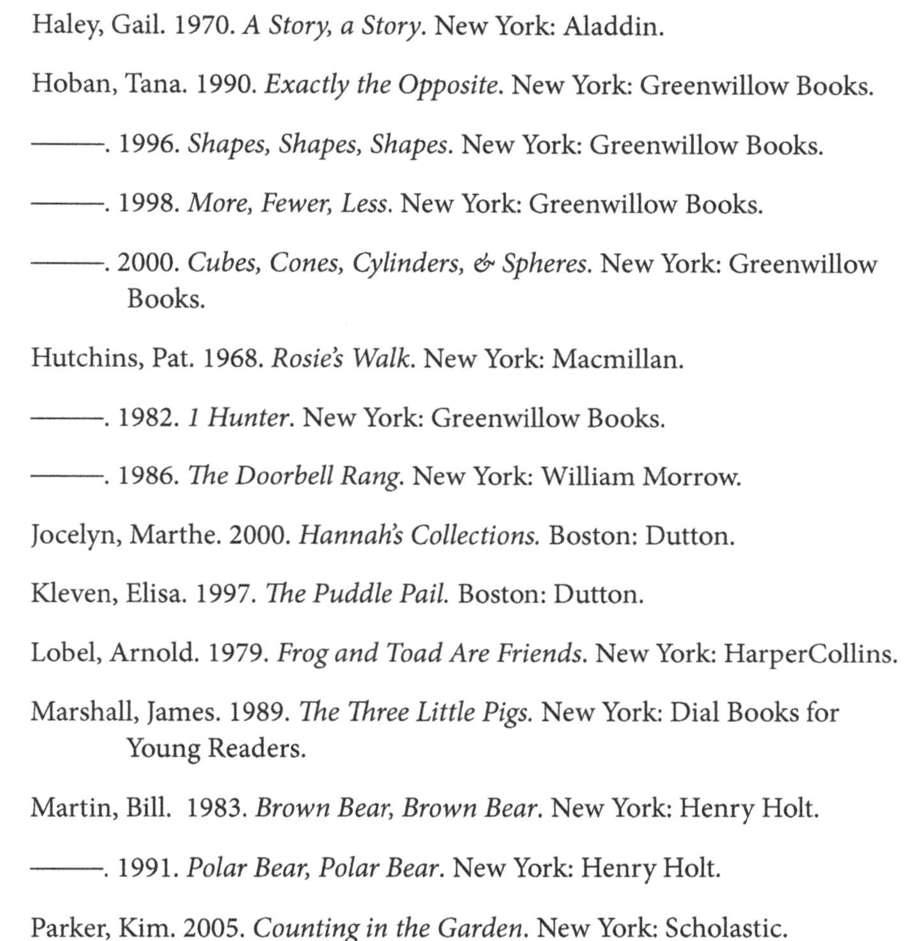

Haley, Gail. 1970. *A Story, a Story*. New York: Aladdin.

Hoban, Tana. 1990. *Exactly the Opposite*. New York: Greenwillow Books.

———. 1996. *Shapes, Shapes, Shapes*. New York: Greenwillow Books.

———. 1998. *More, Fewer, Less*. New York: Greenwillow Books.

———. 2000. *Cubes, Cones, Cylinders, & Spheres*. New York: Greenwillow Books.

Hutchins, Pat. 1968. *Rosie's Walk*. New York: Macmillan.

———. 1982. *1 Hunter*. New York: Greenwillow Books.

———. 1986. *The Doorbell Rang*. New York: William Morrow.

Jocelyn, Marthe. 2000. *Hannah's Collections.* Boston: Dutton.

Kleven, Elisa. 1997. *The Puddle Pail.* Boston: Dutton.

Lobel, Arnold. 1979. *Frog and Toad Are Friends*. New York: HarperCollins.

Marshall, James. 1989. *The Three Little Pigs.* New York: Dial Books for Young Readers.

Martin, Bill. 1983. *Brown Bear, Brown Bear*. New York: Henry Holt.

———. 1991. *Polar Bear, Polar Bear*. New York: Henry Holt.

Parker, Kim. 2005. *Counting in the Garden*. New York: Scholastic.

Peek, Merle. 1981. *Roll Over!: A Counting Song*. New York: Houghton Mifflin/Clarion Books.

———. 1985. *Mary Wore Her Red Dress.* New York: Clarion.

Pfanner, Louise. 1987. *Louise Builds a House.* New York: Scholastic.

Portis, Antoinette. 2011. *Not a Box.* New York: Harper Festival.

Dr. Seuss. 1949. *Bartholomew and the Oobleck.* New York: Random House Books.

(continued)

Reproducible D (Selected Bibiography, *continued*)

———. 1960. *Green Eggs and Ham.* New York: Random House Books.

———. 2007. *Would You Rather Be a Bullfrog?* New York: Random House Books.

Spanyol, Jessica. 2002. *Carlo Likes Counting.* New York: Walker Children Books.

Stevens, Janet. 1995. *Tops and Bottoms.* San Diego: Harcourt Brace.

Scieszka, Jon. 1989. *The True Story of the Three Little Pigs.* New York: Viking Kestrel.

Taback, Simms. 1997. *There Was an Old Lady Who Swallowed a Fly.* New York: Viking.

Van Allsburg, Chris. 1987. *The Z Was Zapped.* Boston: Houghton Mifflin.

Wattenberg, Jane. 2000. *Henny-Penny.* New York: Scholastic Press.

West, Colin. 1986. *"Pardon?" Said the Giraffe.* New York: J.B. Lippincott.

Williams, Sue. 1992. *I Went Walking.* Orlando: Harcourt Brace Jovanovich.

Wood, Audrey. 1984. *The Napping House.* San Diego: Harcourt Brace Jovanovich.

Quick Images: Dot Cards

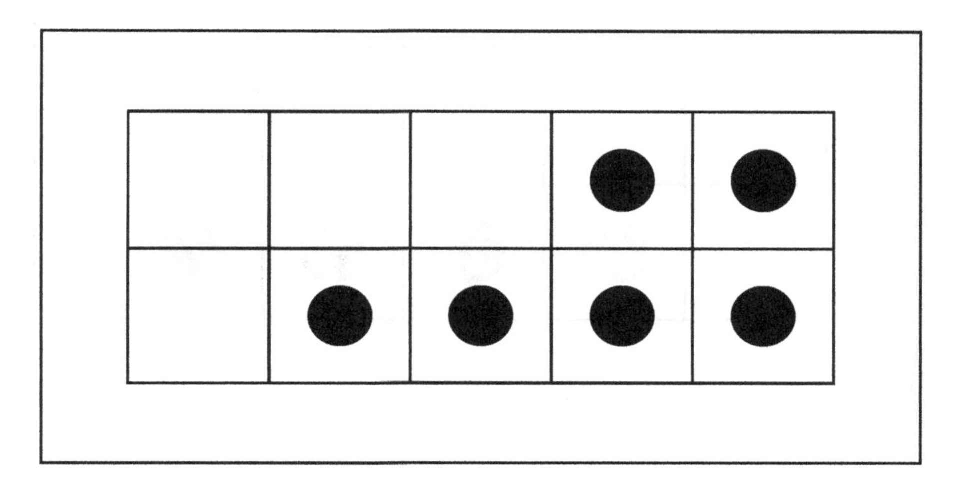

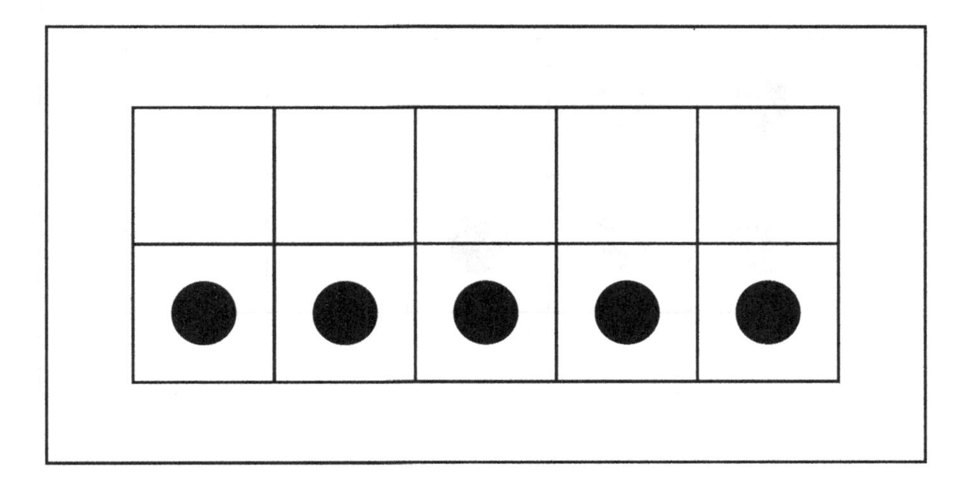

(*continued*)

Reproducible E

(Dot Cards, *continued*)

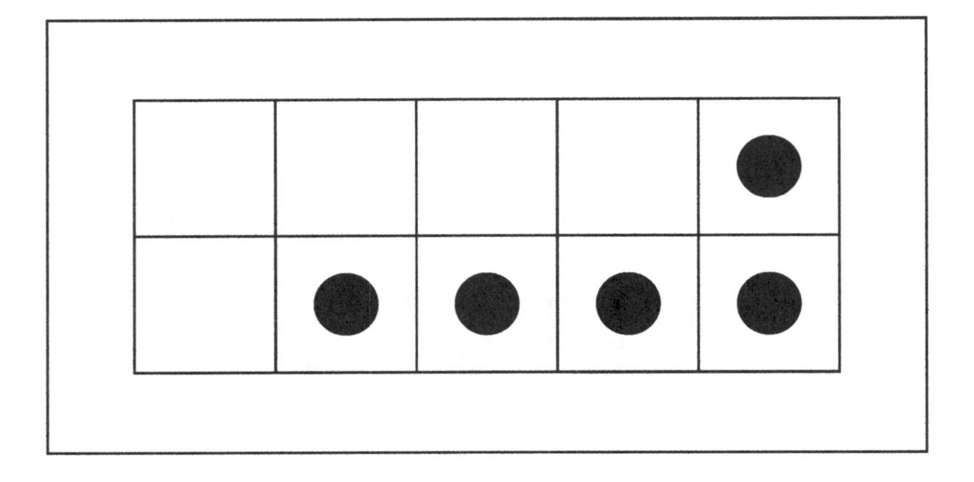

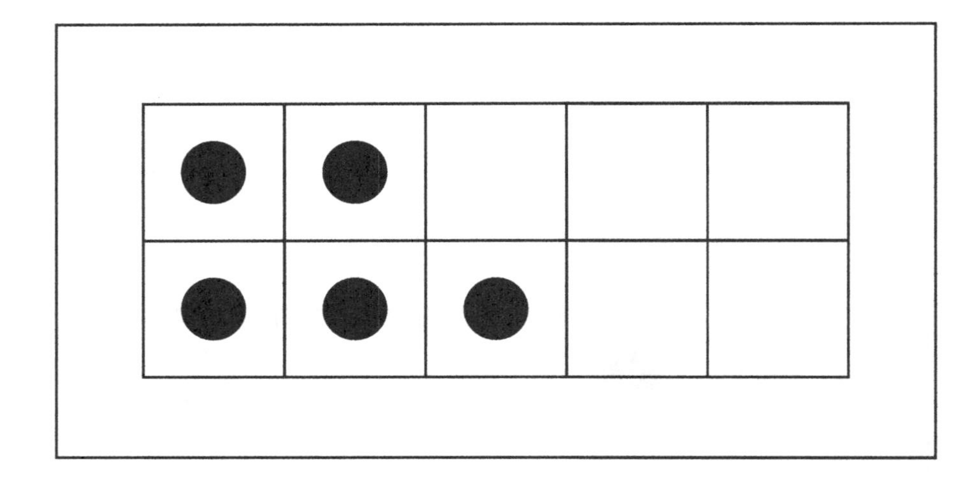

(*continued*)

(Dot Cards, *continued*)

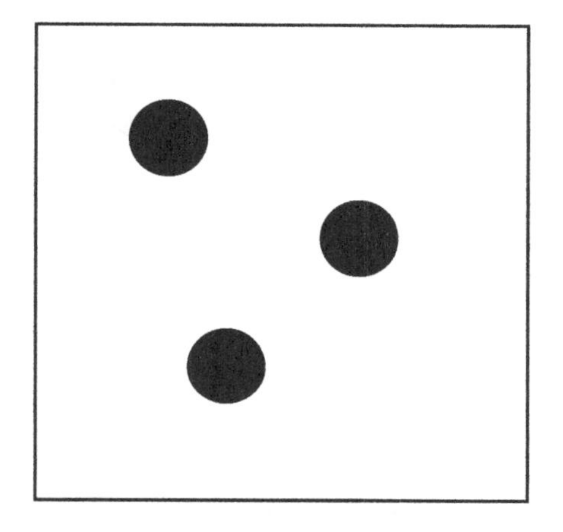

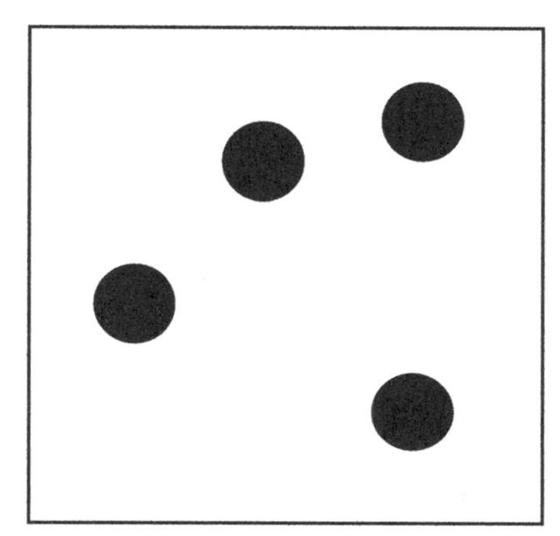

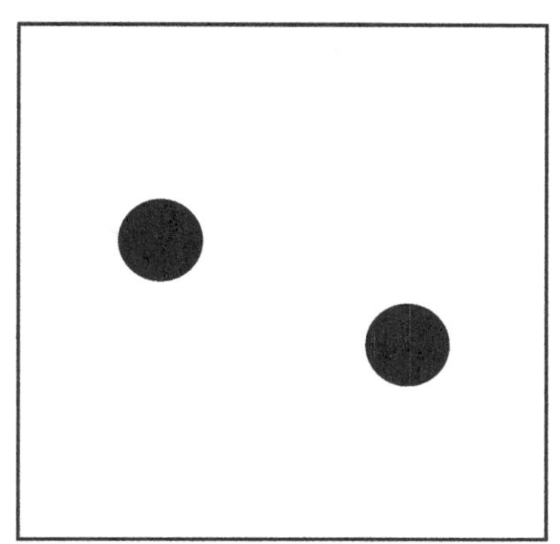

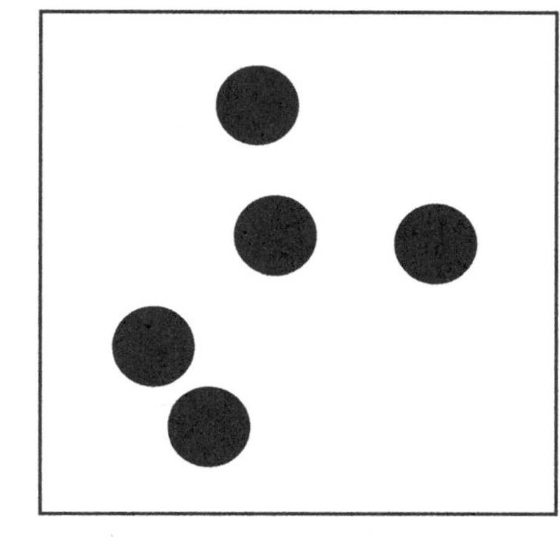

Reproducible F

Number Cards 1–20

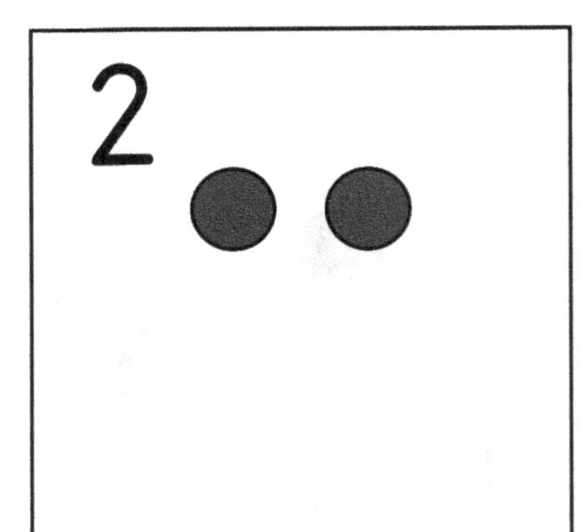

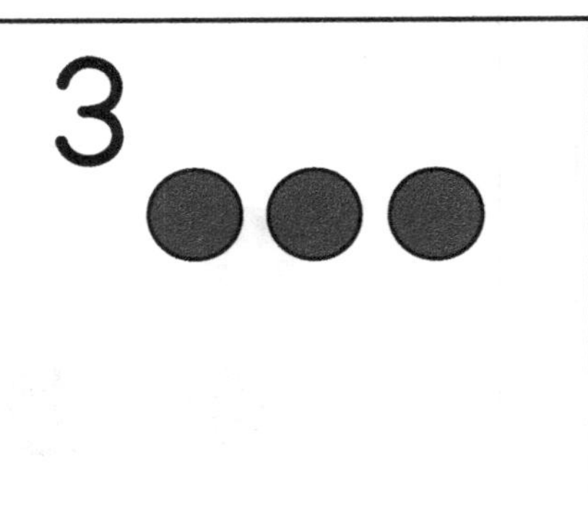

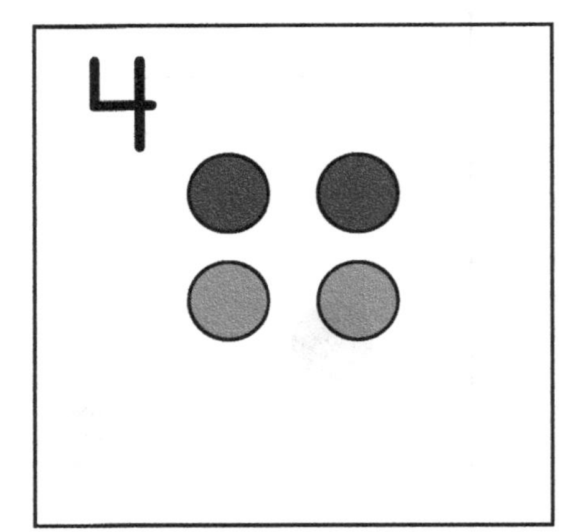

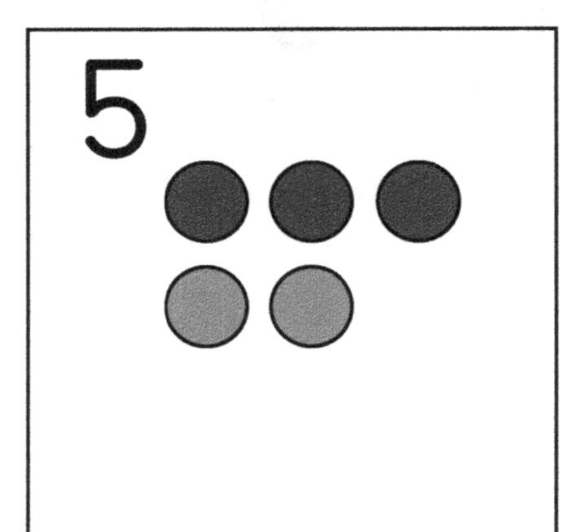

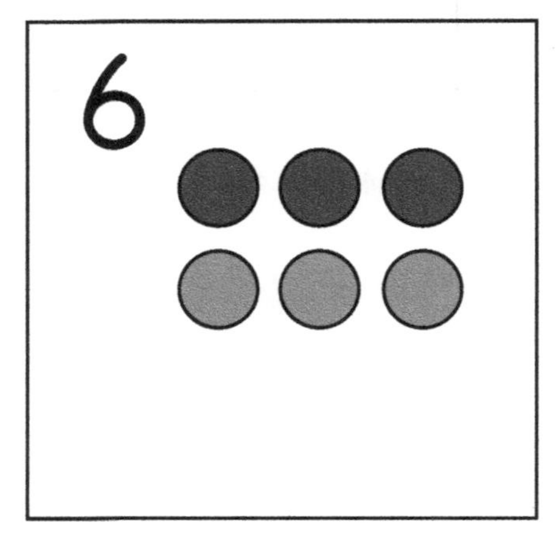

(*continued*)

(Number Cards 1–20, *continued*)

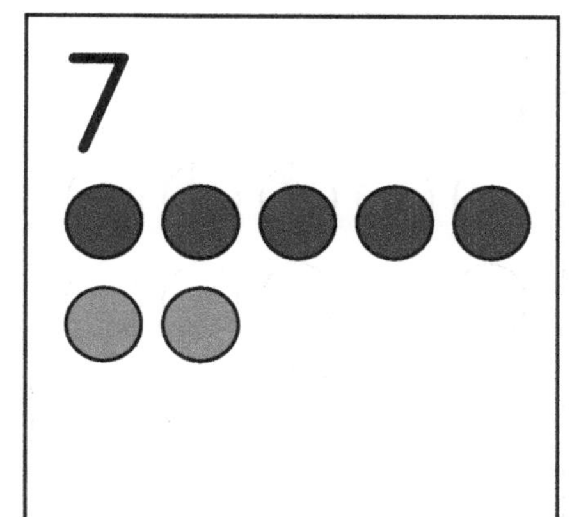

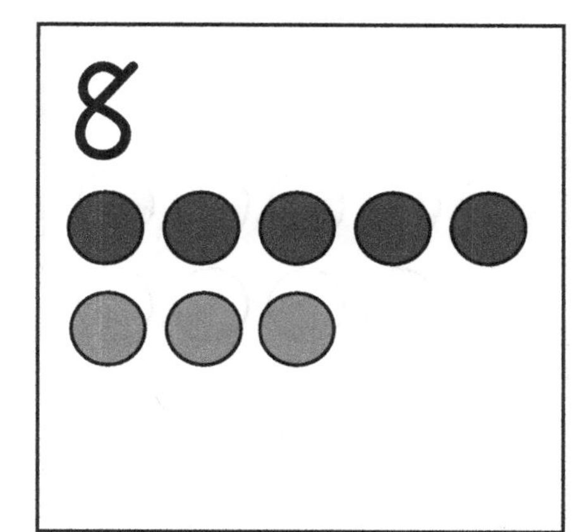

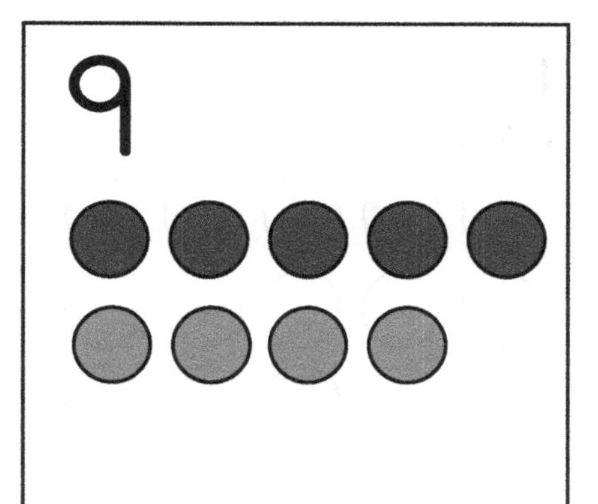

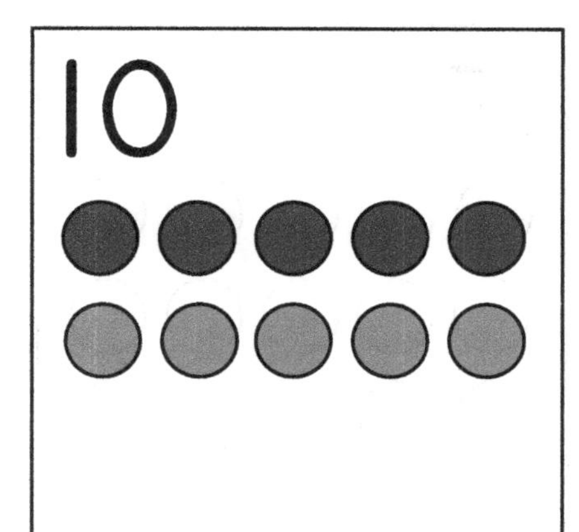

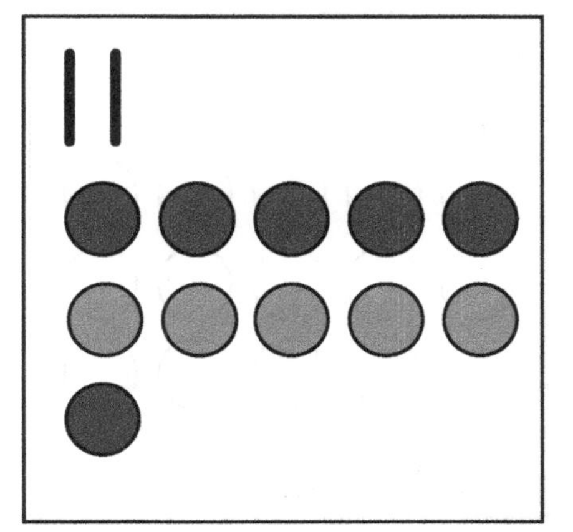

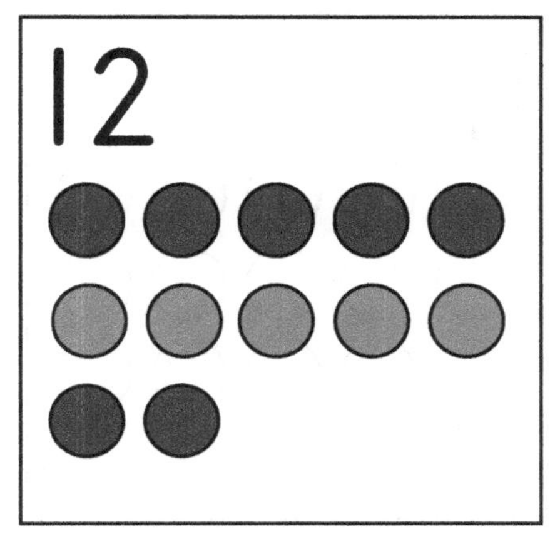

(*continued*)

Reproducible F

(Number Cards 1–20, *continued*)

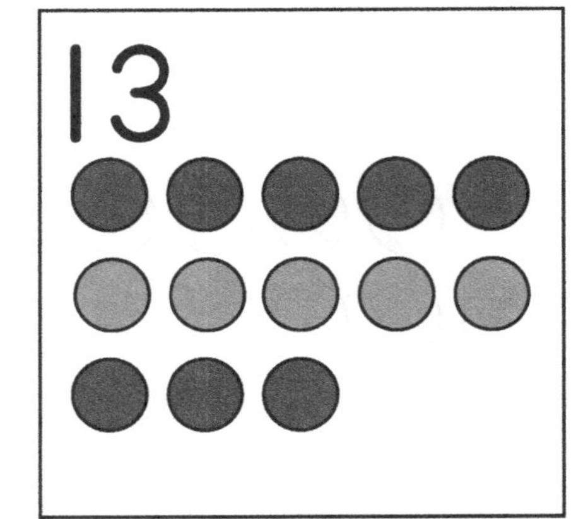

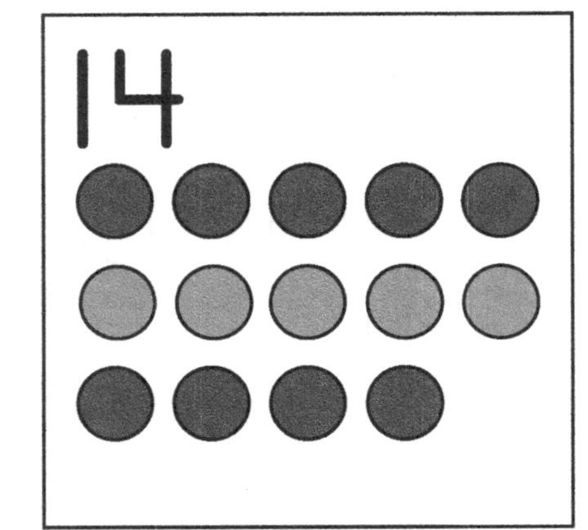

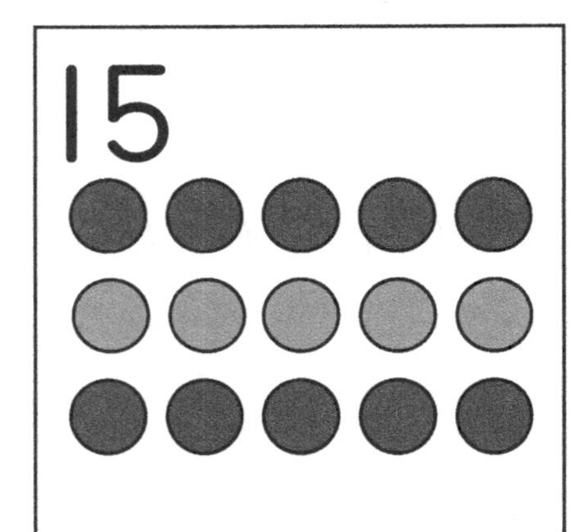

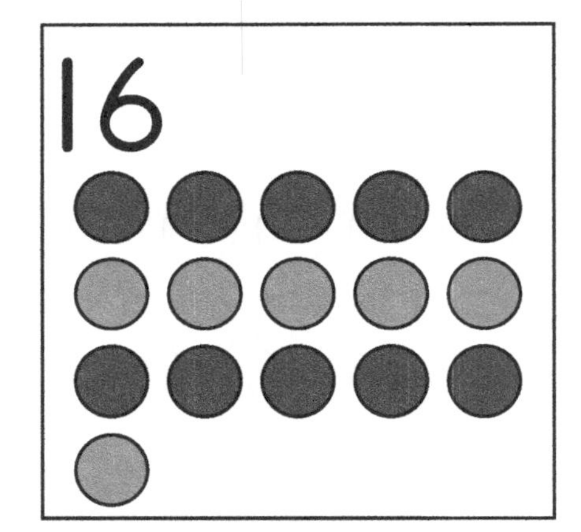

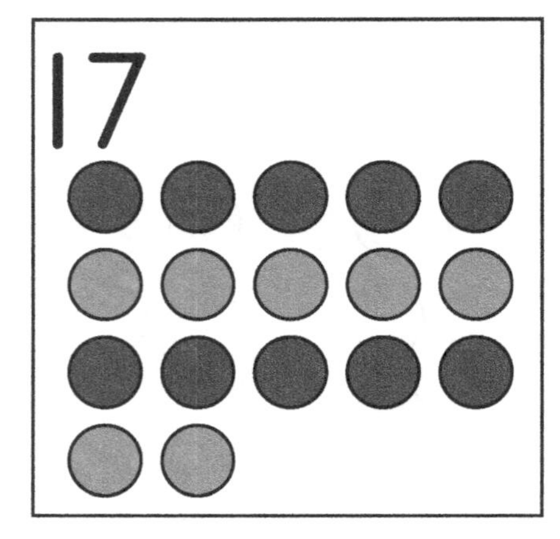

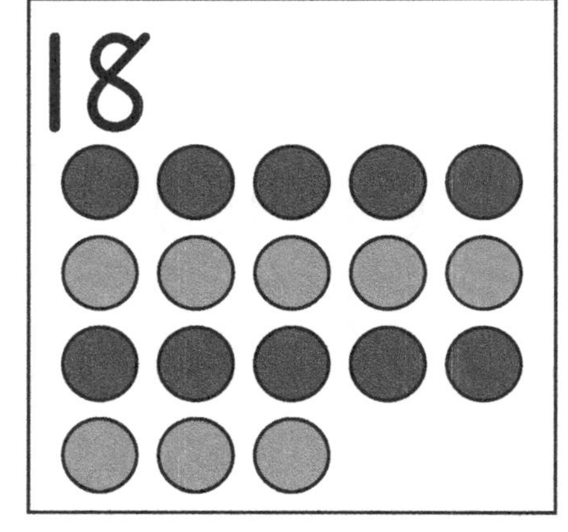

(*continued*)

Reproducible F

(Number Cards 1–20, *continued*)

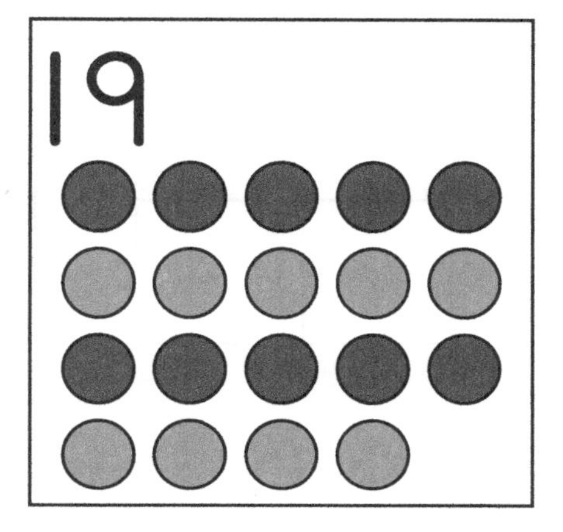

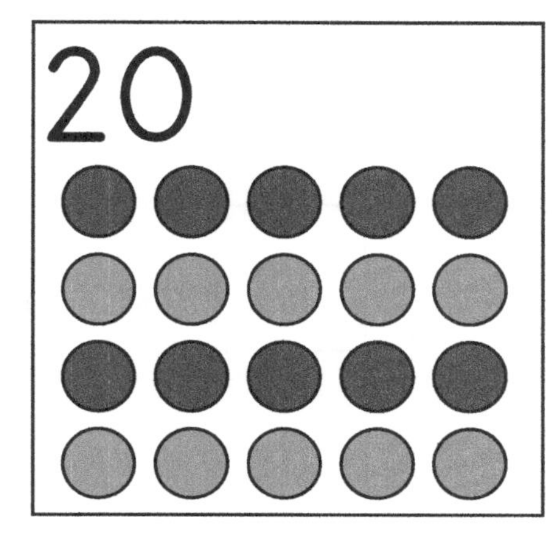

Reproducible G

Matching Picture Cards

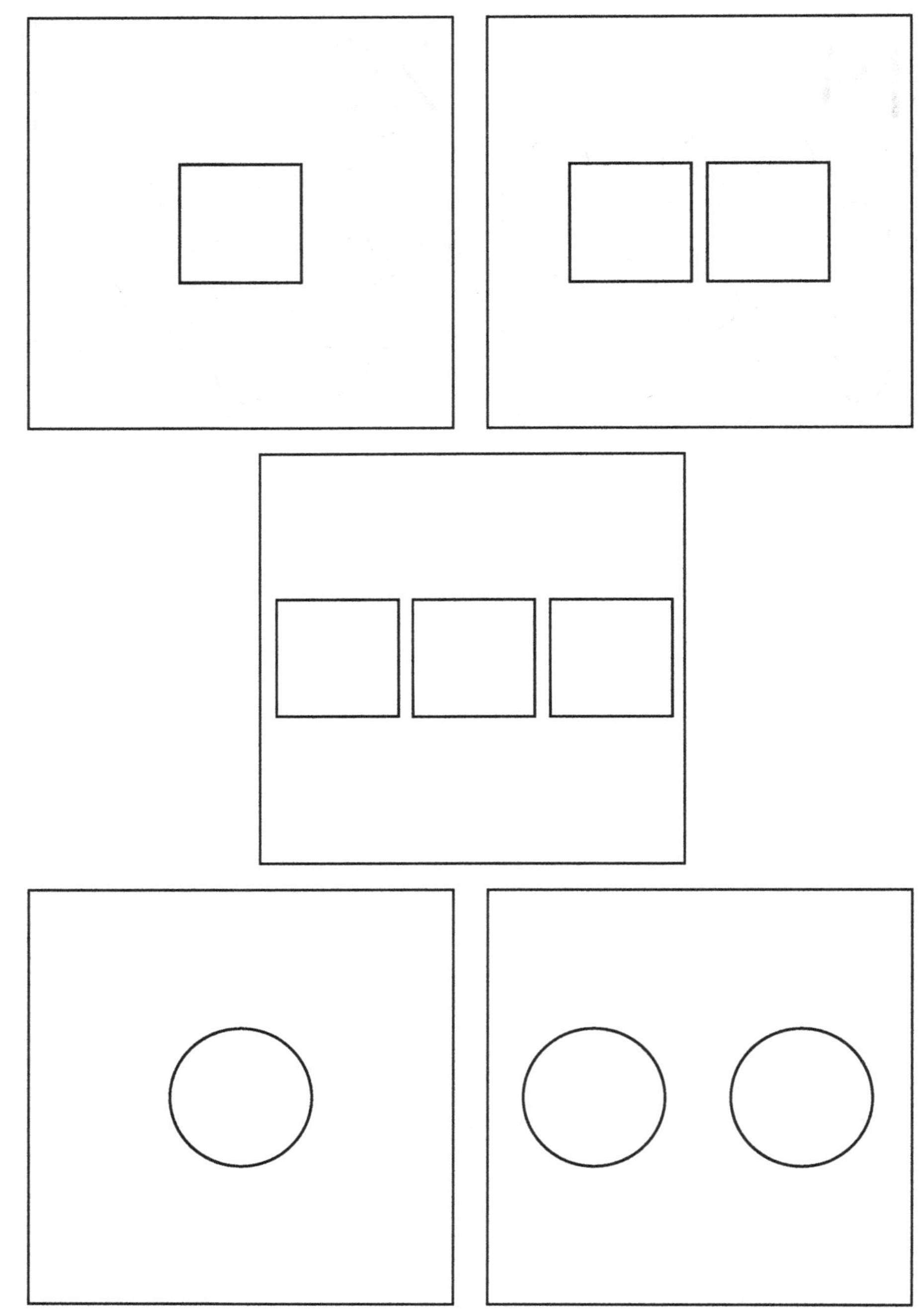

(*continued*)

(Matching Picture Cards, *continued*)

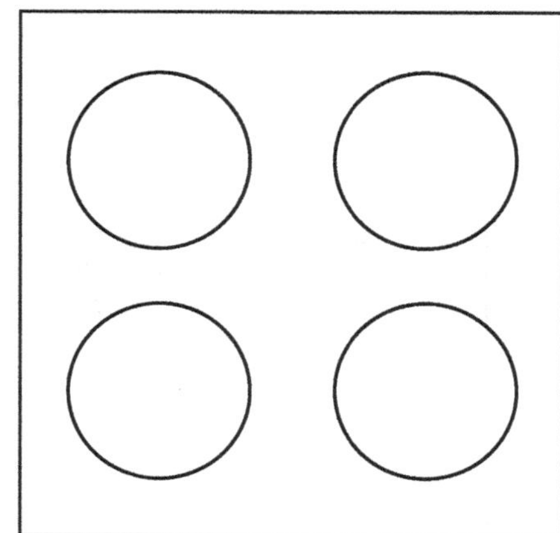

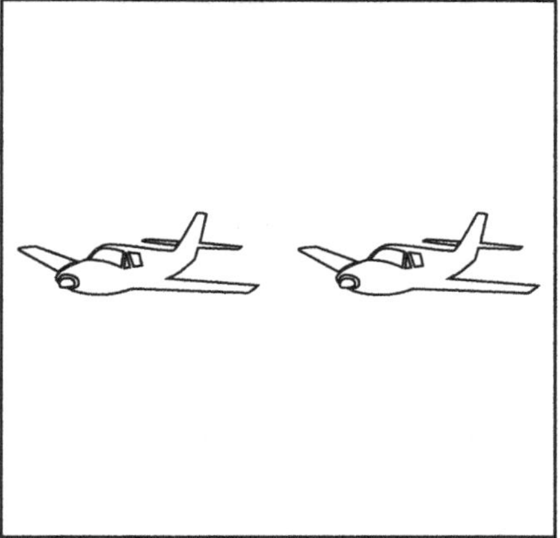

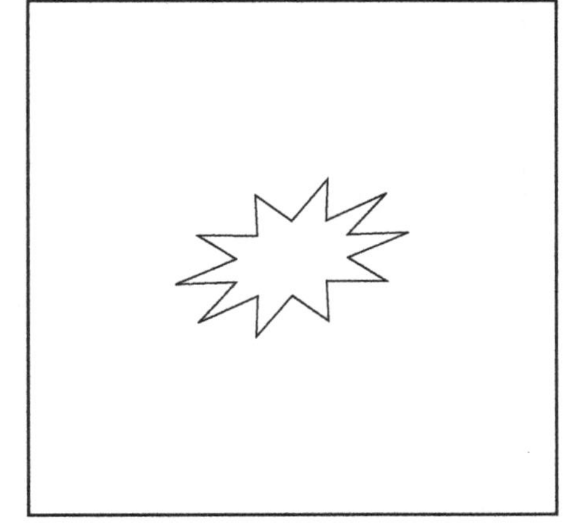

(*continued*)

Reproducible G

(Matching Picture Cards, *continued*)

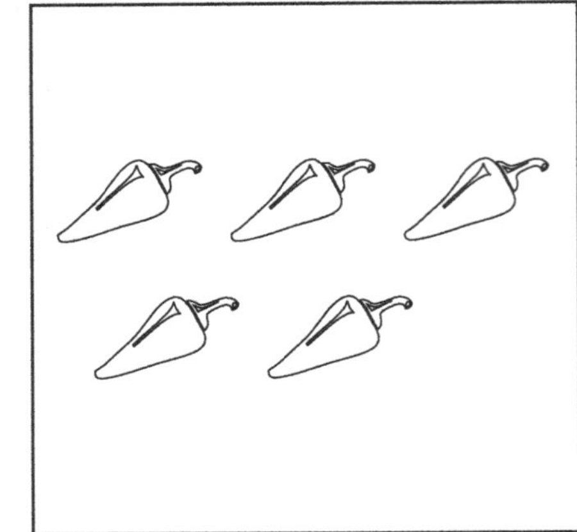

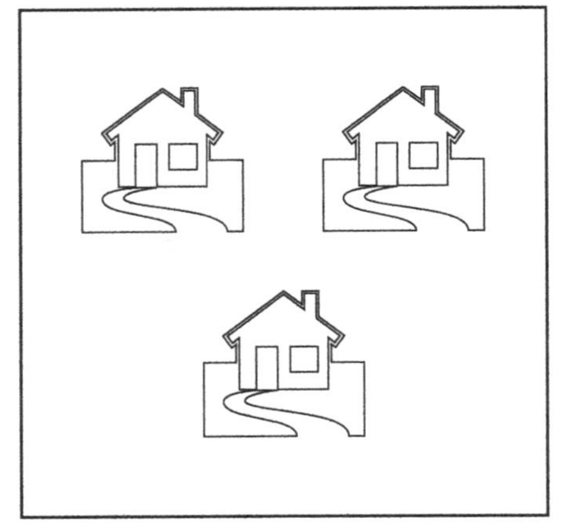

Shapes Placemat

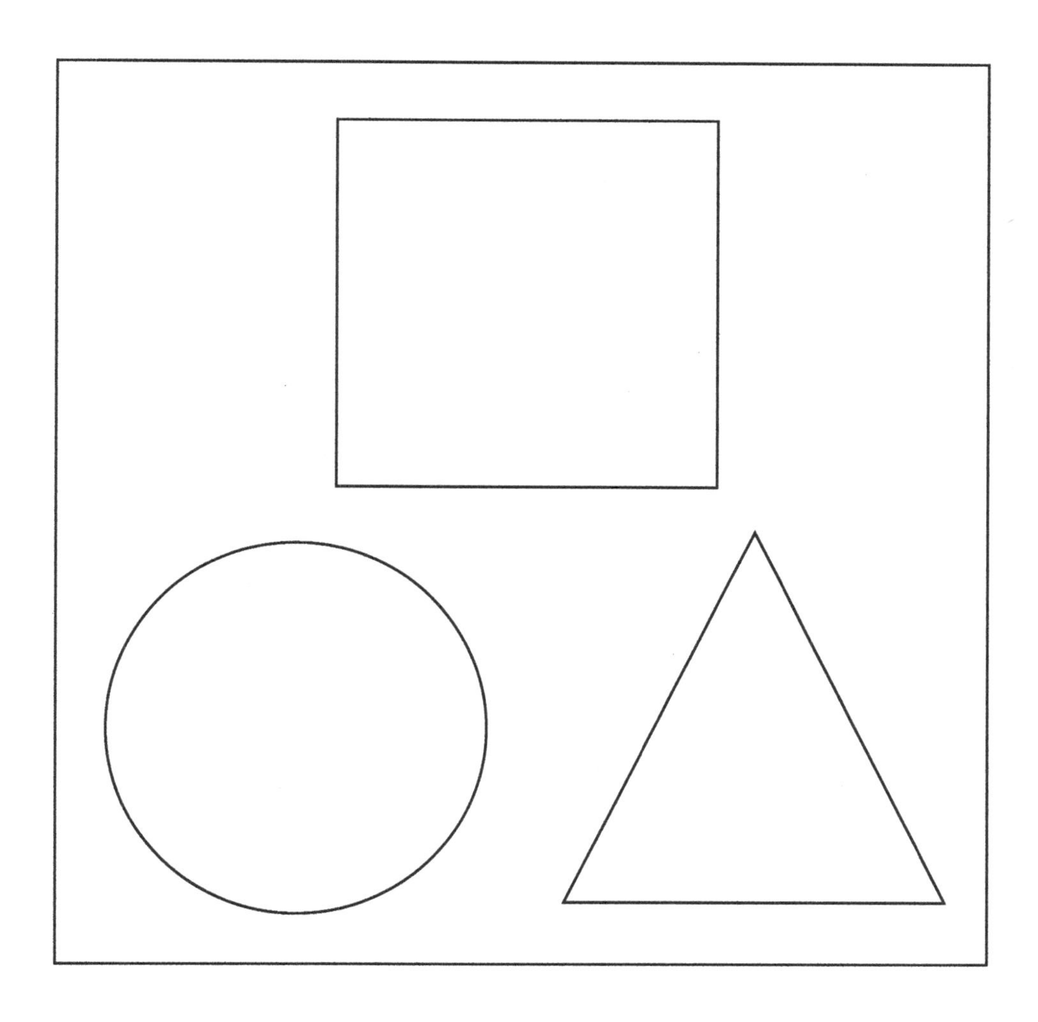

Reproducible I

Apple Template

Five Frame

Reproducible K

Ten Frame

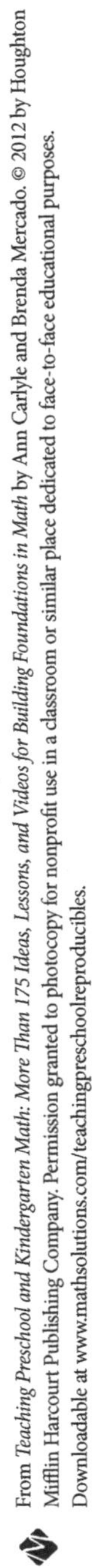

Reproducible L

Number Chart 1–20

1	2	3	4
5	6	7	8
9	10	11	12
13	14	15	16
17	18	19	20

Reproducible M

Shapes Templates

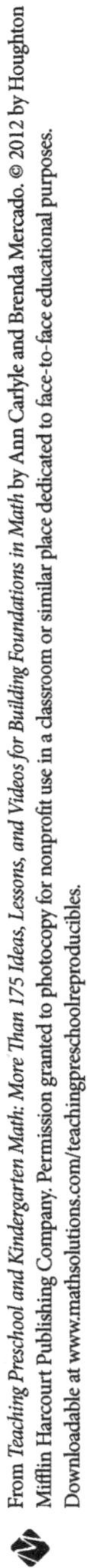

(*continued*)

(Shapes Templates, *continued*)

Rectangle Puzzle Templates

(continued)

(Rectangle Puzzle Templates, *continued*)

(*continued*)

Reproducible N

(Rectangle Puzzle Templates, *continued*)

Hexagon Puzzle Template

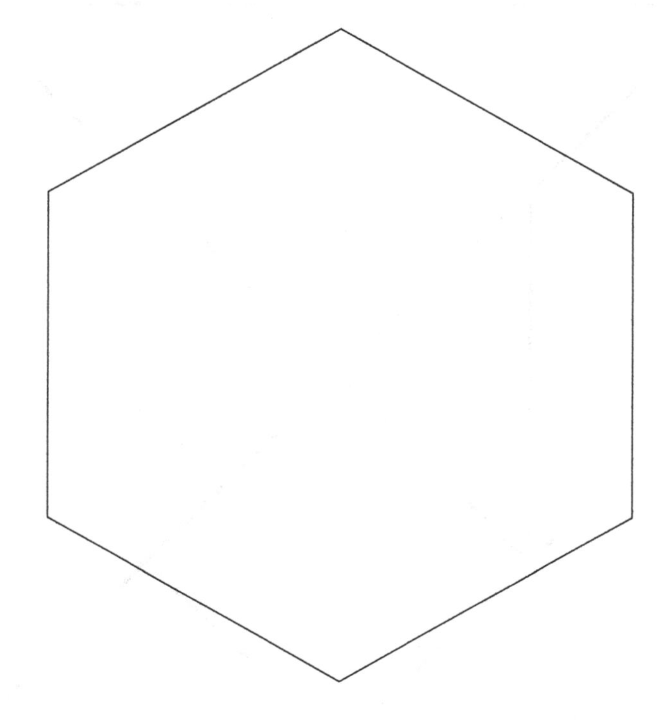

Reproducible P

Tangram Shapes Puzzle

Instructions: Cut along the lines to form seven shapes (pieces).

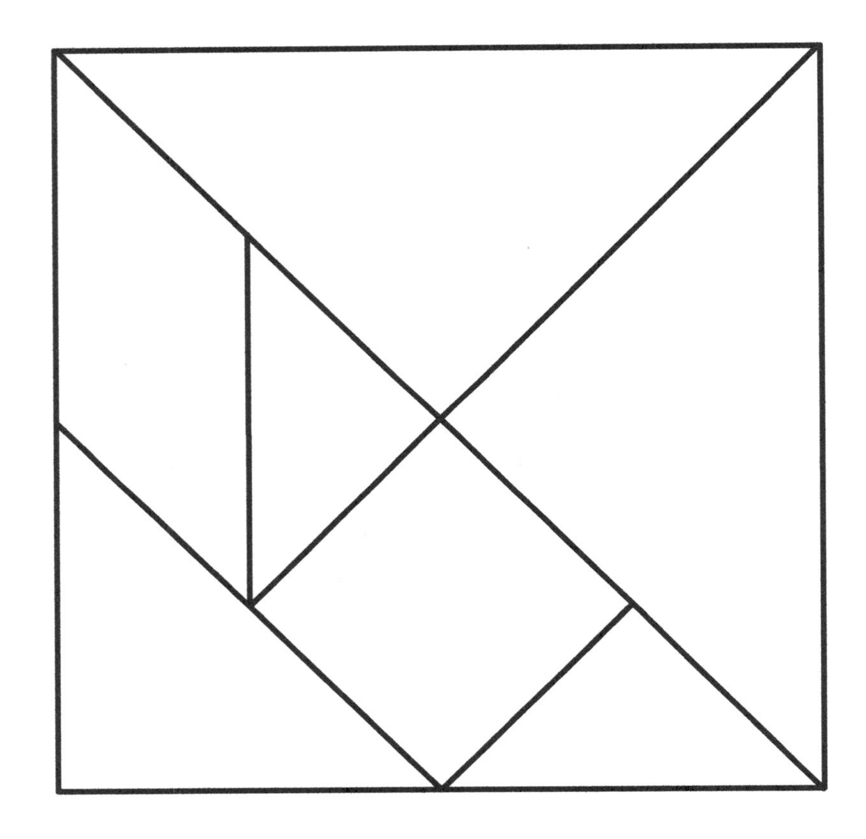

Tangram Puzzle Shapes

Children can create shapes like these with their tangram pieces.

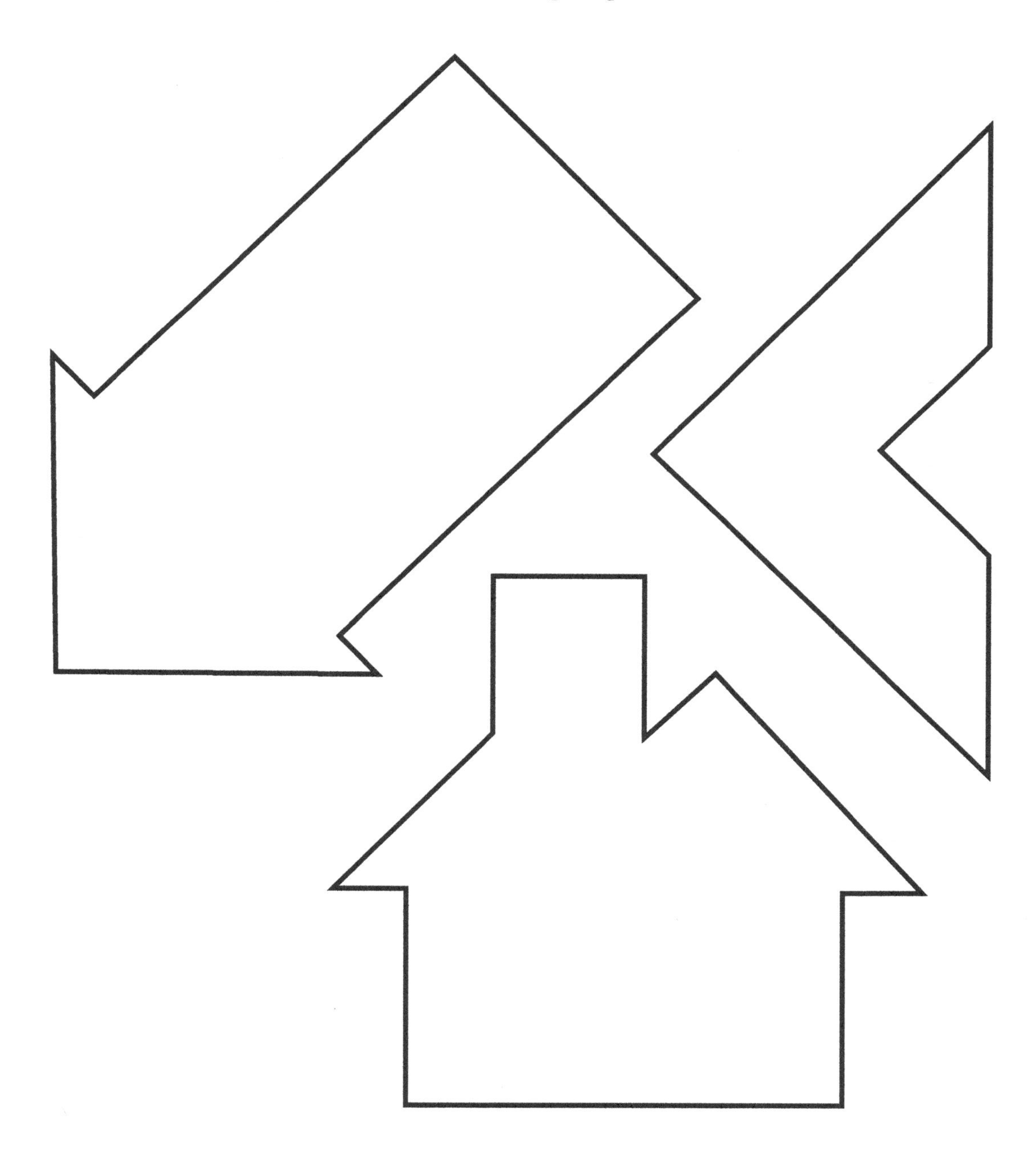

Reproducible R

Pattern Block Triangle Template

Pattern Block Puzzle Shapes

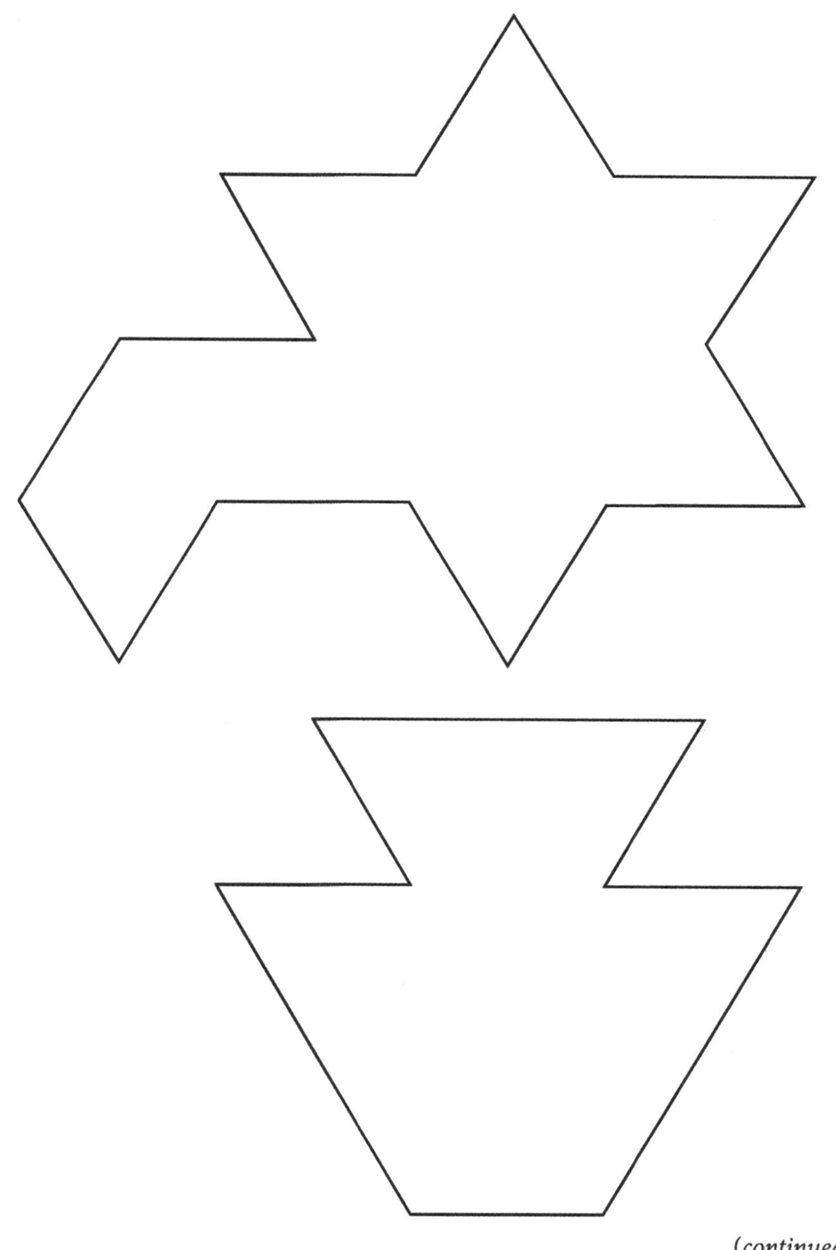

(*continued*)

Reproducible S

(Pattern Block Puzzle Shapes, *continued*)

Hundreds Chart

1	2	3	4	5	6	7	8	9	10
11	12	13	14	15	16	17	18	19	20
21	22	23	24	25	26	27	28	29	30
31	32	33	34	35	36	37	38	39	40
41	42	43	44	45	46	47	48	49	50
51	52	53	54	55	56	57	58	59	60
61	62	63	64	65	66	67	68	69	70
71	72	73	74	75	76	77	78	79	80
81	82	83	84	85	86	87	88	89	90
91	92	93	94	95	96	97	98	99	100

Top Ten Tips for Early Childhood Classroom Setup

Throughout this resource we offer insights on the setup and management of areas in an early childhood classroom; we recognize that teachers have different classroom options and space restraints, and have made our suggestions with this in mind. The following additional tips complement the classroom map and insights throughout this resource.

1. When setting up a classroom, make sure you can see all around the room (for safety's sake) but still have cozy places for children.
2. Organize areas so that children can easily figure out what activities take place in each area. Organize these spaces according to types of materials, which will help children make sense of the areas and keep them orderly.
3. Use natural light and lamps as much as possible; avoid fluorescent lighting.
4. Use flooring that makes sense for the activity going on there—for example, linoleum-type floor is best for places where children paint; carpet is best for places where children sit on the floor.
5. Designate areas so that one side of the room is used for the more quiet activities; for example, arrange the studio, clay, easel painting, writing place, and reading spaces in the same vicinity. The block area can be noisy. Place blocks in a large space designated just for construction. Place a rug or carpet under the blocks to cushion the noise. You need lots of blocks (and lots of space)!
6. Include support shelves in each space; these shelves help to define the space and provide storage; the shelves should be set at a height easily accessible for children (a good measurement is waist-high for adults). Arrange materials so they are clearly visible on the shelves (baskets, glass jars, and other clear containers work especially well).
7. Include moveable tables around the room to support the areas; when movement and dance is involved, use areas that are large and open, and free of tables and other materials.
8. Place "messy" areas, such as clay and painting areas, near sinks to make clean up easier.
9. For small classrooms with very limited space, move some of the activities outside and/or have spaces that can serve several purposes. For example, art activities and construction activities can take place in a work area, dress up and dramatic play can take place in a housekeeping area.
10. Most important, create a classroom that is vibrant, inviting, and visually appealing!

Classroom Map

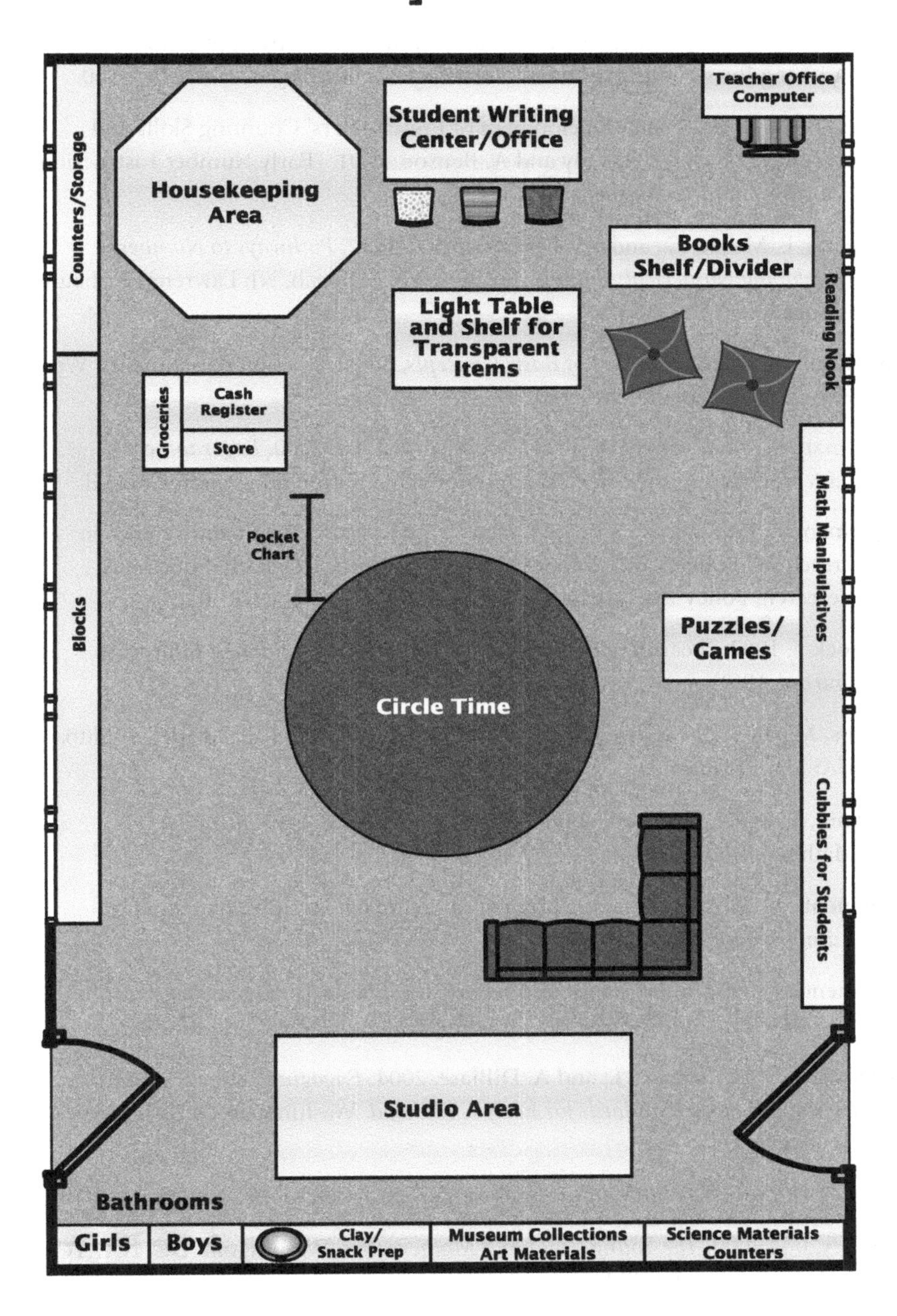

References

Asher, J. 1965. "The Strategy of Total Physical Response: An Application to Learning Russian." *International Review of Applied Linguistics*, 3: 291–300.

Baroody, A. J. 1992. "The Development of Preschoolers' Counting Skills and Principles." In A. J. Baroody and A. Benson. 2001. "Early Number Instruction." *Teaching Children Mathematics*, 3: 154.

Bideaud, J., Meljac, C., and J. P. Fischer. (Eds.). 1992. *Pathways to Number: Developing Numerical Abilities* (pp. 99–126). Mahwah, NJ: Lawrence Erlbaum Associates.

Boehm, A. 2000. *Boehm Test of Basic Concepts*, 3d ed. Pearson Assessments. Web. www.pearsonassessments.com.

Bowman, B., Donovan, M. S., and M. S. Burns. (Eds). 2000. *Eager to Learn: Educating Our Preschoolers*. Washington, DC: National Research Council.

Brenneman, K., Stevenson-Boyd, J., and E. Frede. 2009. "Math and Science in Preschool: Policies and Practice," National Institute for Early Education Research, Policy Brief, Issue 19: 3. New Brunswick, NJ: NIEER.

Bullock, J. 1992. "Learning Through Block Play." *Early Childhood Education Journal*, 19(3).

Burns, M. 2007. *About Teaching Mathematics: A K–8 Resource*. 3d ed. Sausalito, CA: Math Solutions.

Chapin, S., and A. Johnson. 2006. *Math Matters*. 2d ed. Sausalito, CA: Math Solutions.

Clements, D. H. 1999. "Playing Math with Young Children." *Curriculum Administrator*, 35(4): 25–28.

Clements, D. H., and J. Sarama. 2009. *Early Childhood Mathematics Education Research: Learning Trajectories for Young Children*. New York: Routledge.

Clements, D. H., Sarama, J., and A. DiBiase. 2004. *Engaging Young Children in Mathematics: Standards for Early Childhood*. Washington, DC: National Academy Press.

Confer, C. 2005. *Teaching Number Sense*. Sausalito, CA: Math Solutions.

Copley, J. V. 2000. *The Young Child and Mathematics*. Washington, DC: NAEYC and Reston, VA: NCTM.

Crawford, J. 1996. *Math By All Means: Money.* Sausalito, CA: Math Solutions.

———. 2011. *Why Can't I Have Everything? Teaching Today's Children to Be Financially and Mathematically Savvy.* Sausalito, CA: Math Solutions.

Cross, C., Woods, T., and H. Schweingruber (Eds). 2009. *Mathematics Learning in Early Childhood: Paths Toward Excellence and Equity.* Washington, DC: National Research Council.

Espinosa, L. 2002. "High-Quality Preschool: Why We Need It and What It Looks Like." *National Institute for Early Education Research*, Issue 1, Nov.

Faber, A., and E. Mazlish. 1980. *How to Talk So Kids Will Listen and Listen So Kids Will Talk.* New York: Avon.

Fuson, K. C. 1988. *Children's Counting and Concepts of Number.* New York: Springer-Verlag.

———. 1992. "Research on Whole Number Addition and Subtraction." In D. A. Grouws (Ed.), *Handbook of Research on Mathematics Teaching and Learning.* New York: Macmillan.

Fuson, K. C., Clements, D., and S. Beckmann. 2010. *Focus in Prekindergarten, Teaching with Curriculum Focal Points.* Washington, DC: NCTM and NAEYC.

Gelman, R., and C. Gallistel. 1978. *The Child's Understanding of Number.* Cambridge, MA: Harvard University Press.

Ginott, H. 2003. *Between Parent and Child* (rev. ed.). New York: Three Rivers Press.

Gordon, T. 1970. *P.E.T.: Parent Effectiveness Training.* New York: Wyden.

Goswami, U. 1995. "Transitive Relational Mappings in Three- and Four-Year-Olds: The Analogy of Goldilocks and the Three Bears." *Child Development*, 66: 877–892.

Hirsch, E. 1996. *The Block Book.* Washington, DC: NAEYC.

Johnson, H. 1933. *The Art of Block Building.* New York: Bank Street College of Education Publications.

Kamii, C., and J. Rummelsberg. 2008. "Arithmetic for First Graders Lacking Number Concepts." *Teaching Children Mathematics.* Reston, VA: NCTM.

Katz, L. G., and S. C. Chard. 2000. *Engaging Children's Minds: The Project Approach.* Stamford, CT: Ablex

Kilpatrick, J., Swafford, J., and B. Findell. 2001. *Adding It Up: Helping Children Learn Mathematics.* Washington, DC: National Academy Press.

Kinsman, C. A., and L. E. Berk. 1979. "Joining the Block and Housekeeping Areas: Changes in Play and Social Behavior." *Young Children*, 35(1): 66–75.

Mix, K., Huttenlocher, J., and S. C. Levine. 2002. "Multiple Cues for Quantification in Infancy: Is Number One of Them?" *Psychological Bulletin,* 128: 278–294.

National Council of Teachers of Mathematics. 2000. *Principles and Standards for School Mathematics.* Reston, VA: NCTM.

National Governors Association Center for Best Practices and Council of Chief State School Officers. 2010. Common Core State Standards Initiative. Web. www.corestandards.org/the-standards/mathematics.

Piaget, J., and B. Inhelder. 1956. *The Child's Conception of Space.* London: Routledge and Kegan Paul.

Reys, R. E., Suydam, M. N., and M. M. Lindquist. 1995. *Helping Children Learn Mathematics.* Boston: Allyn and Bacon.

Richardson, K. 2003. *Assessing Math Concepts: Hiding Assessment.* Bellingham, WA: Mathematical Perspectives.

Sarama, J., and D. H. Clements. 2009. *Early Childhood Mathematics Education Research: Learning Trajectories for Young Children.* New York: Routledge.

Topal, C., and L. Gandini. 1999. *Beautiful Stuff! Learning with Found Materials.* New York: Sterling.

Quick-Reference Lists: Learning Opportunities by Type

(Circle Time, Small Group Time, and Choice Time)

These lists categorize the learning opportunities offered in this resource by type as another user-friendly way to access them throughout the book.

Circle Time

Circle Time indicates an activity for large groups of children. Use a Circle Time activity when you want children to share their thinking about interesting mathematical ideas and problems with the entire group. Circle Time typically encompasses literature-based opportunities (activities marked with a Literature Connections icon). For more about Circle Time, see page xxv.

Chapter 2: Collecting, Sorting, and Classifying

continued

Chapter 3: Patterning

Activity	Page Number
Repeating Patterns: Candy Canes Cube	41
Growing Patterns: *The Very Hungry Caterpillar*	42
Shrinking Patterns: *Five Little Speckled Frogs*	43
Clothes Patterns	44
People Patterns	45
Showcasing Children's Patterns	48

Chapter 6: Using Counting Books, Rhymes, and Songs

Activity	Page Number
Using Counting Books	97
Using Counting Rhymes and Songs	101
The Counting Song: Video Clip 6.1 ▶	102
The "Me" Rhyme	103

Chapter 7: Using Visual Tools from Bead Boards to Surveys

Activity	Page Number
Dots: What Do You See?	111
Ways We Can Show Five	115
Counting Beads on the Bead Board: Video Clip 7.1 ▶	116
Estimate Jar	118
How Many Days Until My Day?	122

Chapter 8: Using Comparisons and Measurement to Build Number Sense

continued

Chapter 9: Using Geometry and Spatial Skills to Build Number Sense

Chapter 10: Using Foundational Projects to Build Number Sense

Small Group Time

In Small Group Time, groups of four to six children move through rotations until eventually all children have the opportunity to complete a task or receive specific instruction. The activities are planned and either teacher-directed or teacher-supported. For more about Small Group Time, see page xxv.

Chapter 2: Collecting, Sorting, and Classifying

Activity	Page Number
The Sorting Game, Part 1	20
The Sorting Game, Part 2	21
Sorting Various Colored Buttons: Video Clip 2.1 ▶	21
Sorting White Buttons: Video Clip 2.2 ▶	23
Sorting Nuts and Bolts: Video Clip 2.3 ▶	26
Sorting Our Names	28

Chapter 3: Patterning

Activity	Page Number
Repeating Patterns: Candy Canes Cubes	41
Create Your Own Patterns	45
Pattern Snacks	51

continued

Chapter 6: Using Counting Books, Rhymes, and Songs

Activity	Page Number
Making Class Counting Books	101
One More Elephant Rhyme	104
One Less Cookie . . .	106

Chapter 7: Using Visual Tools from Bead Boards to Surveys

Activity	Page Number
How Many Are in the Bag?	125
Matching Picture Cards	126
Make Your Own Board Game	130
Snack Preparation and Counting	132
Counting Snack Cups and Snacks: Video Clip 7.2	133

Chapter 8: Using Comparisons and Measurement to Build Number Sense

Activity	Page Number
Name Comparison Books	166
How Many Pockets Do You Have Today?	172
How Tall Are We?	178
How Many in a Handful?	180
Which Cup Holds More?	184

Chapter 8, *continued*

Chapter 9: Using Geometry and Spatial Skills to Build Number Sense

continued

Chapter 10: Using Foundational Projects to Build Number Sense

Activity	Page Number
What Is Half?	263
Oobleck and Twice as Much	266
Peanut Butter Dough Shapes	267
Shapes and Shadows	270
Puddle Perimeters and the Sun	271
Water to Steam	272
Does It Sink or Float?	273
Does a Magnet Pick It Up?	275
Creating Clay Dinosaurs	278
The Balance Game	279

Choice Time

Choice Time is an opportunity for children to choose where they want to work. During choice time children are self-directed. It is important for children to have these learning opportunities, in which they can truly make a personal choice about how they want to spend their time. For more on Choice Time, see page xxv.

Chapter 2: Collecting, Sorting, and Classifying

Activity	Page Number
Sorting at the Light Table	29
Sorting in the Studio	29

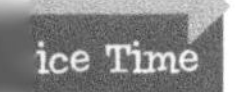

Chapter 3: Patterning

Activity	Page Number
Repeating Patterns: Candy Canes Cubes	41

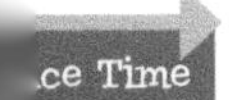

Chapter 7: Using Visual Tools from Bead Boards to Surveys

Activity	Page Number
Using Estimate Jars in Choice Time	122
Commercial Board Games	128
Surveys	135
Taking Surveys: Video Clip 7.3 ▶	138

Chapter 8: Using Comparisons and Measurement to Build Number Sense

Activity	Page Number
Comparing and Measuring at the Multisensory Table	186
Which Is Heavier?	191

continued

Chapter 9: Using Geometry and Spatial Skills to Build Number Sense

Chapter 10: Using Foundational Projects to Build Number Sense

Index

Page numbers followed by a *f* indicates a figure; reproducibles are listed as *R-*, followed by the corresponding letter and/or number.

Q

R